Dirk Meyhöfer

Architekturführer | Architectural Guide

Hafencity
Hamburg
Waterfront

Junius Verlag | ELBE & FLUT Edition

Inhalt
Content

D
**Speicherstadt und
Hafenrand der Altstadt**
Speicherstadt and
Dockside Part of Altstadt 186

Die Speicherstadt im Wandel
der Zeit The Speicherstadt Through
the Ages... 190

E
**Perlenkette: Von der Alster
bis Övelgönne**
The "String of Pearls": from
the Alster to Övelgönne....... 216

Hinter der Waterfront: Eine City für
das 21. Jahrhundert entsteht
Behind the Waterfront:
The Emergence of a Twenty-first-
century City....................................... 252

Perspektivenwechsel
A Change of Perspectives

von by Jörn Walter

Schritt für Schritt hat sich der Hafen vom nördlichen Elbufer zurückgezogen. Schleichend und zunächst fast unbemerkt fielen einzelne Lagergebäude leer und Kräne und Kaianlagen aus der Nutzung. Ungewolltes und auch Unerwünschtes besetzte den freigewordenen Raum. Es war ein langer und tastender Weg bis zur Umsetzung der »Perlenkette« – und ein noch viel längerer und geheimnisvollerer bis zur Verkündung der Hafencity, die erst nach einer Phase ungläubigen Erstaunens auf ungeteilte Begeisterung stieß.

Beide Projekte haben nun konkrete Gestalt angenommen und den Städtebau und die Architektur in Hamburg vor neue Herausforderungen gestellt. Dies ist nicht verwunderlich, denn die Dimension der Aufgabe ist in funktionaler Hinsicht von ebenso großer Bedeutung für das Hamburger Stadtgefüge wie in ästhetischer Hinsicht für die Gestalt der Stadt. Von Övelgönne bis zu den Elbbrücken gibt sich Hamburg über viele Kilometer eine neue Stadtansicht. Es ist die größte Veränderung seit der

Gradually and incrementally the port of Hamburg has retreated from the north bank of the Elbe. This process has occurred by stealth and went largely unnoticed at first as individual warehouses were abandoned and cranes and wharves fell into disuse. The vacuum was filled by a mixture of the inadvertent and the unappreciated. It was a long and tentative process that took us from there to the completion of the "Perlenkette" or "string of pearls" (the line of waterfront buildings that stretches from the beach at Neumühlen to the fish market in Altona)—and an even longer and more mysterious path from there to the announcement of the Hafencity, which, following an initial phase of incredulous surprise, was greeted with unanimous enthusiasm.

Both of these projects have now taken tangible form and have created new challenges for urban planning and architecture in Hamburg. This is hardly surprising, as the sheer dimensions of this project mean that it is both functionally significant for the urban fabric of Ham-

Bebauung der Binnenalster nach dem Großen Brand und der Errichtung der Speicherstadt und vollzieht sich in prominentester Lage und innerhalb weniger Jahrzehnte.

Die Architektur kann sich mit den neuen Nutzungen Wohnen, Büro, Dienstleistungen, Handel und Gastronomie nicht gedankenlos auf die historischen Vorbilder aus Lagerhäusern und Gewerbebauten stützen, und auch die Milieus rund um die Alster sind nicht auf die Maßstäbe und Strukturen entlang der Elbe übertragbar. Es bedarf einer neuen Identität, die die einzigartigen Chancen mit ihren fantastischen Blickbeziehungen ausschöpft und dennoch den Bezug zu ihrer Hafenvorgeschichte nicht verliert. Und es bedarf einer städtebaulichen Dramaturgie, die den Blick nicht mehr vom Land auf das Wasser, sondern vom Fluss auf die Stadt richtet.

Hamburgs Waterfront ist eine Komposition, die nach dem Auftakt des Augustinums in Övelgönne die grüne Geestkante über Neumühlen zeigt, sich mit einem spektakulären Zwischenspiel am neuen Kreuzfahrtterminal ins Wasser der Elbe schiebt, mit der Massivität des Backsteins vom Holzhafen bis zum Stadtlagerhaus an das Fundament des Hamburger Wohlstands erinnert, mit der neuen Hafenkrone entschieden und kompromisslos dem alten Namen unter den veränderten Maßstäblichkeiten Rechnung trägt, den Blick auf die Kirchturmsilhouette der Altstadt freihält, mit der Elbphilharmonie ein neues Wahr-

burg and aesthetically significant for the appearance of the city. From Övelgönne in the west to the Elbbrücken bridges in the east, over a distance of nearly ten kilometres, Hamburg has acquired a new cityscape. This is the greatest change the city has seen since the creation of the Inner Alster lake following the Great Fire of 1842, and the erection of the Speicherstadt warehouse district; both were developed in prominent locations and over just a few decades.

By virtue of the sheer multiplicity of usage—for apartments, offices, services, commerce, and the hotel and restaurant trade—the new architecture of Hafencity simply cannot follow existing historical models; warehouses and commercial buildings. Nor can the architectural milieus that exist around the Alster be made to fit the scales and structures that apply along the Elbe. What's needed is a new identity; one that makes the most of the unique opportunities and fantastic vistas, and yet retains a connection to the architectural antecedents along the Hamburg waterfront. Moreover, this project requires dramatic composition; rather than directing our gaze from land to water, it should encourage us to reappraise the city from the vantage point of the river.

Hamburg's waterfront is an eclectic composition. It kicks off at the exclusive Augustinum retirement home in Övelgönne with its commanding views over the Geest ridge at Neumühlen; sidles up to the water's edge at the spectacu-

zeichen für die Kultur in der Stadt setzt, und schließlich am Magdeburger Hafen aus einem architektonischen Dreiklang den Eingang zu einem neuen Zentrum formuliert und den Raum durch zwei Hochpunkte an den Elbbrücken in Vollendung fasst.

In der Hafencity liegt zugleich der Ausgangspunkt für ein noch längerfristigeres Unterfangen der Hamburger Stadtentwicklung, den »Sprung über die Elbe«. Nach den positiven Erfahrungen mit der »Perlenkette« und der Hafencity zur Erneuerung des Wirtschafts-, Wohn-, Kultur- und Freizeitprofils der Stadt steht der Sprung über die Elbe für einen grundlegenden Paradigmenwechsel in der Hamburger Stadtentwicklung: Von der »Fokussierung der Ränder« auf die »Fokussierung der Mitte«. Es geht nicht nur um die endgültige Abwendung von weiterem Flächenwachstum nach außen, sondern auch um die zentralen sozialen und ökologischen Fragen des künftigen Stadtumbaus in den Metropolen. Dies verlangt einen unvoreingenommenen Blick auf die städtebaulichen und landschaftlichen Realitäten, einen Städtebau und eine Architektur mit Bodenhaftung, aber auch mutigen neuen Perspektiven zugunsten urbaner, stabiler und innovativer Milieus in diesen heterogenen Stadtlandschaften, die vom problematischen Erbe des Industriezeitalters und der Moderne gezeichnet sind.

Das Potenzial der vielseitigen Wasserlagen muss hier erst wieder ins allge-

lar new Cruise Ship Terminal; it reminds us of Hamburg's trading pedigree with the massive red-brick structures at the old timber port and neighbouring Stadtlagerhaus (converted municipal warehouse); it decisively and unapologetically embraces the new architectural scale at the top of St. Pauli, the Hafenkrone (literally "harbour crown"); it retains an open view of the old city's landmark silhouette of church steeples; it gives Hamburg its latest cultural landmark in the Elbphilharmonie; and finally, at the Magdeburger Hafen, an architectural triad forms the entrance to a new urban centre. This spatial denouement is fittingly framed by the twin Elbe Bridges (Elbbrücken).

This is the starting point of an even more extensive urban development venture, the so-called "Leap across the Elbe" (redevelopment of the areas south of the Elbe). Building on positive resonance from the projects on the north bank (the "Perlenkette" and Hafencity) to redevelop the economic, residential, cultural, and leisure profile of the city, the "Leap across the Elbe" represents a paradigm shift in Hamburg's urban development; it is a shift from "focusing on the margins" to "focusing on the centre". This initiative involves not only a definitive departure from further radial expansion of the city, but also raises key social and ecological questions for the future redevelopment of major cities. It demands that we take an impartial look at the architectural and topographical realities, and develop a grounded ap-

meine Bewusstsein gerückt, die Land-schaft zum strukturierenden Element der großräumigen städtebaulichen Be-züge fortentwickelt und das Aufmerk-samkeitsdefizit für qualitätvolle Archi-tektur in weiten Kreisen der Gesellschaft durchbrochen werden. Mit der Interna-tionalen Bauausstellung und der Inter-nationalen Gartenschau im Jahr 2013 konnte Hamburg ein Zeichen setzen, um die überfällige Transformation der fragmentarischen Siedlungsstrukturen zu identitätsstiftenden und merkfähigen Orten, der internationalen Einflüsse und fremden Kulturen zu Motoren für krea-tive Milieus und der Hochwassergefah-ren zum Wandel in einen klimaneutralen Stadtteil einzuleiten.

Dieser Architekturführer geht den vielfältigen Veränderungen an Ham-burgs Wasserrandlagen erstmals syste-matisch nach und zeigt, wie die Heraus-forderungen zu neuen baukulturellen Im-pulsen und architektonischen Höchst-leistungen in Hamburg geführt haben.

proach to architecture and urban plan-ning. It also requires bold new outlooks that will create stable and innovative urban env ronments in heterogeneous cityscapes marked by the difficult leg-acy of the ndustrial and modern eras.

The first challenge is to re-establish awareness among the general public of the potential offered by a wide variety of waterfront locations, then to continue the development of landscape as a key structural element in large-scale archi-tectural planning, and ultimately to break through the "attention deficit" that exists in broad sections of society in relation to high-quality architecture. Through its involvement in the International Building Exhibition and the International Garden Show in 2013, Hamburg has finally taken steps to transform fragmentary settle-ment structures into distinctive locations that foster a sense of identity, taking ad-vantage of international influences and foreign cultures as motors for creative milieus, and turning a flood-prone area into a climate-neutral urban district.

This architecture guide takes a sys-tematic approach to the many changes that have taken place along Hamburg's waterfronts, and shows how this city has succeeded in turning challenges into new cultural and architectural achievements that are a beacon to other cities.

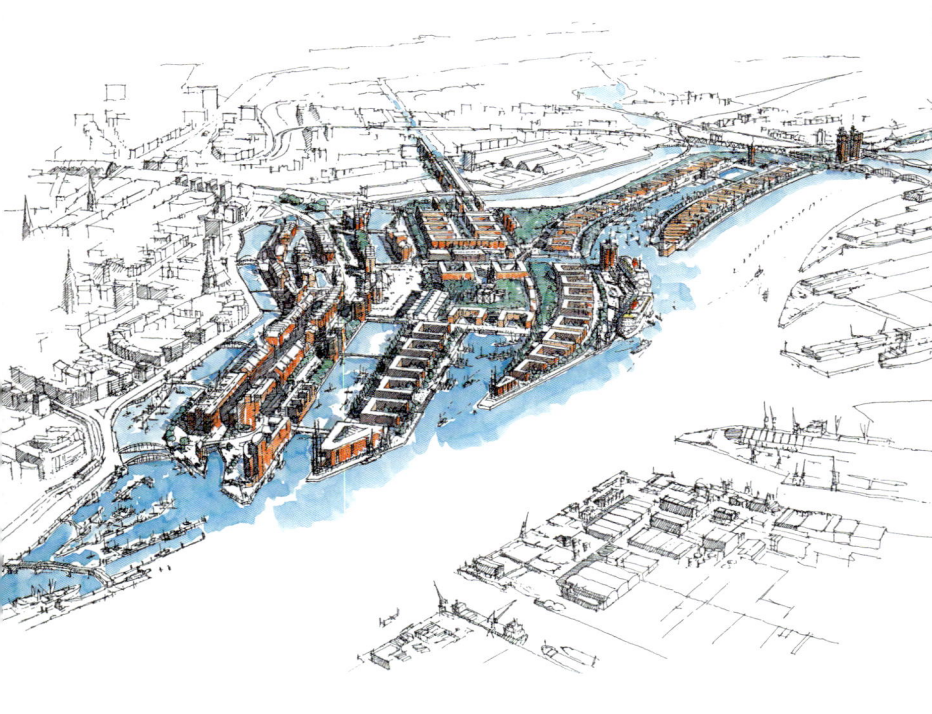

Eine der ersten Skizzen zur späteren Hafencity geht von einer starken Blockstruktur aus (Autor: u.a. Volkwin Marg). An early sketch of the future Hafencity features a dominant perimeter block plan (authors: Volkwin Marg, et al.).

Geschichte der Hafencity

History of Hafencity

Hafencity: Wie alles begann
Hafencity: How It All Began

»Die Feier zum 75-jährigen Bestehen des Hamburger Überseeclubs am 7. Mai 1997 geriet zur Sensation. Der frisch restaurierte große Saal des Hamburger Rathauses war mit gut tausend Gratulanten gefüllt. Vor der eindrucksvollen Kulisse der kolossalen maritimen Historienmalereien beglückwünschte Bundespräsident Roman Herzog die versammelten Hanseaten zur Kontinuität und zum Erfolg ihres kosmopolitischen Handelns. Da ergriff der Erste Bürgermeister Henning Voscherau das Wort und verkündete dem überraschten und staunenden Auditorium seine Vision einer neuen ›Hafencity‹: Das gesamte nördliche Elbufer zwischen dem Sandtorhafen und den Norderelbbrücken werde als Hafengebiet aufgegeben und einer urbanen Mischnutzung aus Wohnen und Gewerbe zugeführt« – eine Sensation, wie der Architekt Volkwin Marg zu Recht feststellt[1], denn selten zuvor war Vergleichbares in Hamburg geschehen, dass Hafenland zu Stadtland wurde. Der Weg war jahrhundertelang genau der umgekehrten Richtung gefolgt ...

"The 75th anniversary celebration of Hamburg's most distinguished private club, the Übersee-Club, on 7 May 1997 became a sensation. The freshly renovated Grand Hall of Hamburg's Rathaus (city hall) was filled with a thousand or so well-wishers. Standing before an imposing backdrop of historical maritime paintings, the German president Roman Herzog congratulated the assembled representatives of Hamburg's business and science communities on the continued success of their cosmopolitan enterprises. The city's mayor Henning Voscherau then took to the podium and announced, to the astonishment of all present, his vision of a new "Dockland City": The entire north bank of the River Elbe—from Sandtorhafen to the bridges crossing the north arm of the Elbe— would no longer be treated as part of the port, but would instead be given over to a mix of residential and commercial usage.[1] Volkwin Marg, one of Hamburg's leading architects, was right this was a sensation, a rare occurrence in Hamburg; the conversion of dockland to

... zum Beispiel mit dem Bau der Speicherstadt ab 1881, als Hamburg unter dem Druck des neu entstandenen Deutschen Reichs zumindest einen Teil seiner Zollprivilegien einer Freien Reichsstadt nur durch die Einrichtung eines Freihafens retten konnte. Hierfür opferte die Stadt intakte Wohngebiete wie das Holländische Viertel auf den Wandrahm- und Kehrwiederinseln, um die Speicherstadt bauen zu können. Noch in den 1980er Jahren war die Entwicklung der Hafengebiete zwischen Innenstadt und Norderelbe ganz anders geplant. Die Hamburger Hafen- und Lagerhaus Aktiengesellschaft (HHLA) hatte unter ihrem Vorstandsvorsitzenden Helmut Kern das Konzept »Speicherstadt 2000« entwickelt. In unmittelbarer Nähe des Lagerhausviertels sollte ein neues Lager- und Distributionsgeschäft mit großflächigen Lagerhallen für den modernen Gabelstaplerbetrieb samt geräumigen Laderampen und Rangierflächen für Lastwagen und Bahn entstehen. Als Standort kamen im Prinzip nur die zugeschütteten Wasserbecken und Kais des Sandtor- und Grasbrookhafens infrage. Dazu ist es nicht gekommen, auch wenn in Hamburg lange mit dieser unsinnigen Idee geliebäugelt, genauer – spekuliert wurde.

urban space. After all, for centuries the process of change had been in precisely the opposite direction.

For example, with the construction of the Speicherstadt warehouse district in 1881. At that time Hamburg, under pressure from the newly unified German Empire, managed to salvage at least some of the customs privileges it had enjoyed as a Free Imperial City through the establishment of a free port. The city willingly sacrificed fully intact residential districts such as the Dutch Quarter on the river islands Wandrahminsel and Kehrwiederinsel in order to build the Speicherstadt. As late as the 1980s the city was planning a very different development of the area between the city centre and the Elbe. The port operator Hamburger Hafen und Logistik AG (HHLA) under its CEO Helmut Kern developed a plan entitled "Speicherstadt 2000". This envisaged a new logistics and distribution centre with immense warehouses designed to accommodate modern forklifts, and complete with large loading ramps and docking areas for trucks and railway carriages. The only feasible way to accommodate this new undertaking was to fill the basins and quays at Sandtorhafen and Grasbrookhafen. This foolish plan never came to fruition, though not for want of investors who flirted with the idea.

Zeichen für den Umbruch: Die Zollhafengrenze wird verschoben

1991 stellte der Senat die Speicherstadt einschließlich ihrer Fleete, Brücken und der Zollgebäude am Zollkanal wegen ihres hohen architektonischen und städtebaulichen Rangs unter Denkmalschutz, was vielleicht ein erstes Zeichen für Wandel und Umdenken war. Schließlich wurde das »bis in die jüngste Vergangenheit vehement verteidigte Tabu gebrochen«, fährt Volkwin Marg fort, »dass die Freihafengrenze unantastbar sei. Insgesamt 155 Hektar Fläche, ein gutes Drittel davon Wasser, standen plötzlich für die notwendige Erweiterung der Hamburger Innenstadt zur Disposition.« Mehr noch – es war eine Geheimaktion: Seit Anfang der 1990er Jahre verfolgte der damalige Erste Bürgermeister Henning Voscherau diese Idee und machte sie zur Chefsache. Er lancierte sie schließlich an seinem damaligen Oberbaudirektor Egbert Kossak vorbei, der schon in den 1980er Jahren Pläne für eine neue Hamburger Waterfront auf ehemaligen Hafenflächen mit einer »Perlenkette«, also einer Rückorientierung der Stadt an die Norderelbe, entwickelt hatte (vgl. S. 220 ff). Voscheraus Vorhaben war hanseatisch-trickreich gedacht: Die überalterten nordelbischen Hafenbecken und -anlagen sollten aufgegeben und die Grundstücke verkauft werden, um mit dem Erlös einen weiteren Containerhafen in Altenwerder zu finanzieren.

A Symbol of Change: The Shifting Boundaries of the Free Port

In 1991 the state government of Hamburg declared the Speicherstadt, with its canals, bridges and the customs building on the Zollkanal, a protected historical area of unique architectural merit. This, perhaps, was the first signal of new thinking and a change of attitude to this section of the city. Eventually, in the words of Volkwin Marg, the "taboo, vehemently defended up to very recently, that the boundaries of the free port were sacrosanct, was broken. A total of 155 hectares, of which roughly a third was water, were suddenly opened up for the much-needed expansion of Hamburg's inner city." What's more, this was all done in secret: From the early 1990s the then-mayor Henning Voscherau made this development a top priority. He pushed the project independently of his own Director of Urban Development Egbert Kossak, who had developed plans for a new Hamburg waterfront—a "string of pearls" as he called it—built on former docklands, and with it a re-orientation of the city towards the Elbe (cf. pp. 220 ff). Voscherau's plan embodied the subtlety and cunning of a Hamburg merchant: The outmoded docks on the north bank would be relinquished by the city and the land sold; the proceeds would then be used to build an additional container port in Altenwerder.

Mit der Wiedervereinigung und dem Zusammenbruch des sozialistischen Ostblocks wurde der alte hamburgische Entwicklungsmotor Hafen wieder angeworfen, der bis dahin zwar höhere Umsätze, aber nie wieder seine Vorkriegsbedeutung erreicht hatte. Mit der Rückgewinnung des traditionellen Hinterlands, das bis Tschechien reicht, und der raschen Globalisierung der Logistik wuchs Hamburg wieder, und der Hafen boomte.

Um zusätzlich zukunftsträchtige Branchen an die Stadt zu binden, benötigte die Stadt attraktive Grundstücke in zentraler Citylage. Denn in Hamburg will man beides: einen modernen Hafen und zentral gelegene Konversionsflächen für zukunftskräftige Branchen wie New Media, IT oder Biochemie, wo gleichzeitig gearbeitet und gewohnt werden soll.

»Die politische Vision der Hafencity wäre freilich eine irreale Utopie für Planspiele auf Architektenforen und für Studentenwettbewerbe geblieben«, meint Volkwin Marg, »wenn nicht in aller Stille durch entschlossene und mutige Vorleistungen ihrer Initiatoren ein praktikables und wirtschaftlich reales Fundament geschaffen worden wäre. Der Grund und Boden im Freihafen befand sich bereits in öffentlichem Besitz, weil die Hamburger Kaufleute vor einem Jahrhundert – obwohl damals, zur Bismarckzeit, keineswegs sozialistisch gesonnen – das Grundeigentum am Baugrund entprivatisiert und somit sozialisiert hatten, um frei von privaten

Following German reunification and the fall of the Eastern Bloc, Hamburg port, which was traditionally the motor of the city's economy but had failed to regain its pre-war stature, experienced a new boom. Thanks to the recovery of Hamburg's traditional economic hinterland— which stretches as far as the Czech Republic—and the rapid globalisation of freight logistics, the city experienced an economic renaissance, and this was nowhere more apparent than in its port.

To attract and retain up-and-coming industries, Hamburg would need to provide attractive office spaces close to the city centre. Hamburgers, after all, like to have it both ways: a modern port and centrally located offices for the industries of the future, such as new media, IT or biochemistry. It was also intended that the new district would accommodate both living and working spaces.

According to Volkwin Marg, "The political vision of the Hafencity would surely have remained an unrealistic and utopian experiment, confined to architecture forums and student competitions, had it not been for the quietly courageous and determined groundwork that was laid by its initiators in creating an economically feasible basis for the entire project. The land on which the free port was built already belonged to the City because a century ago Hamburg's merchant community—a group scarcely inspired by socialist leanings— de-privatised the land so that "their" free port would be able to adapt to changing

Einzelinteressen ›ihren‹ Hafen jederzeit an die sich wandelnden Strukturen anpassen zu können!«

Zur Stunde Null der neuen Entwicklungen musste also niemand enteignet werden. Die Pachtverträge wurden einfach nicht verlängert. 1995 wurde die Gesellschaft für Hafen- und Standortentwicklung mbH (GHS) zunächst als Tochter der stadteigenen Hamburger HHLA gegründet, aus der später die städtische Regiegesellschaft »HafenCity Hamburg GmbH« hervorging, mit dem Ziel, das Anlagevermögen der im Bereich der zukünftigen Hafencity ansässigen Firmen zu erwerben bzw. Beteiligungen mit diesen Unternehmen einzugehen. Denn für die Verfügbarkeit des städtischen Hafengeländes war nicht zuletzt auch die Verlagerung mehrerer großer und vitaler Betriebe wie des Afrika-Terminals oder der beiden Cellpap-Terminals am Baakenhafen und am Magdeburger Hafen unerlässlich, für die in anderen Teilen des Hafens Ersatzflächen zur Verfügung gestellt werden mussten. Außerdem wurde vorsorglich der Beschluss gefasst, das große Kohlekraftwerk der damaligen Hamburgischen Electricitätswerke HEW am Strandkai nicht mehr zu modernisieren, sondern durch ein kleines Erdgas-Heizwerk für das Fernwärmenetz der Innenstadt zu ersetzen und den ursprünglichen Standort zugunsten einer attraktiveren City-Nutzung völlig aufzugeben.

circumstances unfettered by private interests."

This meant that the slate could be wiped clean without resort to expropriation. The City would simply decline to extend the existing leases. In 1995 the GHS—Gesellschaft für Hafen- und Standortentwicklung (Port Area Development Corporation)—was established, initially as a subsidiary of the publically owned HHLA. This company later became the City-owned management company HafenCity Hamburg GmbH. The initial purpose of the GHS was to purchase or acquire a stake in fixed assets belonging to companies based within the zone that would become Hafencity. Making dockland available for redevelopment necessarily meant moving several large and crucial operations such as the Africa Terminal or the two Cellpap terminals at Baakenhafen and Magdeburger Hafen to new sites elsewhere in the port. A cautious decision was also made to forego modernising the coal-burning power station belonging to the public utility HEW at Strandkai, and to replace it with a much smaller natural gas-burning plant that would supply the district heating needs of the inner city. This opened up the site of the original power plant for redevelopment.

The official go-ahead for Hafencity came in August 1997, when Hamburg's state assembly passed the "City and Port Special Assets" law, which re-appropriated and redefined the properties

Der offizielle Startschuss für die Hafencity fiel im August 1997, als die Bürgerschaft das Gesetz über das »Sondervermögen Stadt und Hafen« beschloss, in das die in städtischem Besitz befindlichen Grundstücke am nördlichen Elbufer sowie das Anlagevermögen der Gesellschaft für Hafen- und Standortentwicklung eingebracht wurden.

Volkwin Marg, der schon lange vor der Idee einer Hafencity die Entwicklung dieser Hafengebiete »vorgedacht« hat, gehörte zu den wenigen Mitwissenden: »Es verstand sich von selbst, dass der Erwerb von Hafenbetrieben als Voraussetzung für die sukzessive Umwidmung der nördlichen Freihafenteile nur bei völliger Diskretion über die damit zugleich verfolgten städtebaulichen Ziele möglich war, und nicht zuletzt deshalb musste auch die flankierende städtebauliche Planung für die zukünftige Gestaltung der Hafencity strikt vertraulich vorangetrieben werden. Deswegen wurde nicht riskiert, diese Planung durch den Oberbaudirektor in der sonst üblichen Kooperation mit vielen zuständigen Behördendienststellen entwickeln zu lassen.« Stattdessen wurde an Volkwin Margs Lehrstuhl für Stadtbereichsplanung an der Rheinisch-Westfälischen Technischen Hochschule in Aachen eine Machbarkeitsstudie für die Hafencity erstellt, die – anders als bei der City Süd an den Wasserläufen von Hammerbrook oder dem im Westen der Speicherstadt errichteten Hanseatic Trade Center – nicht den Kardinalfehler

owned by the City as well as the assets acquired by the GHS.

Volkwin Marg, who had foreseen the redevelopment of the docklands well before the idea of Hafencity was first introduced, belonged to the small circle that was privy to the original plan: "It went without saying that the process of acquiring port installations, which was a necessary condition for the gradual re-designation of the northern sections of the free port, needed to be done discreetly, particularly in relation to the accompanying urban planning objectives. For that reason too, the accompanying urban planning for the future design of Hafencity had to be conducted in strict confidentiality. That is why we didn't want to take the risk of planning this project through the office of the Director of Urban Development, which would normally work with numerous different public departments." Instead, Volkwin Marg, who at that time held the Chair of Urban Planning at Aachen Technical University, was asked to conduct a feasibility study of Hafencity. One of the key considerations of this study was that the new project should avoid the cardinal error committed in every commercial development project in Hamburg since the War. Unlike the City Süd district that was built around the canals of Hammerbrook, or the Hanseatic Trade Center to the west of the Speicherstadt this was not to be another mono-functional office district. Instead, Hafencity was to become a var-

aller Hamburger »City«-Planungen nach dem Krieg machte: Es durfte kein monofunktionales Quartier allein für Büroarbeitsplätze entstehen. Stattdessen sollte ein vielfältig gemischter Stadtteil entwickelt werden, der Wohnen, Arbeiten, Freizeit, Kultur und Tourismus als zusammengehörige Teile zu einem Ganzen verschmilzt.

Die Jahrhundertchance: Ein Hafengebiet erweitert die City

Wenn man sich die wesentlichen Entwicklungsparadigmen der Hafen- und Stadtentwicklung während der 1990er Jahre, also der Zeit nach der deutschen Wiedervereinigung, noch einmal vor Augen führt, wird deutlich, wie ein Phänomen, das gern als »geöffnetes Zeitfenster« beschrieben wird, eine große Chance für einen stadtwirtschaftlichen Aufbruch bot. Hamburg erkannte, dass die zentral gelegenen Hafen- und Gewerbeflächen nicht weiter wie gewohnt zu nutzen waren, sondern auf neue Aufgaben warteten. Im Vertrauen auf ein weiter wachsendes Potenzial der Medien- und IT-Branchen entschied sich Hamburg, vertreten durch die Bürgerschaft, nicht nur vorhandene Bedarfe zu decken, sondern durch attraktive Stadtentwicklungsplanung auch neue zu wecken. Die Hafencity wurde auf diese Weise als eine virulente City-Erweiterung in den allgemeinen Entwicklungsprozess der Hansestadt einbezogen, der

ied and mixed urban district that would blend living, working, leisure, culture and tourism.

A Once-in-a-Century Opportunity: Extending the Inner City into the Docklands

If one surveys the significant development paradigms of dockland and urban development since the 1990s, in other words the period since German reunification, it is clear that moments such as these, frequently described as "windows of opportunity", did in fact offer the chance for a new departure in the city's economic and structural make-up. Hamburg realised that centrally located docklands and industrial zones needed a change of usage. Confident of further growth potential in the media and IT sectors, the City, represented by the state assembly, decided not merely to meet existing needs, but to awaken new ones by developing attractive new locations for living and working. In this way, the Hafencity project was included as a vibrant new urban district in Hamburg's general development plans, and was sustained in its early phase by the new spirit of optimism in Hamburg in the late 1990s—for the benefit of the entire city and as an example of successful waterfront development.

In April 1999 a shortlist of eight teams—out of 175 international applicants—was selected to take part in the competition to design Hafencity.

Ende der 1990er Jahre von einer neuen Aufbruchstimmung getragen wurde – zum Wohle der ganzen Stadt und als Beispiel für ein gelungenes Waterfront-Projekt.

Im April 1999 wurden unter 175 internationalen Bewerbern die acht konkurrierenden Teams für den städtebaulichen Ideenwettbewerb Hafencity ausgewählt, der im Oktober desselben Jahres entschieden wurde. Der erste Preis ging an das deutsch-niederländische Team Kees Christiaanse, Astoc Architects & Planners und hamburgplan; Letztere setzten sich aus den Hamburger Büros Schweger & Partner, BPHL Architekten von Bassewitz, Patschan, Hupertz, Limbrock und Kontor Freiraumplanung Möller Tradowsky zusammen.

The winners were chosen in October of that year. First prize was awarded to the German-Dutch team of Kees Christiaanse, Astoc Architects & Planners and hamburgplan. The latter group was composed of the Hamburg firms Schweger & Partner, BPHL Architekten (von Bassewitz, Patschan, Hupertz, Limbrock) and Kontor Freiraumplanung Möller Tradowsky.

1 Der Autor bedankt sich beim Hamburger Architekten und Zeitzeugen Volkwin Marg für die Erlaubnis, dessen Gedanken zu verwenden und zu zitieren.

1 The author expresses his gratitude to the Hamburg architect Volkwin Marg for permission to use and cite his recollection of the above event.

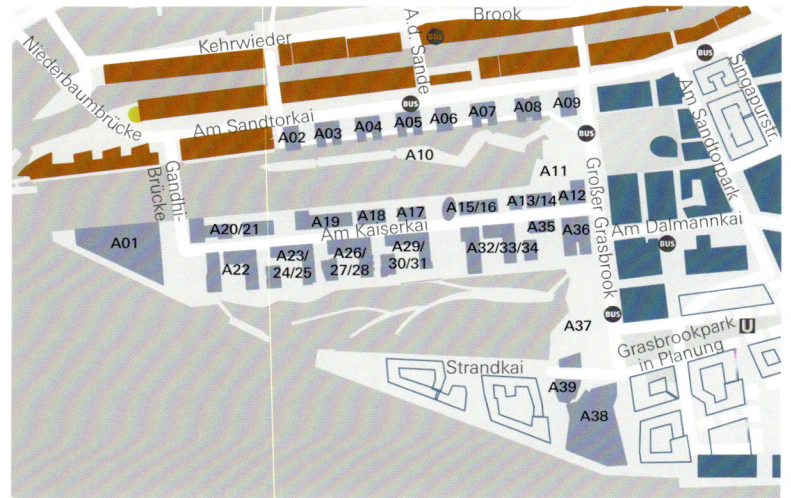

A.01 Elbphilharmonie
A.02 Am Sandtorkai 68
A.03 Ocean's End
A.04 H$_2$O
A.05 Dock 4
A.06 China Shipping
A.07 Harbour Cube
A.08 Harbour-Hall
A.09 Bankhaus Wölbern
A.10 Ponton mit Traditionsschiffhafen
A.11 Magellan-Terrassen
A.12 Marco-Polo-Terrassen
A.13 Pantaenius House
A.14/15 Am Kaiserkai 4–8
A.16/17 Oval und Kontor am Kaiserkai
A.18 home4

A.19 ElbElysium
A.20 Kai 12
A.21/22 Baugemeinschaft 2006
A.23 Johannes-Dalmann-Haus
A.24/25/26 Kaiserkai 47–57
A.27/28/29 Kaiserkai 35–45
A.30/31/32 Quartier am Kaiserkai
A.33/34/35 Dalmann-Carrée
A.36 Baugenossenschaft
        Bergedorf-Bille
A.37 K1
A.38 Unilever-Haus
A.39 Marco Polo Tower

Westliche Hafencity

Western Hafencity

A

Eine Landmarke entsteht – und das braucht Zeit. Luftfoto aus dem Jahr 2012 mit Elbphilharmonie, der westlichen Hafencity und der City – gut sichtbar, wie die Hafencity an der Speicherstadt andockt und wie nah die Innenstadt liegt.

Creating a landmark takes time. Aerial photo taken in 2012 with the Elbphilharmonie, the western Hafencity and the city centre. It is easy to see how Hafencity meets the Speicherstadt warehouse district and how close the city centre is.

Der Masterplan der Hafencity: Eine neue Stadt entsteht

The Hafencity Master Plan: Creating a New City

Das Terrain der heutigen Hafencity bildete im ausgehenden 19. Jahrhundert die Keimzelle des modernen Hamburger Hafens. Die Anlage war damals auf die Dampfschifffahrt ausgerichtet. Das Gebiet liegt direkt an der nördlichen Seite des Stroms, im Schlagschatten der Speicherstadt – gerade 700 Meter vom Jungfernstieg und 800 Meter vom Rathaus entfernt. Zur Jahrtausendwende wurde für die Entwicklung und den Bau der Hafencity ein Masterplan beschlossen. Mit ihm entstand das Drehbuch dieses neu zu entwickelnden Stadtteils, das bestimmt, wie die Stadt komponiert und aus welchen Bausteinen sie sich im Einzelnen zusammensetzen soll.

Genau genommen ist ein Masterplan ein zusammenfassendes und beschreibendes Plan- und Textwerk. Der Hafencity-Masterplan wurde am 29. Februar 2000 vom Senat der Freien und Hansestadt Hamburg beschlossen und später von der Bürgerschaft bestätigt. Er war das Ergebnis eines international ausgeschriebenen Ideenwettbewerbs (1. Preis: Kees Christiaanse und ham-

Hamburg's Hafencity was forced from a landscape of wharves, warehouses, and cranes built to service the steamship trade in the late 19th century. Situated on the northern banks of the River Elbe, just 700 metres from the exclusive shopping promenade of Jungfernstieg and 800 metres from the Rathaus (city hall), this historical site is now home to a panoply of cutting-edge architecture.

The turn of the millennium saw the adoption of the Hafencity Master Plan. This comprehensive urban development plan outlined in detail the steps that would be undertaken to create the new urban district, its architectural composition, and the components that would shape it. The Hafencity Master Plan was approved by the city executive on 29 February 2000 and subsequently adopted by the city's legislative assembly. The result of an international competition in which Kees Christiaanse and hamburgplan claimed first prize (1999), the Master Plan pursued the vision of connecting the city's historical centre with the Hafencity and Speicherstadt

burgplan, 1999). Dieser Masterplan gab das generelle Ziel vor, ein neues südlich anschließendes Stück Innenstadt aus der historischen Situation des (ehemaligen) inneren Wallgebiets mit der direkt gegenüber der Hafencity und der Speicherstadt gelegenen Altstadt zu entwickeln. Eine der wesentlichen Korsettstangen für den langfristigen Erfolg war die Vorgabe, dass dieser neue große Stadtteil von der Vielfalt seiner Quartiere getragen werden soll. Das hat in Hamburg Tradition, weil sich die Hansestadt als Stadtlandschaft vieler eigenständiger Teile versteht. Jeder Bezirk, jeder Stadtteil spricht sein eigenes Idiom, und das wurde in der Hafencity ähnlich angelegt. Trotz aller Komplexität des Planungsprozesses wurde deswegen frühzeitig damit begonnen, die Hafencity in möglichst kleinteiliger Grundstücksvergabe zu planen und zu bauen. Nur so kann eine lebendige und gemischte Nachbarschaft entstehen – mit Büros, mit Einrichtungen für Kultur, Wissenschaft und Bildung sowie einem differenzierten Einzelhandel. Der Bau von mehr als 5500 Wohnungen wurde als zentrales Entwicklungsziel formuliert und wegen der zentralen und wassernahen Lage ein qualitativ hochwertiger Wohnungsbau vorgeschlagen – als Eigentum und zur Miete für Singles, »Dinks« und Familien: Wohnungen für möglichst viele gesellschaftliche Gruppen. Im Fokus standen vor allem die hoch qualifizierten Beschäftigten der Dienstleistungsbranchen, für deren Neu- oder Umsiedlung

developments, expanding the inner city and incorporating in the process Hamburg's historical water defences within the urban landscape. A key aspect of the Master Plan was its insistence on urban diversity and the establishment of a variety of quarters—an approach with a long tradition in Hamburg, where distinct localities largely define the character of the city. Hafencity would carve out its own unique identity just like the city's other districts. The Master Plan eschewed large-scale development in favour of smaller plots, ensuring the creation of vibrant and diverse neighbourhoods with a mix of office and retail spaces alongside cultural, scientific and educational facilities. The construction of more than 5,500 apartments was identified as a central goal in the Master Plan. Hafencity's central location and close proximity to the city's waterways made it a premium location for upmarket residential development, including owner-occupied and rental apartments for single occupants, couples, and families—all the right ingredients for a socially diverse neighbourhood. Designed to appeal to highly qualified employees in Hamburg's flourishing service and creative industries, the residential neighbourhoods would provide firms with an additional incentive to relocate or set up shop in Hafencity. Hamburg was reinventing itself as a metropolis in the making and Hafencity was to be its social and architectural centre. It was a plan with just one minor flaw: Hafen-

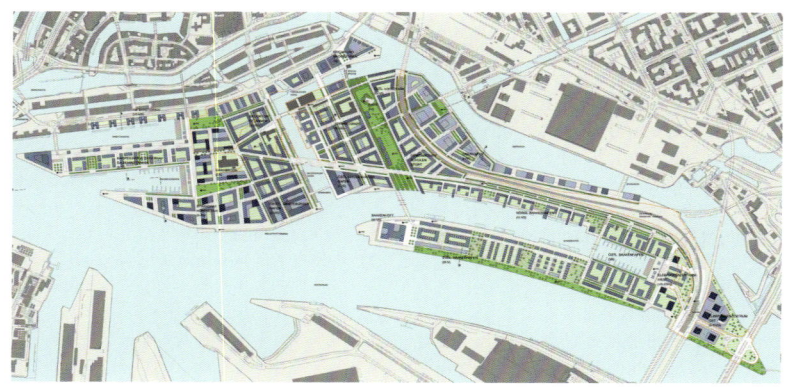

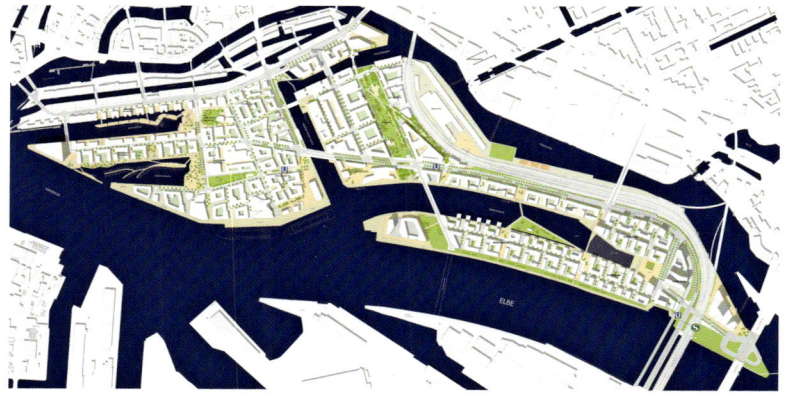

Der ursprüngliche Masterplan der Hafencity aus dem Jahr 2000 (oben) und seine Überarbeitung 2010 The original Hafencity master plan dated 1999 (above) and the 2010 revision

in die Hafencity geworben wurde: Hamburg sieht sich als »wachsende Metropole« und in der Hafencity sollte sie ihren gesellschaftlichen und architektonischen Mittelpunkt finden. Leider besteht das kaum zu beseitigende Manko, dass sich gerade diese Gesellschaftsgruppen die Wohnungen in der Hafencity nicht leisten können.

Urbanität und Dichte

Trotzdem besteht in Hamburg weiter Hoffnung, die Hafencity wirklich im Sinne einer echten Innenstadterweiterung metropolitan zu entwickeln. Planungsrechtlich hat Hamburg städtebaulich für die entsprechende Dichte und eine ausgeklügelte Nutzungsmischung gesorgt. Etwa 1,5 Millionen Quadratmeter Bruttogeschossfläche sollen entstehen, bei entsprechender Bebauung ergibt sich eine Dichte der Bebauung, die man mit einer allgemein zu beschreibenden Grundflächenzahl (GFZ) vergleichen kann, wie sie in der historischen Hamburger Innenstadt erreicht wird.

Dichte wiederum hat auch viel mit der Höhenentwicklung einer Stadt zu tun, und im Fall der Hafencity-Masterplanung sind die Gebäudehöhen weitestgehend an der historischen Innenstadt Hamburgs orientiert – ohne diese vordergründig zu kopieren und zu zitieren. Das ungeschriebene Gesetz, dem zufolge die Türme der Hamburger Hauptkirchen und des Rathauses weiterhin die Stadtkontur beherrschen

city's success would quickly put these neighbourhoods beyond the reach of its envisaged target group.

Urbanity and Density

There are still high hopes that Hafencity will give Hamburg a more metropolitan character as it evolves into an organic extension of the inner city area. The Master Plan was drawn up with an eye to fostering the emergence of a mixed-use development of sufficient density. The project will see the creation of a total of around 1.5 million square metres of gross floor space at a projected density that compares favourably with Hamburg's historical inner city, as demonstrated by a comparison of the respective site ratios (the ratio of gross floor space to actual land area).

Naturally, the density of any given area is heavily dependent on its vertical development. The restrictions on vertical development in the Hafencity Master Plan largely match the relatively uniform building height in Hamburg's historical centre in an attempt to ensure continuity without copying or referencing the existing architecture too closely. In compliance with an unwritten law, the spires of the city's main churches and its towering City Hall (Rathaus) will continue to dominate Hamburg's skyline. Hafencity's design captures the sophisticated restraint for which Hamburg is renowned. The scale, proportion, balance and range of materials applied

sollen, behielt Gültigkeit. Der Städtebau der Hafencity übt sich also in hanseatischer Zurückhaltung. Maß, Proportion, Körnung und Materialien orientieren sich an den städtebaulichen Hamburger Spielregeln aus dem 20. Jahrhundert. Es gibt nur wenige wirklich hohe Bauwerke – eine dieser Ausnahmen ist die Elbphilharmonie.

Wasserstadt

Ihren eigentlichen Charakter bezieht die Hafencity aber aus einer unvergleichlichen, im Sinne eines modernen Stadtmarketings einzigartigen (unique) Stadttopografie, dem Zusammenspiel von Wasser und Stadtraum, in einer beinahe aquatischen Landschaft an der Norderelbe rund um die alten Hafenbecken und an den Kanälen. Irgendjemand hat ausgerechnet, dass die Hafencity allein über zehn Kilometer lange Kaianlagen verfügt. Das Bauen am Wasser, genauer: mitten im Elbstrom, sorgt allerdings für eine ambivalente Situation. Denn die Erweiterung der bestehenden Innenstadt liegt im hochwasserbedrohten Hafengebiet und außerhalb der historischen Deichlinie der Stadt. Der Masterplan hatte auch die Aufgabe, den Hochwasserschutz im Grundsatz zu regeln. Ein zentrales Sperrwerk der Elbe nach holländischem Vorbild war nicht finanzierbar. Eine Eindeichung hätte den großartigen Wasserbezug in den unteren Geschossen und auf den Promenaden zunichtegemacht. Deswegen

across the development reflect the architectural mores of 20th-century Hamburg. Only a handful of buildings have more significant vertical reach—among these giants is Hamburg's audacious Elbphilharmonie.

The Waterfront City

Hafencity derives its distinctive character from its unique urban topography and waterside location. Situated on the banks of the Elbe, with its old harbour basins, canals and industrial flair, this is a paragon of urban redevelopment. According to one industrious statistician, Hafencity has over ten kilometres of waterfront. But waterside construction—especially on the banks of the flood-prone Elbe—is not without its difficulties. Extending the inner city area southwards placed the new development beyond the historical dyke line in the flood-prone harbour area, and required the development of a flood prevention and mitigation strategy within the Master Plan. The construction of a central flood barrier similar to those built in the Netherlands was financially infeasible, while embankment solutions would have destroyed the waterside flair which was to lend the promenades and lower storeys such charm. Instead, the solution outlined in the Master Plan utilises the massive elevated foundations of the historical wharves to create Hafencity's distinctive architectural vernacular.

wurde mit dem Masterplan das Modell der Warftenlösung favorisiert, was in der Folge zu einer ganz spezifischen Grammatik im Städtebau der Hafencity geführt hat.

Der Masterplan von 1999, der im Jahr 2010 für die östlichen Teile der Hafencity feinjustiert und weiterentwickelt wurde, kann als »Vater des Erfolgs« bezeichnet werden. Eine City-Erweiterung mit großstädtischem Gepräge wurde als attraktiver Wohn- und Arbeitsort für die Hamburger angestrebt, ebenso als neuer Erholungs- und Zielort für Millionen von Besuchern. Mit einem gigantischen Freiluftmuseum für hamburgische Architektur des 21. Jahrhunderts, geschmückt mit einigen aufblitzenden Sternchen der großen architektonischen Haute Couture wie der Elbphilharmonie. Und mit vielen guten Ideen für die Baukunst, die sich manchmal erst auf den zweiten Blick erschließen. Mit Promenaden, Parks und Plätzen als Modell für die offene Stadt für alle, mit einer eigenen Universität und vielen weiteren Einrichtungen für Wissenschaft und Bildung. Und natürlich mit einer neuen Schauseite zur Elbe – der Waterfront für das Hamburg des 21. Jahrhunderts.

While a number of changes were made to the plans for the eastern sector of Hafencity in 2010, the Master Plan of 1999 is the "founding document" behind this success story. Its vision: the creation of a greater inner city area with an appealing mix of residential and commercial properties, urban green spaces, recreational areas, and tourist hotspots. Hafencity would be a gigantic open-air museum of twenty-first century architecture, embellished with such haute couture creations as the Elbphilharmonie and a legion of subtly innovative and inspiring designs. With its promenades, parks, and plazas, Hafencity was conceived as a diverse and open urban district with its own university and a host of scientific and educational facilities. And yet the star attraction of the entire ensemble remains the Elbe itself. This is Hamburg's new waterfront for the 21st century.

Elbphilharmonie
Konzerthalle Concert Hall

A.01

Standort Location Kaiserhöft **Architekten Architects** Generalplaner General design contractors: Arbeitsgemeinschaft Herzog & de Meuron, Basel, Höhler + Partner Architekten und Ingenieure, Hamburg **Bauherr Client** ReGe Hamburg Projektrealisierungsgesellschaft mbH als Vertreterin für die on behalf of Elbphilharmonie Hamburg Bau GmbH & Co. KG **Bauzeit Date built** Seit 2007 **Bruttogeschossfläche Gross floor area** 120000 qm (sqm)

Es ist ein Bauwerk, das schon weit vor der Vollendung für Furore sorgte – 2004, als die Architektur noch virtuell und nur als Rendering zu sehen war. Was mit jedem Bautag zunehmend erfahrbar wurde, ist die gewaltige Dimension mit weit über hundert Metern Höhe an der Spitze. Das Konzept ist ebenso einfach wie genial: Der alte Backstein-Kaispeicher A (1966, Architektur: Werner Kallmorgen) bildet die Basis für die drei eigentlichen Philharmoniesäle, für Wohnungen und ein Hotel, für Infrastruktur wie ein Parkhaus und vieles mehr – zum Teil innerhalb der Altbausubstanz, teilweise aufgesattelt. Es ist ein Maßstabssprung, eine neue Dimension der Architektur für Hamburg, die oben gläsern und transparent ist und das Bild eines sich blähenden Segels auf einem Bootskörper vermittelt. Es ist die angestrebte Landmarke geworden, die stolz verkündet: Hamburg ist eine Freie Hafen- und Kulturstadt. Schon während der Bauzeit haben Zehntausende die Elbphilharmonie

When the first rendered images of Hamburg's Elbphilharmonie were released in 2004, this visionary building made headlines long before the construction crews moved in. Standing well over 100 metres tall, the building's awe-inspiring character soon became apparent. The concept is as simple as it is ingenious: the massive brickwork Kaispeicher A (1966, Design: Werner Kallmorgen) forms the foundation for the building's three concert halls, apartments and a hotel, along with additional infrastructure including a multi-storey car park, in a design which incorporates and extends the original architecture. Taking contemporary architecture to new heights a transparent glass façade adorns the upper levels and evokes images of a ship in full sail. The Elbphilharmonie has lived up to its designer's expectations: this is an architectural landmark worthy of a thriving cultural and maritime metropolis. Tens of thousands of visitors flocked to the building during its construction, making

1

2

1+2 Gesamtansicht vom Land und vom Strom Overall view from land and from water

besichtigt; noch zu Fuß, mühsam über Rohbautreppen und ohne die gebogenen Rolltreppen, die auf die öffentliche Plaza in etwa 37 Metern Höhe führt. Diese Rolltreppe ist Teil der Inszenierung, des Ankommens und auch des Staunens. Man gleitet in die Höhe, ohne klares, sichtbares Ziel. Das Geheimnis lüftet sich auf der Plaza-Ebene mit sensationellem – öffentlichem – Ausblick auf die schöne Flusshafenstadt. Darüber liegt der Hauptsaal auf dem Dach des alten Speichers, mit einem großen Rund für 2150 Besucher. Dank seines Akustikers Yasuhisa Toyota stellt er den Anspruch, in die Top Ten der großen Konzertsäle der Welt aufgenommen zu werden. Schon im Stadium des Ausbaus zeigte er Grandezza. Im Vergleich zur Berliner Philharmonie von Hans Scharoun, die wegen ihrer vergleichbaren Asymmetrie und Vieleckigkeit und der Anmutung eines hohen Zelts Vorbild gewesen sein könnte, ist der Saalgrundriss (im Hochhaus der Elbphilharmonie) nur etwa halb so groß. Dafür türmen sich die Zuschauerränge domhoch. Ab 2010 wurde die Glasfassade montiert. Eine solche, vierfach geschichtete und individuell siebbedruckte Glaswand mit über tausend unterschiedlich geformten Paneelen hat es in einer solchen Höhe noch nie gegeben (vgl. S. 72 ff). Ein Baustopp hat den Bauprozess jedoch verzögert. Mit der Eröffnung des Konzertbetriebs ist nicht vor 2017 zu rechnen.

their way up its rough concrete stairs to the plaza some 37 metres above ground. The curving line of the building's escalator – now operational is integral to this architectural performance and invites visitors to glide onwards and upwards into the unknown. All is revealed on arrival at the plaza, where the gallery offers visitors sensational panoramic views of Hamburg harbour and the city beyond. Resting on top of the old warehouse above the gallery lies the Grand Concert Hall. Designed by acoustician Yasuhisa Toyota, this curvaceous auditorium has a maximum capacity of 2,150 and is set to take its place among the top ten performance venues worldwide. Hans Scharoun's angular, asymmetrical design for the Berliner Philharmonie may have been one source of inspiration for this design, but the Elbphilharmonie has aspirations of grandeur that put it in a league of its own. The Grand Concert Hall on the upper level occupies roughly half as much floorspace as its counterpart in Berlin, instead its galleries tower above the performance area creating an almost sacral atmosphere. Outside, work on the building's glass façade began in 2010. Comprised of four layers of over one thousand individually printed glass panels of varying shapes and sizes, the façade's construction high above the waters of the Port of Hamburg is a world first (cf. pp. 72 ff). A temporary halt has delayed the construction process. Concert business is not expected to begin before 2017.

3   4

5

3 Innenraumansicht des Altbaus mit Parkhaus Interior view of the historical building with multi-storey car park **4+5** Perspektiven von Westen und von der Hafencity aus Views from the west and from Hafencity

Am Sandtorkai 68
Bürogebäude Office Building

Standort Location Am Sandtorkai 68 **Architekten Architects** ingenhoven architects, Düsseldorf **Bauherr Client** NOC New Office Company **Wettbewerb Competition** 2001 **Bauzeit Date built** 2003–04 **Bruttogeschossfläche Gross floor area** 6130 qm (sqm)

Das städtebauliche Konzept des Masterplans sah vor, dass die einzelnen Baukörper am Sandtorkai je aus zwei etwa zehn Meter breiten Riegeln bestehen, die in der Mitte durch einen Erschließungskern verbunden sind. Die Gebäuderiegel kragen über die darunter geführte Promenade und den Sandtorhafen aus. Damit wird ein bekanntes historisches Element hamburgischer Architektur am Wasserrand aufgegriffen. Die lichte Höhe ist mit mindestens fünf Metern festgesetzt, was für einen großzügigen Luftraum über der Promenade sorgt. Diese Vorgaben gelten für die gesamte Reihe. Das Bürohaus am westlichen Abschluss fällt insofern auf, als es über nur einen Riegel verfügt, dafür horizontale Fensterbänder auf niedrigen hellen Brüstungen aufliegen und auffällige, diagonale Streben die Konstruktion verstärken: mehr lockeres Rheinland als distinguiertes Elbland, was nicht nur die Autorenschaft, sondern auch den Charakter betrifft.

The urban planning concept outlined in the Master Plan requires that architectural elements on Sandtorkai consist of two blocks, each measuring approximately ten metres across and connected by a central shaft. Overhanging the promenade and the harbour basin below, their design reflects quintessential elements of Hamburg's historical maritime architecture. A minimum clearance height of five metres has been applied across the entire row, lending the promenade a spacious air. The striking office building at the western end of Sandtorkai consists of a single block with horizontal strip windows resting on lightly coloured balustrades. Eye-catching diagonal support struts accentuate the building's façade. Straying from the august style of Hamburg architecture, the building reflects the more nonchalant manner of its Rhenish author.

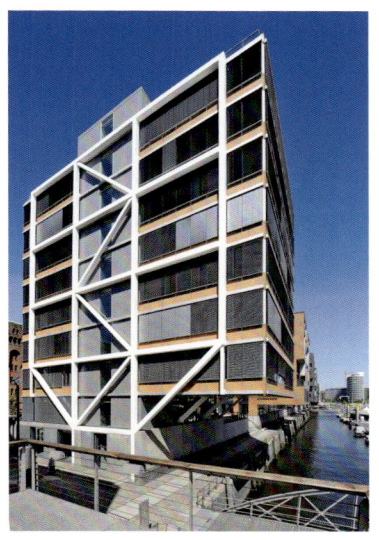

1

2

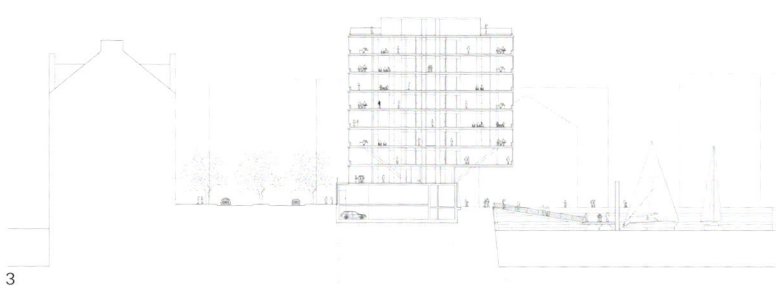

3

1+2 Gesamtansichten von Westen und Süden: Das Haus bildet den Auftakt des neuen Sandtorkais im Westen. Overall views from the west and south: the building marks the beginning of the new Sandtorkai in the west. **3** Schnitt Sectional drawing

Ocean's End
Büro- und Wohnhaus Mixed Use Building

Standort Location Am Sandtorkai 66 **Architekten Architects** BLK2 Böge Lindner K2 Architekten, Hamburg **Bauherr Client** PLUS BAU Projektentwicklungs GmbH **Wettbewerb Competition** 2001 **Bauzeit Date built** 2003–04 **Bruttogeschossfläche Gross floor area** 6710 qm (sqm)

Dem Teilquartier »Am Sandtorkai« mit seinen fünf Wohn- und drei Bürogebäuden ist die Rolle des neuen Gelenkstücks zwischen der Speicherstadt und dem Sandtorhafen zugewachsen, es ist die Inszenierung des stadtseitigen Auftakts der Hafencity zur westlichen Speicherstadt. Obwohl für das ganze Ensemble vornehmlich Rottöne in der Fassade gefordert waren, wurden Ausnahmen wie ein warmer Gelbklinker und korrekt verarbeiteter Sichtbeton für diese kubische Architektur in einer Mischung aus Loos'schem Raumplan und Rietveld'scher Klarheit zugelassen (besonders an der Wasserseite für die Balkone und Fensterbänder der Splitlevel-Loftwohnungen). Konstruktiv ist das Haus vorbildlich, weil das gesamte Bauwerk als offenes räumliches Tragwerk konzipiert wurde – mit der Folge, dass jederzeit Trennwände eingezogen oder entfernt werden können.

Comprised of just five residential buildings and three office blocks, "Am Sandtorkai" lies between the Speicherstadt and Sandtorhafen, forming a natural interface between the Hafencity and the Speicherstadt developments. While red tones dominate the ensemble's façades, they are set off by the use of warm yellow clinker bricks and architectural concrete in a design that blends the spatial planning of Adolf Loos with the clear lines of Gerrit Rietveld (particularly facing towards the water where the balconies and window strips of the split level residential lofts are located). The building's exemplary design utilises an open space frame, allowing for the uncomplicated insertion and removal of partition walls.

1

2

3

1 Loos oder Rietveld – Reminiszenzen an die Frühmoderne vor der Kulisse der Speicher-stadt Loos or Rietveld – reminiscences of early modernism against the backdrop of the Speicherstadt **2** Wohnraum mit Galerie Living room with gallery **3** Grundriss 5. OG Floor plan of 5th storey

H₂O
Büro- und Wohnhaus Mixed Use Building

Standort Location Am Sandtorkai 64 **Architekten Architects** Spengler Wiescholek Architekten und Stadtplaner, Hamburg **Bauherr Client** Wernst Immobilien AG **Wettbewerb Competition** 2001/02 **Bauzeit Date built** 2002–05 **Bruttogeschossfläche Gross floor area** 5300 qm (sqm)

Wohnen und Arbeiten unter einem (Flach-)Dach: Die Wohnungen befinden sich in einem Ziegelkörper mit feiner Lochfassade, die Büros hinter einer gläsernen Hülle mit markanten Schrägstützen. Der Eingangsbereich des Hauses ist zweigeschossig, der Luftraum wird durch eine gläserne Brücke durchstoßen, die die obere Ebene der Halle und den oberen Eingang verbindet, der wegen des möglichen Hochwassers zusätzlich zu dem auf Straßenniveau liegenden Haupteingang erforderlich ist. Die Wohngrundrisse wurden weitgehend frei von den Zwängen des Bürorasters und dessen technischen Anforderungen entworfen und erhielten u.a. durch Erker an der Ost- und Westseite freien Wasserblick. Ernste Marginalie: Dieses Niedrigenergiehaus sollte in Shanghai für die Expo 2010 als nachhaltiges Vorbild und Hamburger Pavillon noch einmal gebaut werden. China war im Expo-Stress nicht in der Lage, deutsche Standards zu erreichen. Es lebe das Original!

Residential and office space under a single (flat) roof: the apartments are housed in a brickwork structure with a fine perforated façade, while the offices are enclosed within a glass exterior mounted on prominent diagonal support struts. The lobby spans two storeys, with a glass bridge cutting across the open area and connecting the upper level with the upper entrance, complementing the entrance at street level and providing alternative access in case of flooding. Unfettered by the technical requirements of the building's office facilities, the residential tower trumps with bay windows on the eastern and western faces affording tenants magnificent views of the water. A copy of this low-energy design was to have housed the Hamburg Pavilion at the 2010 Shanghai Expo, but the project went off the rails when China, scrambling to complete an avalanche of Expo projects, was unable to fulfil German engineering standards. All the more reason to celebrate the prototype!

1

2   3

1 Wohnen und Arbeiten finden hier hinter unterschiedlichen Fassaden Platz, zum Beispiel im rechten Flügel unten. Living and office space is housed behind different façades, e.g. in the lower right wing. **2** Bürogrundriss 3. OG Office floor plan, 3rd storey **3** Wohngrundriss 6. OG Residential floor plan, 6th storey

Dock 4
Büro- und Wohnhaus Mixed Use Building

Standort Location Am Sandtorkai 62 **Architekten Architects** ASP Schweger + Partner, Hamburg **Bauherr Client** Bau-Verein zu Hamburg AG **Wettbewerb Competition** 2001 **Bauzeit Date built** 2003/04 **Bruttogeschossfläche Gross floor area** 5000 qm (sqm)

Auch bei diesem Beispiel darf man von dem gelungenen Versuch sprechen, eine moderne Variante des historischen Hamburger Speicherhauses, das auch zu Wohnzwecken genutzt wurde, neu zu erfinden: Im Prinzip ist es ein Misch-bauwerk. 18 Wohnungen wurden im Südflügel untergebracht. Die Grund-risse darf man konventionell nennen, aber wegen der neutralen Zuschnitte sind sie gut zu nutzen: In den größeren Wohnungen sind Essräume über gro-ße Schiebetüren mit den Wohnräumen verbunden. Typologisch fällt auch hier das U im Grundriss auf (Es wird in der ganzen Reihe thematisiert und variiert, mit dieser Form können Belichtung und Ausblick auf das Wasser vergrößert werden). Was die Kleiderordnung be-trifft: Dock 4 ist als hanseatisch zurück-haltend einzustufen.

Hamburg's maritime heritage is revisited in this accomplished modern interpreta-tion of northern German warehouse architecture. Essentially a mixed-use development, the structure houses 18 apartments in its south wing. While its floor plan is conventional, the neutral layout provides enhanced functional-ity, with large sliding doors connecting the dining and living rooms in the more spacious apartments. The building's U-shape is replicated with variations across the entire row, improving light-ing conditions and affording occupants extensive views of the water. As for the façade, Dock 4 is a succinct example of North German understatement.

1

2

3

1 Wohnen mit Hafenblick Harbourview living **2** Grundriss EG und 3. OG Floor plan, ground floor and 3rd storey **3** Südfassade Southern façade

China Shipping
Bürohaus Office Building

Standort Location Am Sandtorkai 60 **Architekten Architects** BRT Architekten LLP
Bothe Richter Teherani, Hamburg **Bauherr Client** Aug. Prien Immobilien, Gesellschaft
für Projektentwicklung mbH, Hamburg **Wettbewerb Competition** 2001 **Bauzeit Date
built** 2004–05 **Bruttogeschossfläche Gross floor area** 6300 qm (sqm)

Oft sind es die kleinen Tricks, die große
Wirkung zeigen. Wie hier, wo die laszi-
ve Art, mit der dieser »Hauscontainer«
an ein rostrotes Stahlgerüst gehängt
scheint, auf den Ort hinweist: Hier war
Hafengebiet. Diese Geste korrespon-
diert sehr schön mit dem maroden
Charme des gegenüber gelegenen historischen Kesselhauses. Zwei Etagen
wurden herausgeschoben und erinnern
an Kranbrücken oder Helgen – nach dem
Gruner + Jahr-Gebäude (Steidle/Kiess-
ler, vgl. S. 226) ist hier ein weiteres starkes Bauwerk entstanden, das hanseatische Assoziationen und Erinnerungen
weckt. Und für die Qualität des Sandtorkais steht die Erkenntnis: Die Architektur der Hafencity braucht Individu-
alisten, die teamfähig sind. Deswegen
gehört dieses Ensemble zu den besseren der Hafencity.

In architecture, it's often the little tricks
that pack the biggest punch. In a rever-
ential nod to the area's maritime past,
this "container building" appears to
hang in space from a rust-red steel
frame. This gesture resonates with the
dilapidated charm of the historical boiler
house (Kesselhaus) opposite. Following
in the footsteps of the Gruner + Jahr
building (Steidle/Kiessler, cf. p. 226),
two floors protrude from the statuesque
crane bridges, presenting a unque vision of Hanseatic style and tradition.
One of Hafencity's most accomplished
ensembles, this design demonstrates
that architectural excellence is the stuff
of individualists with a flair for team-
work.

1

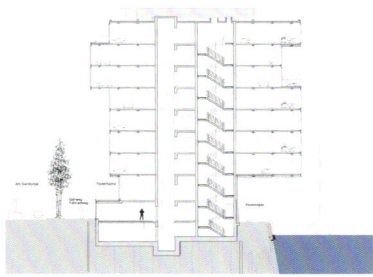

2

1 Motiv aus dem Containerhafen auf der anderen Elbseite: Stahl gestapelt oder gehängt Image from the container port on the opposite side of the Elbe: stacked and overhanging steel **2** Schnitt Sectional drawing

Harbour Cube
Büro- und Wohnhaus Mixed Use Building

Standort Location Am Sandtorkai 58 **Architekt Architect** Marc-Olivier Mathez, Hamburg **Bauherr Client** Cantina Bau & Boden Projektentwicklung GmbH zusammen mit and HTG Hoch- und Tiefbau Gadebusch GmbH **Wettbewerb Competition** 200ʹ **Bauzeit Date built** 2004–05 **Bruttogeschossfläche Gross floor area** 5400 qm (sqm)

In den ersten Jahren der Hafencity, noch zwischen Sandgruben und Baukränen, wurde es zum Treppenwitz: Die unverputzten Kohlebrand-Steine erweckten den Eindruck, dass – wie in südlichen Teilen Europas üblich – das Haus noch unvollendet sei und, noch ein bis zwei Jahre zum Austrocknen verurteilt, auf den endgültigen weißen Putz warten müsse. Der Eindruck täuscht. Diese Lösung ist endgültig und in ihrer geometrischen – starken und überzeugenden – Plastizität aus einem Material, das häufig für die Hintermauerung gebraucht wird, und in einer Rohheit, die an den Brutalismus der 1950er Jahre gemahnt, das eigenwilligste Gebäude der Reihe. So sorgt es immer noch für eine gewisse Kritik bei Besuchern, die nicht wissen, dass man dieses Haus als eine Hommage an Gustav Oelsners plastische Ziegelfassaden in Bahrenfeld sehen kann.

In the days when construction cranes still dominated Hafencity's skyline, this building was something of a running gag: its raw coal-fired brickwork lent the structure all the charm of a building site in southern Europe—condemned to dry out in the sun for a year or two while awaiting its finishing touches. But looks can be so deceiving. The building's rugged exterior is here to stay. Its strong geometric lines and compellingly solid form lend it a rawness that evokes associations with the Brutalist school of the 1950s, making it the most idiosyncratic structure in its row. Today, visitors continue to debate the building's pros and cons, largely unaware that it represents an homage to Gustav Oelsner's three-dimensional brick façades in Bahrenfeld.

1

2

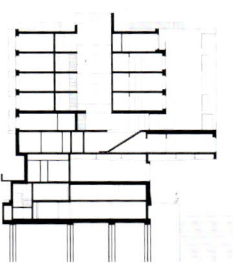

3

1 Unverputzte Plastik mit guter Ausstrahlung Sculptural plasticity with striking appeal
2 Eingangshalle Foyer **3** Schnitt Sectional drawing

Harbour-Hall
Büro- und Wohnhaus Mixed Use Building

Standort Location Am Sandtorkai 56 **Architekten Architects** APB Architekten, Hamburg **Bauherr Client** DDS Unternehmen für Eigenheim- und Wohnungsbau GmbH **Wettbewerb Competition** 2001 **Bauzeit Date built** 2004–05 **Bruttogeschossfläche Gross floor area** 5888 qm (sqm)

Alle Wohnhäuser am Sandtorkai unterlaufen auf ihre jeweils eigene Weise sensibel die vielen anderen Hamburger Geschäftshäusern verordnete Kleiderordnung, den üblichen Backsteinlook. Die Fassaden der Harbour-Hall wirken sogar ausgesprochen mediterran und scheinen immer in Bewegung, weil die Ziegelwände mit Holzschiebeelementen für den Sonnenschutz ausgestattet wurden. Das erinnert an Südeuropa, generiert aber immer wieder neue Wandbilder. Zwei Wohnflügel nehmen die Eingangs- und Zugangshalle in die Mitte, womit das Gebäude hervorragend den vorgegebenen U-förmigen Hausgrundriss entwickelt. Erker und vertikale Fensterschlitze führen zusätzliches Licht von der Halle in die Wohnungen. Schöne Besonderheit am Rand: Die fragilen Stützen sind schräg in den Kaimauerbestand gesetzt. Das wirkt doch sehr dynamisch.

The residential buildings on Sandtorkai represent a subtle break with the brickwork that has defined Hamburg's traditional commercial buildings. There is something distinctly Mediterranean about the Harbour-Hall's façade, where adjustable wooden sunshades mounted on brickwork create an impression of constant motion. More than just an allusion to Southern European architecture, the façade's shifting texture generates an endless series of images. Following in the footsteps of its predecessor, the U-shaped structure is comprised of two residential wings flanking a central lobby. Bay windows and vertical window slits direct additional light to the apartments from the lobby, while fragile struts extending at an angle from the quay wall lend the building a dynamic aspect.

1

2

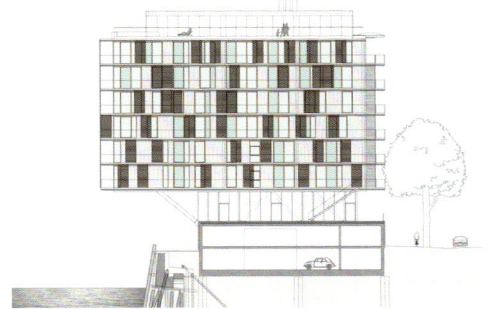

3

1 Zwei Wohnflügel nehmen die Eingangshalle in ihre Mitte. Two residential wings flank the central lobby. **2** Erker und vertikale Fensterschlitze führen zusätzliches Licht von der Halle in die Wohnungen. Bay windows and vertical window slits direct additional light to the apartments from the lobby. **3** Schnitt/Ansicht Sectional drawing/view

Bankhaus Wölbern
Banking and Commercial Building

Standort Location Am Sandtorkai 54 **Architekten Architects** Störmer Murphy and Partners, Hamburg **Bauherr Client** Bayern-Versicherung, Lebensversicherung AG **Wettbewerb Competition** 2002 **Bauzeit Date built** 2003–05 **Bruttogeschossfläche Gross floor area** 4300 qm (sqm)

Das Bank- und Geschäftshaus Wölbern besetzt aus Richtung Osten gesehen die Poolposition der Hausreihe. Dabei gelingt es, einer heute gängigen Bankhausarchitektur aus viel Glas durch rötliche Einfärbung der Betonbrüstungen etwas entgegenzusetzen, das zum Auftritt der Speicherstadt im Speziellen und Hamburgs im Allgemeinen passt. Das Gebäude entwickelt dabei Vielfalt, ja, fast ein janusköpfiges Erscheinungsbild: Nach Westen unterstreichen die horizontalen Betonbänder den eleganten, weil schwebenden Charakter, im Osten überzeugt eine klassische Lochfassade. Weit in die Magellan-Terrassen hereinragend, entstand mit dem Bankhaus auch ein Standort für ein Restaurant im öffentlichen Stadtraum des Sandtorhafens.

Viewed from the east, the Bankhaus Wölbern takes pole position in this row. The building's glass elements, really of contemporary bank architecture, are counterbalanced by the red tone of the concrete balustrades, resulting in a visual design that reflects the aesthetics of both Hafencity in particular and Hamburg in general. Like the Roman god Janus, this multifaceted design looks ahead to the future while celebrating the past: to the west, horizontal concrete ribbons underscore the building's elegant aura of weightlessness, while a classical perforated façade faces eastward. Extending far into the Magellan Terraces, the building is also home to a restaurant along Sandtorhafen.

1

2

3

1 Horizontale Bänder im Westen Horizontal ribbons to the west **2** Lochfassade nach Osten Perforated façade facing eastward **3** Öffnung zu den Magellan-Terrassen mit Restaurant und Bar Opening into the Magellan Terraces with restaurant and bar

Ponton mit Traditionsschiffhafen
Traditional Ship Harbour Pontoons

Standort Location Sandtorhafen **Architekten Architects** EMBT Arquitectes Associats, Barcelona **Bauherr Client** HafenCity Hamburg GmbH **Wettbewerb Competition** 2002 **Bauzeit Date built** 2007–08 **Bruttogeschossfläche Gross floor area** 5600 qm (sqm)

Das Sandtorhafenbecken war das erste, dessen Wasserflächen in das vorbildliche Freiraum- und Freizeitkonzept der Hafencity einbezogen wurden. Acht geschwungene Schwimmpontons bilden den Kern eines Traditionsschiffhafens und erschließen dem Besucher buchstäblich neue Perspektiven, weil man hier, fast auf Höhe des Wasserspiegels stehend, die neuen Hafencity-Bauwerke anders erlebt als von den Promenaden aus. Gewaltig türmt sich am westlichen Ende die Elbphilharmonie als Kulisse in den Himmel, die Pontons sind die Bühnen, und es bleibt unklar, wer die Hauptdarsteller sind – die Menschen oder die Schiffe. Ehemalige Landungsbrücken aus dem Hafen führen (unter anderem von den Magellan-Terrassen) hinunter zu den speziell für diesen Hafen gefertigten Pontons. Sie heben und senken sich mit den Gezeiten, gewähren so stets direkten Zugang und Nähe zum Wasser – und bieten einen festen Liegeplatz für rund zwanzig alte Dampfer und Segler.

Sandtorhafen was the first harbour basin to feature in Hafencity's pioneering recreational usage plan. Eight gently curved pontoons traverse the historical harbour basin, enabling visitors to appreciate Hafencity's architecture from a water-level perspective. To the west, the towering Elbphilharmonie forms a postcard-perfect backdrop. While the pontoons form the stage in this visual drama, it is as yet unclear who will play the lead role—people or ships. Gangways once used to unload ships now descend from the Magellan Terraces (to name just one point of access) to the basin's custom-built pontoons. Rising and falling with the tides, the pontoons provide easy access to the water and a safe haven for approximately twenty historical steamships and yachts.

1

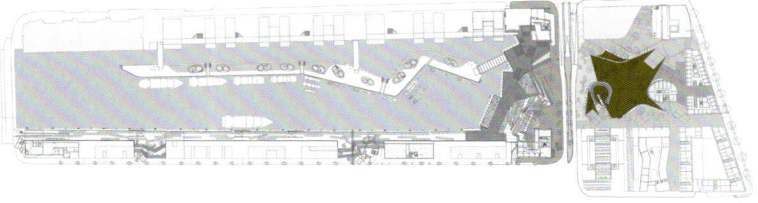

2

1 Blick nach Osten zum Sandtorpark View to Sandtorpark development towards the east
2 Übersichtsplan: Rechts ist der Übergang zu den Magellan-Terrassen zu sehen, hinter der Straße liegt der Sandtorpark. Layout plan: on the right is the transition to the Magellan Terraces; Sandtor Park is located behind the street.

Magellan-Terrassen
Magellan Terraces

Standort Location Sandtorhafen **Architekten Architects** EMBT Arquitectes Associats, Barcelona **Bauherr Client** HafenCity Hamburg GmbH, Sondervermögen Stadt und Hafen **Wettbewerb Competition** 2002 **Bauzeit Date built** 2004–05 **Bruttogeschossfläche Gross floor area** 5000 qm (sqm)

Kunstvoll gestalteten die Planer ein Wechselspiel von Land und Wasser, denn die strengen kubischen Bauwerke am Sandtorkai stehen jetzt im spielerischen Kontrast zu einer schwungvollen Terrassenlandschaft: mit hellen Steinplatten, aber herausgefordert durch Applikationen aus Backstein. Hier ist Hamburg! Und wie es das raue Hamburger Winterklima manchmal erfordert, mit eisbrechenden Strukturen an den neuen Kaimauern am Kopf des Sandtorhafens. Die berechtigte Befürchtung, dass Hamburger Wetter nicht immer gütig sind, wird durch poetische Inszenierungen an den Sommertagen vergessen gemacht: Platzleuchten sind so fantasievoll gestaltet, dass man sie als flüchtige Dreiecke von Segelbooten am fernen Horizont interpretieren könnte! Oben am Straßenrand steht ein auffälliger Kubus, mit einem Modell im Maßstab 1:10 des großen Saals der Elbphilharmonie (Architektur: Studio Andreas Heller).

Sandtorkai is the setting for an accomplished dialogue between land and water. The quadratic form of the buildings positioned along the quay contrasts playfully with the sweeping lines of the terraces, where lighter tilework is set off by brickwork details. This could only be in Hamburg! Special icebreakers mounted on the quay walls at the mouth of the harbour basin testify to the bitterly cold northern winters that afflict the city from time to time. But come the summer, Hamburg's Arctic season is soon forgotten thanks to the harbour's delightful outdoor light installations, which could easily be mistaken for the distant sails of approaching yachts. Meanwhile, an eye-catching cube at street level is home to a 1:10 scale model of the Elbphilharmonie's Grand Concert Hall (Architecture: Studio Andreas Heller).

1

2

3

1 Blick auf die Magellan-Terrassen mit dem Ensemble der Häuser am Kaiserkai View of the Magellan Terraces with the ensemble of buildings on Kaiserkai **2** Detail mit Backsteinapplikationen Brickwork detail **3** Temporärer Pavillon mit dem Modell der Elbphilharmonie Temporary pavilion with Elbphilharmonie model

Marco-Polo-Terrassen
Marco Polo Terraces

Standort Location Kleiner Grasbrook **Architekten Architects** EMBT Arquitectes Asso-ciats, Barcelona **Bauherr Client** HafenCity Hamburg GmbH, Sondervermögen Stadt und Hafen **Wettbewerb Competition** 2002 **Bauzeit Date built** 2006–07 **Bruttogeschoss-fläche Gross floor area** 6400 qm (sqm)

Andere Akzente als die von weitgehend harten Oberflächen geprägten Magel-lan-Terrassen setzen die Marco-Polo-Terrassen, die im Jahr 2007 die Hafen-landschaft ergänzten: Weich und grün – Grasinseln mit Holzdecks laden hier zum Sitzen, Liegen und Verweilen ein. Schatten oder Regenschutz bieten Am-berbäume, Sumpfzypressen und Wei-den. 6400 Quadratmeter misst diese Mischung aus Park und Platz, mit Aus-sichten auf Elbe und Grasbrookhafen, auf die Phalanx der neuen Wohnhäuser am Kaiserkai, auf die »Bauskulpturen« von Unilever und Marco Polo Tower sowie auf Land und Wasser, wo eine moderne Sportboot-Marina geplant ist. Früher haben sich solche vielfältigen Orte ganz langsam als Spiegel vorhan-dener Handelsströme und Verkehrs-knoten gebildet. Dieser neue Ort ist von Anfang an generalstabsmäßig geplant – als ein Treffpunkt für Stadtflaneure, um Lust zu machen auf Stadt und ihre Frei-räume. Das Konzept geht auf!

Created in 2007, the Marco Polo Ter-races form a fetching contrast to the hard surfaces of the Magellan Terraces. Here soft grassy knolls with wooden decks invite visitors to relax and unwind in the sun. Willows, sweet gums, and bald cypresses dotted about the Ter-races offer shade and protection from the occasional sun shower. Extending across 6,400 square metres, the Ter-races combine the lush greenery of park landscapes with the urban flair of the plaza. Views of the Elbe and nearby Grasbrookhafen are complemented by a phalanx of new residential buildings on Kaiserkai and the sculptural forms of the Unilever Building and the Marco Polo Tower. To top it off, planning has already begun for a new pleasure craft marina. In the past, diverse urban envi-ronments tended to develop slowly over time around trade and transport hubs. This site will emerge within a few years as a verdant meeting place with urban flair for all.

1

2

1 Park und Platz zugleich: die am Marco Polo Tower gelegenen Marco-Polo-Terrassen
Park and plaza at once: the Marco Polo Terraces at the Marco Polo Tower **2** Rasen
und Holzdecks im Wechsel; EMBT Architekten entwarfen hier auch ein Restaurantgebäude (vgl. S. 95). Alternating grassy spots and wooden decks, EMBT Architekten
also designed a restaurant pavilion here (cf. p. 95).

Pantaenius House
Bürogebäude Office Building

Standort Location Großer Grasbrook 10 **Architekten Architects** David Chipperfield Architects, London/Berlin **Bauherr Client** Sandtor GmbH **Wettbewerb Competition** 2002 **Bauzeit Date built** 2002–05 **Bruttogeschossfläche Gross floor area** 7200 qm (sqm)

Er galt zunächst als schwächerer »Chipperfield«-Entwurf. Hatte der Meister ein B- oder C-Team angesetzt? Mitnichten, wie bei all seinen Bauten muss man genauer hinschauen, um Qualitäten in der Proportionierung zu sichten, um zu erkennen, wie ein einfacher zu einem guten Bau geworden ist. Mit jedem fertiggestellten Bauwerk im Quartier gewann dieses Geschäftshaus an Achtung, Qualität und Wirkung: als Mitspieler einer Straße – ganz wie früher – und Vorbild für viele ein wenig überdrehte Nachbarn: weil er ruhig geblieben ist. Bei bestimmten sonnigen Wettersituationen erwacht die helle Klinkerfassade zum Leben und wird zur echten Herausforderung der Architekturkritik: Weniger ist hier mehr, besonders an der Seite zum Hafenbecken lohnt die Begutachtung, wo die dunklen Fensterbänder ganz sinnig tief in der hellen Wand das Schweben lernen ...

Initially seen as the lesser of David Chipperfield's designs, this building caused pundits to wonder whether the master had opted to field his B-team. But here, as always, the genius is in the detail. It takes a patient eye to recognise the quality of the building's subtle proportions and intelligent design. The completion of nearby structures has brought both to the fore, and this building now commands the respect it deserves. Its reserved style has made it integral to the street's wider impact and sets an example to some of its more exuberant neighbours. On sunny days its light clinker brick façade comes to life, throwing down the gauntlet to critics: less is more. The contrast between the dark band of sunken windows and the light surface of the wall makes the windows appear almost weightless.

1

2

3

1+2 Einfache Struktur, jedoch mit überzeugender Detailqualität: Pantaenius House als östlicher Auftakt zum Kaiserkai Simple structure with powerful details: Pantaenius House marks the eastern end of Kaiserkai. **3** Übersicht des Kaiserkais mit Zeilenbebauung (Nordseite) und Hofbildung (Südseite) Layout plan of Kaiserkai with ribbon development (northern side) and courtyards (southern side)

Am Kaiserkai 4–8
Wohn-und Geschäftshaus Mixed Use Building

Standort Location Am Kaiserkai 4–8 **Architekten Architects** Marc-Olivier Mathez (Lph 1–5), Mevius Mörker Architekten (Lph 1–9), Hamburg **Bauherr Client** Bauherrengemeinschaft Dalmannkai Fläche 5 GbR c/o Pfadt & Pfadt Immobilien GmbH & Co. **Wettbewerb Competition** 2006 **Bauzeit Date built** 2006–07 **Bruttogeschossfläche Gross floor area** 5500 qm (sqm)

Diesem Doppel-Ensemble gelingt es, mit einer ausgefeilten Grundrisstypologie auf die Beziehung von Wohnen und Wasser einzugehen. Besonders reizvoll ist ein durchlaufendes Deck, das die beiden Häuser auf der Höhe des ersten Obergeschosses miteinander verbindet. Wie ein Balkon bietet es Ausblicke auf die Magellan-Terrassen und auf die Traditionsschiffe. Die Wohnungen sind zum Teil über zwei Ebenen angelegt und großflächig verglast. Blick und Balkone bleiben den Bewohnern vorbehalten, aber auch unten auf der Straße lohnt das Verweilen mit dem Blick auf den Kaiserkai in Richtung Elbphilharmonie. Gut sichtbar ist das Hafencity-Prinzip eines hohen Erdgeschosses, das innen jeweils mit einer Galerieebene multifunktional zu nutzen ist. Bleibt zu hoffen, dass die vielen kleinen Läden eine Keimzelle für langfristigen urbanen Einzelhandel sind.

The elaborate floor plan of this two-piece ensemble presents a vision of waterside living that has few peers. A continuous deck connecting the two buildings on the first storey adds a charming feature, and offers generous views of the Magellan Terraces and the nearby historical ships. Some of the apartments, which feature extensive glazing, are split across two storeys, and while the balcony views are reserved for tenants, at street level visitors enjoy views of Kaiserkai and the Elbphilharmonie. Spacious ground floors and high ceilings are par for the course in Hafencity; here mezzanine galleries take things one step further and allow for multiple uses. And if all goes according to plan, the small shops that have already opened here will be the beginning of a bustling retail cluster.

1

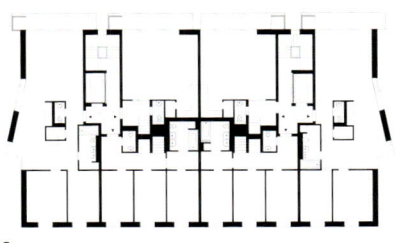

2

3

1 Die beiden Hausteile mit 42 Wohnungen der Baugemeinschaft (links Mathez, rechts Mevius Mörker) sind über ein durchlaufendes Deck miteinander verbunden.
The two parts of the building with 42 apartments (left Mathez, right Mevius Mörker Architekten) are connected by a continuous deck. **2** Grundriss 4. OG (Mathez) Floor plan, 4th storey (Mathez) **3** Ansicht vom Kaiserkai View from Kaiserkai

Oval und Kontor am Kaiserkai
Residential Tower and Office Building

Standort Location Am Kaiserkai 10–12 **Architekten Architects** ingenhoven architects, Düsseldorf **Bauherr Client** d.quai GmbH c/o imetas property services GmbH, Hamburg **Wettbewerb Competition** 2002 **Bauzeit Date built** 2006–08 **Bruttogeschossfläche Gross floor area** Oval: 5500 qm (sqm), Kontor: 6600 qm (sqm)

Der ovale Wohnturm überragt die übrige Zeile am Kaiserkai und bildet einen provokanten Kontrapunkt zur braven Riegelbebauung in direkter Nachbarschaft. Sehr gut sichtbar ist »das Runde im Eckigen« auch von der Altstadt aus, als Leuchtturm eines architektonischen Aufbruchs. Auf elf Etagen bieten lichtdurchflutete Wohnungen einen privilegierten Ausblick über die Hafencity, die Speicherstadt, die Elbe und die Hamburger Innenstadt. Die Einheiten sind zwischen 58 und 300 Quadratmeter groß. In den unteren Geschossen sind gewerbliche Nutzungen erwünscht. Dieser Turm beweist im Detail die Qualität des Masterplans, der an wichtigen Orten der Hafencity solche Hingucker gefordert hat, die auch von der Speicher- und Innenstadt oder anderen Nachbarbereichen der Hafencity aus gut sichtbar sein sollen. Zur Anlage gehört ein straßenbegleitender Riegelbau.

This oval-shaped apartment tower looms above Kaiserkai, forming a provocative counterpoint to the more conventional block buildings in the neighbourhood. A beacon of architectural transformation, its eye-catching curved form is easy to make out from Hamburg's Altstadt. Standing eleven storeys tall, the building trumps with bright, airy apartments and stunning views of Hafencity, the Speicherstadt, Elbe and city centre. Individual units range in size from 58 to 300 square metres. The lower floors will be dedicated to commercial use. The tower highlights the strength of the Master Plan, which called for the construction of eye-catching features at key sites that would be visible from the Speicherstadt, city centre, and other parts of Hafencity. A block building that runs parallel to the street rounds off this world-class ensemble design.

1

2

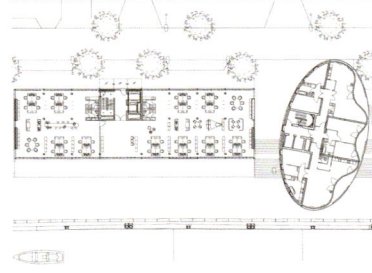

3

1 Eine der kleineren Landmarken in der westlichen Hafencity: Wohnturm und Büro-
riegel One of the smaller landmarks in western Hafencity: residential tower and office
block **2** Die aufgeständerte ellipsoide Konstruktion ruht auf kräftigen Betonscheiben.
The elevated ellipsoidal structure rests on strong concrete slabs. **3** Grundriss OG Floor
plan, upper floors

home4
Wohn- und Geschäftshaus Mixed Use Building

Standort Location Am Kaiserkai 26/28 **Architekten Architects** BRT Architekten LLP Bothe Richter Teherani, Hamburg **Bauherr Client** Home 4 Hamburg GmbH & Co. KG **Bauzeit Date built** 2007–08 **Bruttogeschossfläche Gross floor area** 4460 qm (sqm)

home4 ist ein offenes Bausystem, das individuell jedem Standort und den konkreten Bedürfnissen der Nutzer angepasst werden kann – dieses Wohn- und Geschäftshaus fungiert als Modellhaus. Merkmale: lichtdurchflutete Räume mit Höhen von mindestens 2,80 Metern, eine geschosshohe Verglasung mit großformatigen Terrassentüren, die für einen fließenden Übergang vom Innenraum zum großzügigen privaten Außenraum sorgen. Der Nutzer entscheidet nach seinen individuellen Bedürfnissen und dem ihm zur Verfügung stehenden Budget: lieber mehr Raum? Dafür ein einfacherer Ausbau? Basisversion oder Sondermodell? Großzügige, nutzungsneutrale Grundrisse bieten eine hohe Nutzungsflexibilität. Klassisch, modern oder vielleicht mediterran eingerichtet – die Loftwohnung von heute könnte schon morgen in eine Vier-Zimmer-Wohnung verwandelt werden. home4 entwickelt sich jeweils flexibel mit.

home4 is an open building system which can be configured to meet the demands of each location and user. This dual-use office and residential building also functions as a show-house. The building features bright rooms with natural lighting and a minimum ceiling height of 2.8 metres. Floor-to-ceiling glazing and large French windows make for a natural flow between the interior and the building's spacious outdoor areas. Users can customise their apartments according to their needs and budgets: More room? Exclusive furnishings? Standard or premium designs? Whatever your preferences, the spacious and neutral floor plans ensure a high degree of flexibility. home4 is designed to adapt to changing needs, and transforming a Mediterranean style loft into a four-room apartment is as easy as 1-2-3.

1

2

3

1 Straßenseite mit beispielhafter Umsetzung hoher Erdgeschosszonen für hybride Nutzungen Street side with exemplary implementation of higher ground-floor zones for hybrid uses 2 Ansicht nach Norden mit Blick auf den Traditionshafen View to the north overlooking the traditional ship harbour 3 Grundrisse 3. OG und 4. OG Floor plans, 3rd and 4th storeys

ElbElysium
Seniorenwohnen Retirement Residence

Standort Location Am Kaiserkai 42–46 **Architekten Architects** BLK2 Böge Lindner K2 Architekten, Hamburg **Bauherr Client** PLUS BAU Kaiserkai GmbH, Hamburg **Wettbewerb Competition** 2005 **Bauzeit Date built** 2007–09 **Bruttogeschossfläche Gross floor area** 10870 qm (sqm)

Einfach komponiert: zwei Quader, einer hoch-, der andere quergestellt – mit Fassaden, die durch einen hohen Glasanteil geprägt werden (Hafenbeckenseite). Mehr braucht es nicht für ein gescheites Haus, das auf die Bedürfnisse von Senioren zugeschnitten ist, die im Alter aktives Stadtleben bevorzugen. Dazu gehören flexible Wohnungstypologien mit zwei oder drei Zimmern. Begleitende Dienstleistungen im Erdgeschoss sollen das Angebot abrunden – zum Beispiel ein Café, ausgewählte Fachgeschäfte, Arztpraxen, eine Apotheke oder Wellness. Insgesamt sind etwa siebzig Wohnungen entstanden, teils zur Miete, teils zum Kauf. Betreiber der Mietwohnungen ist die diakonische Martha Stiftung, die als modernes Dienstleistungsunternehmen im Bereich Sozial- und Gesundheitswesen auftritt.

This simple composition is comprised of two cuboid forms with extensive glazing towards the harbour basin—one extends into the vertical plane, while the other is positioned horizontally. That's all it takes to create an intelligent building especially tailored to the needs of senior citizens who want to lead an active life in an urban environment. The buildings feature two- and three-room apartments with flexible layouts. A range of service outlets on the ground floor, including a café, shops, medical practices, a pharmacy and spa services, will complete the picture. The complex contains approximately seventy apartments, with a mix of rental and owner-occupied apartments. The rental apartments are owned and run by the Martha Stiftung, a healthcare and social welfare foundation affiliated to the Lutheran Church.

1

2

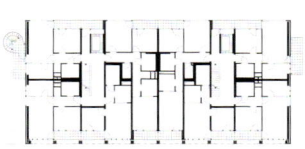

3

1 Wasserseite des Sandtorhafens Sandtorhafen facing towards the water **2** Fantasievoll ausgebildet: Balkone und Loggien am Kaiserkai Creatively designed: balconies
and loggias on Kaiserkai **3** Grundriss 1. OG: flexible Wohnungstypologien mit zwei oder
drei Zimmern Floor plan, 1st storey: flexible apartment types with two or three rooms

Kai 12
Wohn- und Geschäftshaus Mixed Use Building

Standort Location Am Kaiserkai 30 **Architekten Architects** nps tchoban voss | Architektur und Städtebau **Bauherr Client** Baugemeinschaft Kai 12 GbR c/o Buegerbau AG
Bauzeit Date built 2007 **Bruttogeschossfläche Gross floor area** 3700 qm (sqm)

Das Besondere hier: ein gemeinsames Treppenhaus, das durch ein Fenster zum Museumshafen geöffnet ist. Besucher und Bewohner erreichen es über eine fünf Meter hohe, repräsentative Eingangshalle, dort startet ein gläserner Aufzug in die Höhe – mit bewundernswertem Blick auf Museumsschiffe und Magellan-Terrassen. Das »Himmelsauge« über der Treppe verstärkt die lichte Wirkung des Raums. Zu den Wohnungen und ihrem Wohnwert: Die Raumhöhe liegt bei überzeugenden 2,85 Metern, große Loggien bieten Aus- und Überblick. Bodentiefe Fenster liefern Reminiszenzen an beliebte Altbauwohnungen wie in Eppendorf. Warme Farbtöne außen und innen sowie ein rhythmischer Wechsel zwischen Ziegel und anderen Materialien zeichnen das Haus außerdem aus.

This building trumps with a shared stairwell featuring a window opening onto Museumhafen. Access to the stairwell is through a spacious foyer with a spectacular five-metre-high ceiling, while a glass elevator offers splendid views of the museum ships docked near St. Pauli Landungsbrücken, and of the Magellan Terraces. A skylight positioned above the stairs augments the bright and airy atmosphere of the interior. As for the apartments, a ceiling height of 2.85 metres combined with spacious loggias makes for great views and a clean style. The floor-length windows are reminiscent of the stately fin-de-siècle apartments in Eppendorf, one of Hamburg's most fashionable residential districts. The building's warm exterior and interior colour schemes combine with the rhythmic play of brickwork and other materials in a distinctive visual design.

A.20

1

2

3

1 Ansicht von Norden: Jede Wohnung hat einen Blick auf das Wasser und den alten Hafen-kran. View from the north: each apartment has a view of the water and the old port crane.
2 Straßenseite: Wechsel zwischen hellem Ziegel und anderen Materialien Street side: inter-play of light brick and other materials **3** Wohnungsgrundrisse Apartment floor plans

Baugemeinschaft 2006
Residential Building

Standort Location Am Kaiserkai 56 **Architekten Architects** LOVE architecture and urbanism ZT GmbH, Graz / üNN–überNormalNull, Hamburg **Bauherr Client** Bürgerstadt AG Hamburg als Vertreterin der Baugemeinschaft on behalf of a cooperative housing group **Wettbewerb Competition** 2005 **Bauzeit Date built** 2006–08 **Bruttogeschossfläche Gross floor area** 3150 qm (sqm)

Wegen der provokant gerundeten Erker, Loggien und Balkone ist dieses Haus nicht aller Hamburger Liebling (Stiehlt es vielleicht der benachbarten Elbphilharmonie die Schau?). Tatsächlich erscheint es auf den ersten Blick wahlweise zu mondän oder zu schlicht, zu »retro« auf die 1970er Jahre angelegt. Architekturkritisch betrachtet erfüllt das Gebäude jedoch eine wichtige Aufgabe: Es beweist, dass inmitten der ansonsten treu eingehaltenen hamburgischen Bekleidungsvorschriften ein »Glitterjäckchen« tolerabel, ja, vielleicht sogar notwendig ist. Dank seiner Wohn- und Grundrissqualität nimmt das Innenleben des Hauses Bewohner wie Besucher gleichermaßen gefangen. Was außen vielleicht aus Gründen der städtebaulichen Zwänge nicht zugelassen war, durfte innen passgenau auf die jeweiligen Wohnwünsche zugeschnitten werden. (Nicht näher beschrieben: Am Kaiserkai 60–62 von Meurer Architekten, Frankfurt a.M.)

This building, with its provocatively contoured bay windows, loggias, and balconies, has divided commentators. While it has been lauded by some, others fear that it upstages the nearby Elbphilharmonie. At first glance, its design comes across as somewhat overwrought with a splash too much of 1970s "retro" chic. But critics have noted that the building fills an important gap in the Hafencity skyline—where nearly every other building has stood by Hamburg's traditional dress code, it takes a "dandy" to put the icing on the cake. With its intelligent residential design solutions and floor plans, this building has delighted both visitors and tenants alike. While urban planning restrictions did place constraints on the exterior, the apartments within are carefully tailored to meet the needs and wishes of each occupant. (Not described: Am Kaiserkai 60–62, Meurer Architekten, Frankfurt a.M.)

1

2

3

1+2 Das komplexe Innenleben sowie die Wohn- und Grundrissqualität teilen sich außen schwungvoll mit. The building's complex inner life and intelligent residential design solutions and floor plans are exuberantly evident from the outside. **3** Grundrisse EG und 1. OG Floor plans, ground floor and 1st storey

Johannes-Dalmann-Haus
Bürogebäude Office Building

Standort Location Am Kaiserkai 67–69 **Architekten Architects** Schenk + Waiblinger Architekten, Hamburg **Bauherr Client** Deutsche Immobilien AG, Hamburg **Wettbewerb Competition** 2003 **Bauzeit Date built** 2007–08 **Bruttogeschossfläche Gross floor area** 6300 qm (sqm)

Vis-à-vis der Elbphilharmonie – das ist ein vergoldeter Bauplatz, und hier wurde er entsprechend genutzt: Der metallisch glänzende Baukörper hat sich formal ganz aus der Bestimmung der Sichtlinien im Zusammenspiel mit den Nachbargebäuden ergeben und liefert dem Platz vor der Elbphilharmonie einen starken baulichen Rahmen. Die Fassaden in den Obergeschossen bestehen aus sägezahnartig versetzten Fensterelementen mit schmalen Alupaneelen und umlaufenden Deckenrandverkleidungen aus Alublechkassetten. Als Sonnenschutz dienen hochtransparente, außen liegende Edelstahl-Stablamellen, die bündig in die Fassaden integriert wurden. Soweit es geht, wechselt die Architektur Temperatur und Farbe der Fassade, mal wirkt sie geschlossen, mal offen. Weitere Häuser des westlichen Hofs: an der Straßenseite Nr. 63–67 von Bieling Architekten und quer zum Wasser Nr. 59–61 von Wacker Zeiger Architekten.

Designed to live up to its prominent location, this building is a nuanced response to the surrounding structures and lines of sight, and its gleaming metallic form provides a powerful architectural counterweight to the shimmering beauty of the Elbphilharmonie. The offset window elements adorning the façade on the upper floors are reminiscent of saw teeth and are embellished with delicate panels finished with sheet aluminium edge protectors. Sunshades with style: the highly transparent stainless steel louvres mounted on the building's exterior sit flush against the façade. The façade varies in temperature and colour, producing a mercurial countenance. Other buildings adjoining the western courtyard: at the roadside No. 63–67 (Bieling Architects) and, sitting at a right angle to the water: No. 59–61 (Wacker Zeiger Architekten).

1

2

3

1 Westfassade zur Elbphilharmonie und zum neuen Vorplatz des entstehenden Kulturtempels Western façade facing the Elbphilharmonie and the forecourt of the cultural flagship under construction 2 Lageplan Site plan 3 Sicht von der Uferpromenade (verdeckt dahinter: die Elbphilharmonie) View from the waterfront promenade (concealed behind it: the Elbphilharmonie)

Geschichte der Elbphilharmonie: Erste Adresse der Musikwelt

The Elbphilharmonie: New Diva of the Music World

Die neue Hamburger Elbphilharmonie steht auf dem Kaiserhöft – mitten im Strom an der westlichen Spitze des ersten Hamburger Dampfschiffhafens am Nordufer der Norderelbe. Es wurde 1875, passend zum Grundstück und zur Zeit, mit dem Kaiserspeicher von Johannes Dalmann, dem früheren Hamburger Wasserbaudirektor, bebaut: 19 000 Quadratmeter Speicherfläche in einem Baukörper, den man als Mischung aus Burg, Rathaus und Kirche beschreiben kann, in einer mittelalterlichen Bildsprache von Macht und Einfluss. Die Weltkriege hat der Speicher überstanden, allerdings eher als Mahnmal mit Turm und nur fragmentarisch stehengebliebenen Seitenwänden.

1963 wurden diese Reste gesprengt, obwohl eine Rekonstruktion möglich gewesen wäre. Aber die modernen Ansprüche eines Hafens standen dagegen und ebenso die Möglichkeit, einen viel größeren Speicher zu bauen. Der neue Kaispeicher A wurde mit 30 000 Quadratmetern Fläche von Werner Kallmorgen als großer, purer Backsteinquader in die

Hamburg's new Elbphilharmonie is located at Kaiserhöft, the site of Hamburg's earliest steamship docks. Like the Kaiserspeicher (designed by Hamburg's former Director of Waterway Engineering, Johannes Dalmann), the Kaiserhöft was built in 1875. With 19,000 square metres of warehouse facilities, the Kaiserhöft's architecture takes its cue from town halls, churches and fortresses, and its medieval idiom exudes an aura of power and influence. Only the tower and some of the side walls survived the Second World War, leaving little more than a grim memorial.

Planners considered reconstructing the complex, but the changing face of maritime transport and the demand for larger warehouse facilities led to its demolition in 1963. It was replaced by Werner Kallmorgen's massive brickwork cube: the 30,000-square-metre Kaispeicher A building. Some critics—particularly those involved with the publication series "Hamburg und seine Bauten" (Hamburg and its Buildings)—lauded its imposing form, heralding it

Er prägte viele Jahre die Skyline Hamburgs: Der Kaiserspeicher A prominent feature of Hamburg's skyline for many years: the Kaiserspeicher

Hafenlandschaft implantiert. Die einen – etwa die Architekturkritiker der großen Bauchronik »Hamburg und seine Bauten« – bewunderten ihn als eindrucksvoll, geschlossen und sahen ihn als würdigen Nachfolger des ehemaligen Kaiserspeichers. Anderen galt er als Kiste, die als erster Speicher Hamburgs auch von Gabelstaplern beschickt werden konnte. Leider waren da aber die Zeiten der Lagerung in Säcken schon gezählt, und der Standardcontainer hielt Einzug.

Und doch schlich sich dieser »Brocken« – nachdem er sich für den modernen Hafenbetrieb endgültig als unbrauchbar erwiesen hatte – mit seinen

as a worthy successor to the original Kaiserspeicher (imperial warehouse). Others suggested that it was little more than a quadratic box designed for fork-lift operations—albeit the first of its kind in Hamburg. Moreover, the advent of containerisation was about to change maritime logistics forever.

The building's detractors were right. The monolithic giant soon proved to be entirely unsuitable for modern port operations. Yet for whatever reason, most people in Hamburg associate the building's picturesque quayside semi-portal cranes and rows of hatches with the golden age of the city's port. Unlike its

wohl hundert grafisch perfekt gesetzten Luken an der Südwand und den Halbportalkränen in das kollektive Hamburger Gedächtnis an die großen, vergangenen Hafenzeiten. Er galt als einer der letzten Zeugen, der durch seine Wucht und seine unbeschreiblichen Gerüche als Kaffee- und Kakaospeicher die rohe Arbeitswelt des Hafens lebendig hielt – obwohl oder vielleicht gerade, weil er anders als die Bauten in der Speicherstadt nur eine schlichte, moderne Gebrauchsarchitektur war. In den 1990er Jahren mutierte der Speicher endgültig zum Kulturdenkmal. In der Masterplankonzeption der Hafencity von 1999 wurde der Kaispeicher A als Gebäude mit hohem Denkmalwert eingestuft.

In einem internationalen Wettbewerb, an dem die Architektenelite (u.a. Coop Himmelb(l)au) teilnahm, sollte die Zukunft dieses monumentalen Ortes geklärt werden. Das Ergebnis des Wettbewerbs (Sieger Benthem und Crouwel, Amsterdam) berücksichtigte die denkmalpflegerischen Schutzaspekte des alten Kaispeichers A von Werner Kallmorgen nicht genügend und plädierte für einen Abbruch der Speichermauern. Das geplante Medienzentrum passte ebenfalls nicht mehr so recht in die Zeit.

Die Idee für die Elbphilharmonie beruht auf der Initiative des privaten Projektentwicklers Alexander Gérard, der gemeinsam mit dem Basler Architekturbüro Herzog & de Meuron das Projekt initiierte. Es war der richtige Platz für eine zweite Philharmonie in der

peers in the Speicherstadt, the building is a solid example of modern functional architecture. Its sheer size and the heady blend of coffee and cocoa scents that once wafted from within have ensured its lasting status as a cultural icon; not surprisingly, the warehouse was declared a listed building in the 1990s. The Hafencity Master Plan of 1999 identifies Kaispeicher A as a building of particular historical and cultural significance.

An international competition that was held to decide the future of this monumental structure attracted the elite of the architectural world (including, for example, Coop Himmelb(l)au). Disregarding the heritage value of Werner Kallmorgen's Kaispeicher A, Benthem & Crouwel's (Amsterdam) winning design called for the demolition of the building's walls. Later plans for a media centre also fell by the wayside.

The inspiration for the Elbphilharmonie came from private project developer Alexander Gérard, who initiated the project together with Basel-based architects Herzog & de Meuron. Gérard recognised that this was the ideal location for the construction of a philharmonic concert hall to complement the neo-Baroque Laeiszhalle on Johannes-Brahms-Platz. The design concept developed by architects Herzog & de Meuron proposed building a new complex crowned with dramatic spires directly on top of the existing Kaispeicher, which would, in effect, "support" the Elbphilharmonie (cf. pp. 30–33).

Stadt, als Ergänzung der bestehenden Musikhalle (Laeiszhalle) am Johannes-Brahms-Platz. Die Planung der Architekten Herzog & de Meuron sah vor, auf den bestehenden Kaispeicher einen neuen Gebäudekomplex mit hoch schwingenden Spitzen zu setzen – der Kaispeicher »trägt« nun die Philharmonie (vgl. S. 30–33).

Hamburg wollte eine Landmarke mit der Strahlkraft des Opernhauses von Sydney. Es bekommt sie, auch wenn der Preis vielen Hamburgern viel, viel zu hoch ist. Die Elbphilharmonie wirkt mit ihrer gut hundert Meter hohen Spitze selbstbewusst als neues städtebauliches und kulturelles Wahrzeichen Hamburgs in den Elbraum hinaus. Für die Waterfront, für die Hafencity entwickelt sich so ein baulicher Dreiklang auf den Landspitzen Kehrwiederspitze, Sandtorhöft und Kaiserhöft – die modernen Hochhäuser stehen sinnbildlich für den Aufbruch zur Entwicklung eines neuen Stadtteils an der Elbe. Die engen Bezüge von Zukunft und Vergangenheit dokumentieren die geretteten Kaispeichermauern und ebenso drei alte Halbportalkräne, die wieder die Südfassade des Speichers – inzwischen auf hochwassersicherem Niveau – schmücken.

Der Kaispeicher A von Werner Kallmorgen
The Kaispeicher A designed by Werner Kallmorgen

Hamburg wanted a landmark with all the panache of the Sydney Opera House, and the Elbphilharmonie is certainly in a class of its own—although many fear that the price tag may be too high. Soaring over one hundred metres above the waterline, the Elbphilharmonie is a contemporary cultural landmark. The buildings on Kehrwiederspitze, Sandtorhöft and Kaiserhöft form a triangle of architectural excellence which defines the waterfront and the wider Hafencity development—these modern skyscrapers herald the advent of a new and vibrant era on the banks of the Elbe. Before this dramatic backdrop, three historical half-gantry cranes adorn the southern façade—an eye-catching reference to the building's maritime past.

Kaiserkai 47–57
Wohnhäuser Residential Buildings

Standort Location Am Kaiserkai 47–57 **Architekten Architects** KBNK Architekten (47–49), APB Architekten (51–55), spine architects GmbH (57) **Bauherr Client** Behrendt/Lehmann/Garbe/Privatinvestoren, c/o Lehmann & Partner **Wettbewerb Competition** 2005 **Bauzeit Date built** 2006–08 **Bruttogeschossfläche Gross floor area** 12 000 qm (sqm)

Auf dem Baufeld 22 realisierten mehrere Bauherren zusammen mit drei Architektengruppen einen Block und setzten damit ein Hafencity-Prinzip vorbildlich um: Unterschiedliche architektonische Handschriften stehen für individuelle Häuser, lassen diese aber durch abgestimmten Maßstab, Materialaussage und Textur zu einer »Haus-Familie« verschmelzen. Die zwei Wohnhäuser von KBNK fallen durch brillante Farbigkeit der Außenhaut aus Torfbrandziegeln auf. Die Grundrisse sind klar strukturiert und als Zweispänner organisiert. Die Erdgeschosswohnungen sind durch kleine Privatgärten an den intimen Wohnhof angeschlossen. Mit jugendlichem Schwung bildet Haus 57 (spine architects) einen Kontrast: Der Name Taille Vent bezieht sich auf den formalen Trick, das Haus an einem Punkt wie durch ein Korsett eingeschnürt erscheinen zu lassen. Der Dritte im Bunde – klassisch, steinern, hamburgisch – stammt von APB Architekten.

A number of developers and three groups of architects contributed to the development of Site 22; the result is a pitch-perfect realisation of the Hafencity vision. While the individual components reflect the varied architectural idioms of their creators, the scale, materials, and texture of the buildings have been carefully balanced to create a harmonious whole. KBNK's two residential buildings are notable for their striking colours and the texture of their peat-fired brick exteriors. Two units per storey provide clear and uncluttered floor plans. The ground floor apartments open onto private gardens within an enclosed courtyard. spine architects' House 57 provides an exuberant contrast: the name Taille Vent refers to the technique used to create the building's sleek corseted waistline. Designed by APB Architekten, the third building combines classical elements with plenty of stonework—this is quintessentially Hamburg.

1

55 53 51
49
57 47

Grasbrookhafen

2

3

4

1 Blick vom Strandhöft, Hochbau vorn links: spine architects; Ziegelbauten rechts anschlie-
ßend: KBNK Architekten View from Strandhöft, tall building front left: spine architects;
adjacent brick buildings to the right: KBNK Architekten **2** Übersicht Overview **3** Projekt
spine gesehen vom Kaiserkai View of spine project from Kaiserkai **4** Metropol Dock von
APB Architekten Metropol Dock designed by APB Architekten

Kaiserkai 35–45
Wohnblock Residential Block

Standort Location Am Kaiserkai 35–45 **Architekten Architects** Léon Wohlhage Wernik, Berlin (35–37), SEHW Architekten, Hamburg (39–43), Benedikt Schmitz und Maike Lück in SML Architekten, Hamburg (45) **Bauherren Clients** Groß & Partner Grundstücksentwicklungsgesellschaft mbH/Aug. Prien Immobilien/Yoo Deutschland GmbH/Vivacon AG **Wettbewerb Competition** 2004/2005 **Bauzeit Date built** 2006–08 **Bruttogeschossfläche Gross floor area** 13000 qm (sqm)

Auch dieser Abschnitt lebt von der Vielstimmigkeit seiner Architekten, Formen und Materialien. Leider entsteht der Eindruck von zu viel Durcheinander. Weil es sich im Wesentlichen um luxuriöse Eigentumswohnungen handelt (Nr. 35–37 zum Beispiel nach einem Design von Philippe Starck), verstärkt sich der Verdacht, dass hier Häuser wie eine Marke ihr eigenes Wesen entwickeln und zeigen sollen. Das bekommt dem Ensemble, ja, dem Quartier, nicht – besonders, wenn man es vom gegenüberliegenden Strandkai betrachtet. Das Haus Nr. 35–43 (architektonischer Entwurf SEHW und Léon Wohlhage Wernik) und sein Nachbar mit seinen dunkelbraunen Paneelen und den stehenden Formatem finden keine vernünftige optische Bindung zueinander. Allerdings hatten die Architekten auch keine Möglichkeit, sich nach dem Wettbewerb untereinander abzustimmen.

A diverse range of architects worked on this block, combining a variety of forms and materials. Sadly, the impression given is not one of consistency. Most of the buildings feature luxury freehold apartments (some featuring Philippe Starck design, No. 35–37), and one cannot help but gain the impression that too much emphasis was placed on creating a distinct visual identity for each building. The approach has proven detrimental to the ensemble as a whole—especially when viewed from the nearby Strandkai. Building No. 35–43 (architectural design by SEHW and Léon Wohlhage Wernik) and its neighbour, clad in dark brown façade panels and sporting an upright format, form a conspicuously odd couple. Sadly, the architects were not granted the opportunity to coordinate their efforts following the competition.

1

2

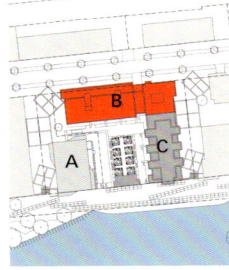

3

4

1 Ansicht vom Strandhöft im Süden: links das Haus von SML, rechts der Block von SEHW und Léon Wohlhage Wernik View from Strandhöft to the south: on the left the building by SML, on the right the block designed by SEHW and Léon Wohlhage Wernik **2** Ansicht von der Straße (B) View from the street (B) **3** Blick in den Hof (C) View of the courtyard (C) **4** Lageplan: A SML Architekten, B SEHW, C Léon Wohlhage Wernik Site plan: A SML Architekten, B SEHW, C Léon Wohlhage Wernik

Quartier am Kaiserkai
Residential Development

Standort Location Am Kaiserkai 23–31 **Architekten Architects** Loosen, Rüschof² + Winkler, Architekten und Stadtplaner, Hamburg (23); Carsten Lorenzen, Kopenhagen (25–27); KBNK Architekten, Hamburg (29–31) **Bauherr Client** H. Fischer & Co. und Viterra Development GmbH als Vertretung für on behalf of five housing cooperatives fünf Hamburger Wohnungsbaugenossenschaften (Altonaer Spar- und Bauverein, Baugenossenschaft Dennerstraße-Selbsthilfe eG, Bauverein der Elbgemeinden eG, Allgemeine Deutsche Schiffszimmerer-Genossenschaft eG und Baugenossenschaft Fluwog-Nordmark eG) **Wettbewerb Competition** 2003 **Bauzeit Date built** 2005–07 **Bruttogeschossfläche Gross floor area** 12 000 qm (sqm)

Die nordische Allianz aus dänischen und Hamburger Architekten zeigt mit ihren Bauten, worum es an dieser Stelle vorwiegend gehen sollte: um Wohnungen, die weder als überteuert noch als elitär gelten können; um einen Wohnungsbau, der in seiner ausnehmend kultivierten Detaillierung akkurat zu nennen ist. Trotz der weitgehenden Freiheit bei der Auswahl des Fassadenmaterials ist hier etwas entstanden, das der gesamten Anlage Form und Format verleiht. Die begrünten Innenhöfe aller U-förmigen Gebäude stehen ausschließlich den Bewohnern zur Verfügung. Familien mit Kindern wird so ein weiteres Argument für den Umzug in die Hafencity geboten.

The fruit of a Nordic alliance of Danish and Hamburg architects, this modern ensemble was developed with a focus on providing residential apartments at a reasonable price and combines cultivated designs with attention to detail. The architects enjoyed a remarkable degree of freedom in their choice of materials for the façade and the result ends the ensemble both form and format. Access to the grassed courtyards nestled snugly within the U-shaped buildings is restricted to residents, making the ensemble particularly appealing to young families keen to settle in Hafencity.

1

2

3

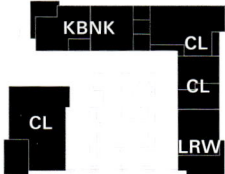

4

1 Ansicht aus der Luft, im Vordergrund der Entwurf von Loosen, Rüschoff + Winkler Aerial view, in the foreground the design by Loosen, Rüschoff + Winkler **2** Entwurf KBNK Architekten Design by KBNK Architekten **3** Entwurf Carsten Lorenzen Design by Carsten Lorenzen **4** Übersicht Overview

Dalmann-Carrée
Häuser mit hybrider Nutzung Hybrid Houses

Standort Location Am Kaiserkai 9–19 **Architekten Architects** MRLV Architekten – Markovic Ronai Lütjen Voss, Hamburg (9–11, 15), Prof. Bernhard Winking Architekten BDA mit Martin Froh, Berlin (13), Spengler Wiescholek Architekten und Stadtplaner, Hamburg (17–19) **Bauherr Client** DS-Bauconcept GmbH/Wernst Immobilien **Wettbewerb Competition** 2002 **Bauzeit Date built** 2003–07 **Bruttogeschossfläche Gross floor area** 12 900 qm (sqm)

Sechs »Zinshäuser« sind auf diesem Hochwassersockel am Kaiserkai miteinander verwoben – so sah es der Wettbewerb vor. Dabei wurde u.a. das Grundrissprinzip sogenannter Schlitzbauten aus der Hamburger Gründerzeit angewendet, das MRLV Architekten hier durch Einschnitte auf die einzelnen Hauseinheiten übertragen. Das mehrfarbige Klinkermuster der Kaimauer und der dunkle Ziegel für die Wände aus dem Freiraumkonzept wurden für das Projekt aufgenommen. Die Häuser und der Hochwassersockel bilden eine Einheit; das verleiht dem Block den Eindruck von Kraft. Auf die besonderen Anforderungen im Umgang mit den erhöhten Lärmemissionen durch die Lage am Vasco-da-Gama-Platz, auf dem zu bestimmten Zeiten öffentlich Basketball gespielt werden darf, wurde mit »Architektur« geantwortet: Die Loggien sind mit schlanken Klappschiebeelementen ausgestattet. Dazu gibt es Gewerbeflächen im Erdgeschoss des Eckhauses.

Also located on the Kaiserkai, this ensemble of six interwoven apartment buildings is perched on an elevated flood-proof foundation. By means of incisions to the building, MRLV Architekten invoke the geometric design of Hamburg's Schlitzbauten, a residential design that was popular prior to the First World War. The pattern of the dock's brickwork and the building's dark walls reflect the visual design guidelines detailed in the open-space plan. The buildings form a unified whole with their elevated foundation, underscoring the block s commanding aspect. The nearby Vasco da Gama Plaza is home to a public basketball court, and the designers have come up with an ingenious solution to cope with unwanted noise: foldaway sliding elements mounted on the balconies provide shelter when needed from wind and allow residents to enjoy all the privacy of a conservatory. The ensemble includes commercial space on the ground floor of the corner building.

1

2

3

1 Links der Bau von Prof. Winking Architekten (Am Kaiserkai 13), rechts (querab) der von MRLV Architekten (9–11) On the left the building by Prof. Winking Architekten (Am Kaiserkai 13), on the right (at a right angle) that of MRLV Architekten (9–11) 2 Der quer stehende Block von Spengler Wiescholek (17–19) ragt weit über die Promenade hinaus. The transversely positioned block by Spengler Wiescholek (17–19) extends far beyond the promenade. 3 Das Eckhaus The corner building (MRLV Architekten, 15)

Baugenossenschaft Bergedorf-Bille
Cooperative Residential Buildings

Standort Location Am Kaiserkai 3–7 **Architekten Architects** Prof. Jörg Friedrich PFP Architekten BDA, Hamburg **Bauherr Client** Baugenossenschaft Bergedorf-Bille eG **Wettbewerb Competition** 2003 **Bauzeit Date built** 2006 **Bruttogeschossfläche Gross floor area** 7800 qm (sqm)

Diese beiden Häuser für den genossenschaftlichen Wohnungsbau lassen sich sehr stark auf den Ort ein, zum Beispiel die Fassaden: Sie könnten unterschiedlicher kaum sein – zugeknöpft, wo sie die Wohnungen im Block vor Einblicken schützen, und mit vollständig verglasten Loggien an den Wasser- und Hofseiten. Die Zwei- oder Dreispänner-Wohnungen werden durch ein zentral gelegenes Treppenhaus erreicht, mit einzelnen Wohnräumen, die nach Hamburger Tradition durch das Öffnen der Türen optisch zusammengelegt werden können. Das sind flexible Grundrisse für sehr unterschiedliche Wohnwünsche. Für den Betrachter ist dieses Haus, wie das benachbarte Bürohaus von David Chipperfield, ein Gebäude, das sich mit seiner Fassadengestaltung zurückhält. Nichts Aufgeregtes, sondern Normalität als Gestaltungslinie. Das ist präzises architektonisches Handwerk.

Commissioned by a housing cooperative, these two buildings are splendid examples of site-specific design: the façade adopts a reserved aspect to protect residents from prying eyes where necessary, while elsewhere glass balconies offer generous views of the water and courtyards. Two or three apartments are located on each storey, and can be accessed through a central stairwell. Inside, connecting doors between the individual rooms create a more spacious atmosphere. A common feature in many of Hamburg's historical buildings, the connecting doors allow residents to add a personal touch to the layout of their apartments. Like the adjoining office block designed by David Chipperfield, the building is clad in a reserved and balanced façade. An exercise in unpretentious design—this is rock-solid architectural craftsmanship.

1

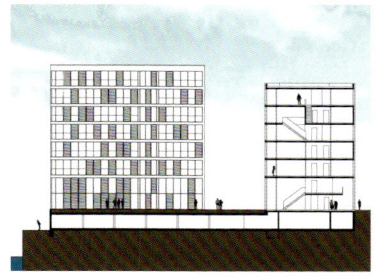

2

3

1 Ansicht vom Strandhöft, also von Süden, offen und transparent View from Strandhöft, i.e. from the south: open and transparent 2 Gebäudequerschnitt Cross section of the building 3 Sehr verschlossen und introvertiert: die Fassade zur Straße Extremely closed and introverted: the façade facing the street

K1
Bürohaus Office Building

Standort Location Am Kaiserkai 1, Großer Grasbrook **Architekten Architects** nps tchoban voss | Architektur und Städtebau **Bauherr Client** ABG Allgemeine Beteiligungsgesellschaft für Gewerbeimmobilien mbH & Co. **Wettbewerb Competition** 2003 **Bauzeit Date built** 2006–08 **Bruttogeschossfläche Gross floor area** 15 000 qm (sqm)

Das achtgeschossige Haus besetzt die östliche Kopfposition am Hafenbecken. Die durchaus mächtige Kubatur wird vielfältig aufgelockert – im Westen beispielsweise durch ein »Fenster zum Hof« mit Durchblicken und einem Stück »gerahmter« Hafenlandschaft. Prägende Merkmale sind Stützen und Fenstersprossen, die betont eng gesetzt wurden und auf diese Weise das Haus optisch nach oben streben lassen. An der Wasserseite schieben sich drei mehrgeschossige Gebäudepartien sanft vor die Fassade – ein alter, aber guter Trick, um von innen einen 180-Grad-Panoramablick auf das maritime Hafenumfeld zu liefern. Am Grasbrook reagiert der Zugang zum Haus exakt auf die Straßenflucht von Osten, öffnet sich über fast acht Meter Höhe, überdacht durch einen nach außen geschlossenen stählernen »Tisch«. Die gläserne Lobby ist »meetingpoint« und Auftakt mitten im Haus, abgeschirmt durch einen hochstämmigen Bambusgarten zum westlich gelegenen Wohnhof.

This eight-storey building sits at the head of the harbour basin. Its powerful form is softened by a "window to the world" on the western side, flooding the courtyard with light and affording spectacular views of the harbour through its frame. Eye-catching support struts and dark window glazing bars set close together heighten the building's vertical flow and create a striking image. Three multi-storey sections protrude from the façade facing the water—a well-proven trick that provides panoramic 180-degree views of the building's maritime environs. The building's entrance on Grasbrook extends the natural line of the road, channelling visitors under an overhanging steel "tabletop" nearly eight metres in height. Shielded from the residential courtyard to the west by lush stands of bamboo, the glass lobby provides a meeting point and a central reception area.

1

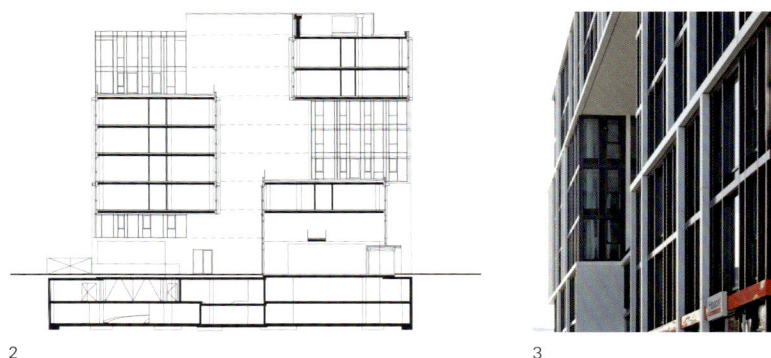

2   3

1 Gesamtansicht von den Marco-Polo-Terrassen aus General view from the Marco Polo
Terraces **2** Schnitt Cross section **3** Fassadendetail Façade detail

Der öffentliche Raum: Mediterran und traditionell zugleich

Public Space: Mediterranean Flair Meets Northern Tradition

Bereits im Westen, wo die Entwicklung der Hafencity mit dem Sandtorkai begann, musste ein topografisches Problem der neuen Hafencity grundsätzlich gelöst werden: der Höhenunterschied zwischen den hochwassergeschützten Freibereichen und den Wasserspiegeln. In der Regel schwankt in einem tideabhängigen Hafen der Wasserstand stark. Häufig liegt der Wasserspiegel tief unten. In der Hafencity werden die Besucher an vielen Orten näher ans Wasser herangebracht – u.a. mit den begehbaren Schiffspontons im Sandtorhafen (vgl. S. 50–51). Ein weites Netz von Kaipromenaden erschließt zusätzlich die Wasserflächen. Und im Spiel mit den auf den Warften höher gelegenen Platzflächen beginnt so ein reizvolles Auf und Ab inmitten der besonderen Hafencity-Topografie. Darüber hinaus sind in der westlichen Hafencity zwei große terrassierte Plätze entstanden: am Kopf des Sandtorhafens die zuerst vollendeten Magellan-Terrassen und danach am Grasbrookhafen die Marco-Polo-Terrassen (vgl. S. 52–55).

When work began on the redevelopment of Hafencity's Sandtorkai, the planners soon realised that the harbour's topography would pose a significant challenge—in particular the variations in elevation of the development's flood-proof outdoor areas and the tidal harbour's constantly changing water level. The marina pontoons on Sandtorhafen add to Hafencity's charm and allow easy access to the water, while an extensive network of promenades criss-crosses the waterfront (cf. pp. 50–51). In combination with the raised buildings on the harbour's massive elevated foundations, the promenades and pontoons make for a playful and unique topography. Two large terraced areas in the western section of Hafencity add to the development's appeal. Situated at the head of Sandtorhafen, the Magellan Terraces were completed first, and were soon followed by the Marco Polo Terraces neighbouring Grasbrookhafen (cf. pp. 52–55).

These terraces exemplify Hafencity's concept of tiered public spaces

Eine der wichtigsten Eigenschaften der Hafencity: Sie ist öffentlich und wird durch schöne Plätze, Promenaden und Parks geprägt. A critical feature of Hafencity: it is full of public spaces including many beautiful plazas, promenades and parks.

Diese Terrassen sind die Musterbeispiele für ein tief gestaffeltes System von öffentlichen Angeboten zur Begegnung, aber auch für Ruhe und Konzentration. Obwohl oder gerade weil diese Plätze, Parks und Promenaden neu geplant, also nicht vorhanden waren, konnten sie nach allen Regeln der architektonischen (Verführungs-)Kunst gestaltet werden. Design, Material, Topografie und vor allem der offene Horizont mit dem Blick aufs Wasser sind in dieser Konzentration nicht häufig im Hamburger Stadtbild anzutreffen.

Zwischen den Wohnbauten am Grasbrookhafen, sozusagen im Hoch-

designed to facilitate communication while providing visitors and residents with a place to relax. Working with what was essentially a blank canvas, the planners were invited to dip into their bag of architectural tricks to create a series of parks, promenades, and plazas that will seduce visitors and residents alike. The result: few places in Hamburg can match Hafencity's dazzling blend of world class design, innovative materials, undulating topography and spectacular water views.

A series of promenades winds its way along Dalmannkai, connecting several smaller plazas looking out on

parterre und auch den höchsten denkbaren Wasserständen entzogen, liegen kleinere, private Plätze, Promenaden und Treppen am Dalmannkai. Auf dem Vasco-da-Gama-Platz, einem Quartiersplatz für Bewohner und Besucher, wurde ein Basketballspielfeld angelegt, auf der Dalmannkai-Promenade wachsen Kirschbäume. Vereinendes Element für viele Stadträume in der Hafencity sind die Sockelwände der Warften. Sie wurden an vielen Stellen mit artifiziellen Mustern verziert. Manchem Besucher mag das zu viel sein, Langeweile kommt jedenfalls nicht auf.

Den zweiten Freiraumwettbewerb zur Gestaltung der zentralen Hafencity, der Flächen westlich und östlich des Magdeburger Hafens, gewann die Architektin Beth Galí gemeinsam mit ihrem Büro BB + GG arquitectes aus Barcelona. Sie entwirft auch die Stadträume im Überseequartier, am Magdeburger Hafen und am St. Annenplatz. Der erste von ihr gestaltete Platz liegt vor dem Internationalen Maritimen Museum Hamburg im Kaispeicher B. Mit der Materialwahl nimmt er Bezug zur Backsteinarchitektur des Speichergebäudes: Streifenförmig zieht sich brauner und rötlicher Granitstein durch Asphaltterrazzo.

Der Sandtorpark (vgl. S. 110–111), der im Frühjahr 2011 eröffnet wurde, ist Teil des Freiraumkonzepts von EMBT. Ebenso der Grasbrookpark, der später angelegt wird. Bereits 2008 wurde der 850 Quadratmeter große Schatzinsel-

Grasbrookhafen from vantage points well above the high water mark. Vasco da Gama Plaza, which is open to residents and visitors, is home to a public basketball court, while cherry trees line the promenade on Dalmannkai. The walls of the harbour's massive elevated foundations are a conspicuous element in Hafencity's various urban spaces, and in some areas their surfaces have been embellished with decorative patterns. While some visitors might find this all a bit too much, the effect is anything but dull.

A second spatial design competition was held to identify a suitable design for the centre of Hafencity, which extends across the areas to the west and east of Magdeburger Hafen. The competition was won by architect Beth Galí—also responsible for the design of the urban spaces in the Überseequartier, around Magdeburger Hafen and at St. Annenplatz—and her Barcelona office BB + GG arquitectes. The first of her designs was implemented outside the International Maritime Museum Hamburg in Kaispeicher B and features an asphalt terrazzo surface with ribbons of brown and red granite in a sophisticated allusion to the building's brickwork architecture.

Sandtor Park (cf. pp. 110–111) opened in early 2011 and is part of the urban space concept developed by EMBT, along with Grasbrook Park, which will be established at a later date. Covering 850 square metres, the Treasure Island Play-

Spielplatz am Kreuzfahrt-Terminal eröffnet; später wird der Spielplatz ersetzt durch eine neue, wesentlich größere Spielfläche im Grasbrookpark. Östlich des Magdeburger Hafens wird der Lohsepark mit 3,5 Hektar die mit Abstand größte Grünfläche der Hafencity bilden; er erstreckt sich zwischen Baaken- und Brooktorhafen und ist der große »Central Park« der Hafencity.

Insgesamt muss man das Angebot an öffentlichen Freiräumen, an Plätzen, Parks und Promenaden großzügig nennen. Das musste so sein, weil die Hafencity so dicht bebaut ist, wie man das von Innenstädten kennt. Aber es gibt noch einen zweiten, wichtigeren Grund: Die vielfältige Mischung aus Wohnen, Arbeiten, kulturellen und touristischen Angeboten bringt viele Bevölkerungsgruppen in die Hafencity – nicht nur die Bürger Hamburgs, sondern auch viele Besucher von auswärts. Hier treffen sie sich, hier können sie miteinander erleben, was die aktuelle Fortsetzung des »Hamburg-Gefühls« ist: Leben am Wasser und ein bisschen Fernweh im Herzen. Das Geflecht aus Wasser- und Grünflächen ist eine Reverenz an die Hamburger Stadtlandschaft der Außen- und Binnenalster – ein Stückchen Lombardsbrücken-Blickfreiheit in der Hafencity.

ground opened in 2008. Located at the Cruise Center Terminal, the playground will eventually be replaced by a larger facility in Grasbrook Park. The proposed Lohse Park to the east of Magdeburger Hafen will eventually form the largest green space in Hafencity. A sprawling 3.5-hectare park extending from Baakenhafen through to Brooktorhafen—Lohse Park is destined to become Hafencity's Central Park.

The numerous public spaces, plazas, parks, and promenades scattered about Hafencity have been carefully designed to ensure that even in the heart of an inner-city development residents and visitors can always find a place to unwind. With its unique blend of residential areas, office blocks, cultural hotspots, and tourist attractions, Hafencity is in a league of its own and will appeal to people from all walks of life, both from Hamburg and farther afield. Hafencity is contemporary Hamburg at its best: a vibrant melting pot that combines waterside living with a touch of wanderlust. Generous waterfront access and countless green spaces bring the wide open vistas of Hamburg's Lombardsbrücke to Hafencity and pay homage to the legacy of Hamburg's beloved Inner and Outer Alster.

Unilever-Haus
Bürohaus Office Building

Standort Location Strandkai 1 **Architekten Architects** Behnisch Architekten, Stuttgart **Bauherr Client** Hochtief Projektentwicklung GmbH/RREEF Waterfront GmbH & Co. KG (Besitzer seit Owner since 2010) **Wettbewerb Competition** 2006 **Bauzeit Date built** 2007–09 **Bruttogeschossfläche Gross floor space** 38 000 qm (sqm)

Um das Unilever-Haus richtig begreifen zu können, sollte man es von der südlichen Seite der Norderelbe betrachten. Oder eine Kreuzfahrt oder Oberelbe-Schifffahrt buchen. Dann wird klar, dass der Auftakt der Hafencity-Perlen am Strandkai Maßstäbe für andere setzt, die folgen werden. Zu verdanken ist das auch der zusätzlichen Kunststoffhülle (aus Polyurethan) als Schutz für den außen liegenden Sonnenschutz gegen starke Hafenwinde – eine locker umgeworfene Stola für das kleine Schwarze. Eine Amöbe in der Wirkung, eine erste feine Landmarke für die Hafencity. Das angestrebte Frei- und Wasserraumkonzept der Hafencity geht hier wunderbar auf. Das Haus übt durch seinen Eingang eine Sogwirkung aus, holt die Besucher und Passanten schon am maritimen Terrassenpark Marco Polo ab und fordert sie zum Eintreten auf. Und sofort besteht im Haus eine Sichtbeziehung zur Elbe. Hier soll das Bürohaus den Bewohnern und Besuchern nicht den

To truly grasp the genius of Hafencity's Unilever Building, one must either find a suitable vantage point on the southern banks of the Northern Elbe, take a tour of the harbour or, better yet, book a passage on a cruise ship. Occupying a prominent position on Strandkai, the Unilever Building sets the standard for others to follow. A delicate membrane protects the building's exterior sunshades from the harbour's strong winds, creating a fascinating organic form that has made the Unilever Building a Hafencity landmark. The vision of a city criss-crossed by open urban spaces that access and engage with the Elbe has become a reality here. The building's stunning entranceway is clearly visible from the nearby Marco Polo Terraces and mesmerises both visitors and passers-by, picking them up and sweeping them into its dazzling interior. Inside, views of the Elbe awat. But this isn't just more of the same—the elegant design is an invitation to take

1

Uferblick und -besuch stehlen, sondern neue Ein- und Ausblicke liefern. Die Stadt ist auch »drinnen«, und diese Stadt ist Vorbild und Organisationsmodell für das Organigramm des Bürobetriebs von Unilever. Der Besucher kreuzt diese gebaute Matrix in der Erdgeschossebene, bevor er am Elbufer das Haus wieder verlässt und die Uferterrassen betritt. Die Büroflächen werden in bis zu sechs Etagen für 1200 Mitarbeiter organisiert (Empfang im 1. OG). Der Bürobetrieb findet allerdings zum Teil auch im Luftraum statt. Dafür schwingen sich Rampen und Stege quer durch die innen liegende Halle nach oben und unten. Die Arbeitsplätze werden zum großen Teil als große Gruppenbüros mit bis zu 400 Quadratmetern angeboten. Sie zählen zu den schönsten in Hamburg: Räume mit Aussicht ins Hafenland, nach innen ins Behnische Raumgefüge. Dort umfassen sie den Lichthof, in dem die Farbe Weiß die Richtung und Stimmung bestimmt. Grüne und rote Paneele aus Heraklith hinter Gitterrosten betonen die Balustraden.

in the harbour from a new and unique perspective. If ever there was an office building that sought to make the urban experience its organisational principle, then this is it. Visitors are offered a glimpse of the building's matrix from the ground floor, before exiting to approach the Elbe across the adjacent terraces. Extending over six storeys, Unilever's offices accommodate a staff of around 1,200 employees (reception on the first floor). But this is no ordinary office building; instead of corridors and stairways, bridges and ramps traverse the building's central atrium in an office landscape dominated by open spaces of up to 400 square metres. These offices are among the best that Hamburg has to offer, combining spectacular views of the harbour with a compelling interior. White sets in the tone in the atrium, while the balustrades above are decked out in cheerful green and red Heraklith compressed wood panels in a protective meshwork sleeve.

1 (Vorseite) Blick von Norden über die Marco-Polo-Terrassen auf das Ensemble von Unilever-Haus und Marco Polo Tower (Previous page) View from the north over the Marco Polo Terraces towards the duo of the Unilever Building and the Marco Polo Tower 2 Die Büros umrahmen das öffentliche Atrium, der eigentliche Bürobereich beginnt erst in der +1-Ebene. The offices surround the public atrium, the actual office space starts at the +1 level. 3 Zwischen Tower und Terrassen ist ein neues Restaurantgebäude entstanden (Entwurf: EMBT, Barcelona). A new restaurant building has been erected between the Tower and the terraces (design: EMBT, Barcelona). 4 Grundriss Erdgeschossebene Floorplan, ground level 5 Bürogrundrisse Ebene 3 Office floor plans, level 3

2

3

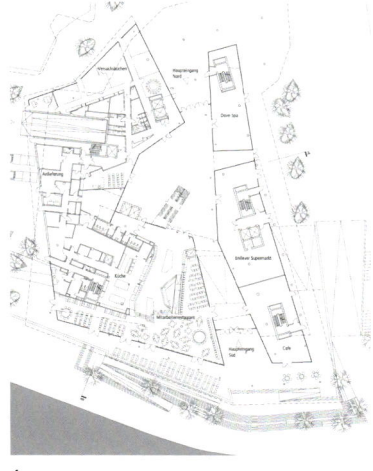

4

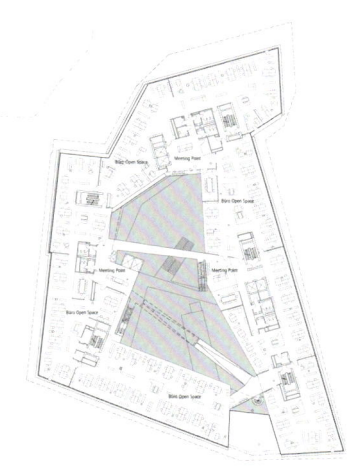

5

Marco Polo Tower
Wohnhaus Residential Building

Standort Location Hübenerstraße 1 **Architekten Architects** Behnisch Architekten,
Stuttgart **Bauherr Client** Projektgesellschaft Marco Polo Tower GmbH & Co. KG
Wettbewerb Competition 2006 **Bauzeit Date built** 2007–10 **Bruttogeschossfläche
Gross floor space** 12 500 qm (sqm)

14 Etagen, 58 Wohnungen, eine Mischung aus Blues und Swing – das ist der Marco Polo Tower. Außen aus Glas und Beton, eine Kontur leicht und logisch wie ein Federstrich. Innen herrscht Exklusivität, und die kündigt sich durch die gegeneinander verdrehten und sich hinauslehnenden Geschosse schon außen formal an. Diese Hausskulptur stellt an seine Betrachter die in der Architektur selten gestellte Frage: Darf man das? Ja. Denn die Kontur des Marco Polo Towers ist überall in der westlichen Hafencity der Eyecatcher, wegen seiner mutigen und ausgedrehten Form. Er animiert andere Architekten, daran anzuknüpfen. Die Wohnungen sind neben denen in der Elbphilharmonie die teuersten in der Hafencity. Auch die Planung des Gebäudeinneren ist ein Experiment. Der Wohnturm entstand zunächst als sogenannter veredelter Rohbau, der weitere Innenausbau liegt bei den einzelnen Wohnungseigentümern.

14 storeys, 58 apartments—the Marco Polo Tower is a sizzling blend of blues and swing. The gentle curve of its glass and concrete exterior is light and decisive like the stroke of a pen. Oozing style, the building's provocatively sinuous sculptural form sets it apart from its surroundings. Is this art or architecture? Answer: it's both. The Marco Polo Tower's serpentine contour makes it the signature landmark in Hafencity's West End—this is a building which will challenge other architects to follow its lead. Together with the Elbphilharmonie, the Marco Polo Tower is one of Hamburg's most exclusive residential addresses and a daring experiment in "design ready construction". The individual units will be handed over as semi-finished shell structures, enabling their new owners to implement an interior fit-out of their choice.

1

2

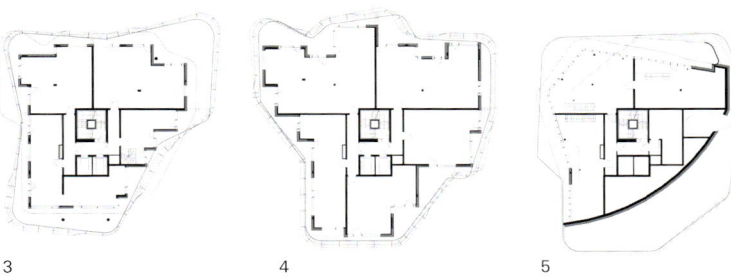

3   4   5

1 Gesamtansicht: mutig geformt, gedreht und weit sichtbar General view: boldly designed and visible from afar **2** Detail mit Wohnungen und Terrassen Detail with apartments and terraces **3–5** Wohnungsgrundrisse Apartment floor plans

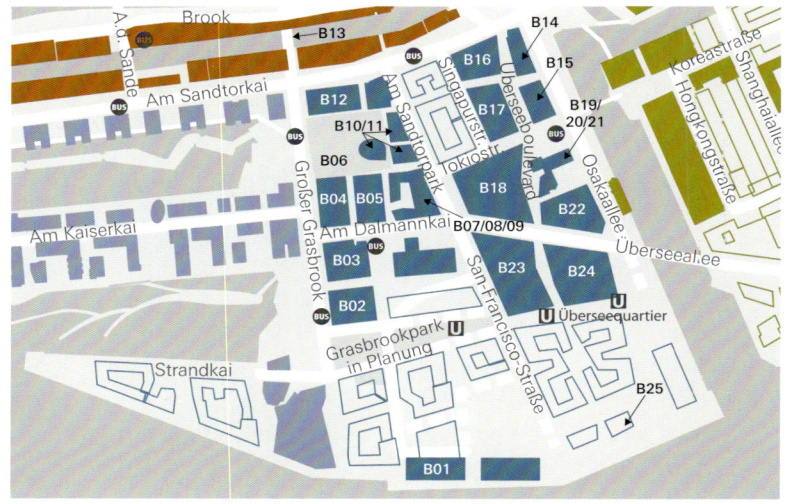

B.01 Hamburg Cruise Center
Terminal 1

B.02 SAP Schulungs- u. Bürogebäude

B.03 Kühne+Nagel Hauptquartier

B.04 Commercial Center

B.05 Katharinenschule in der Hafencity

B.06 Sandtorpark

B.07/08 Hofquartier

B.09 Baugemeinschaft Hafenliebe

B.10/11 Hamburg-America-Center und
Coffee Plaza

B.12 SKAI

B.13 Kibbelsteg-Brücken

B.14/15/16 Arabica, Ceylon und Java

B.17 Pacamara

B.18 Sumatra-Kontor

B.19/20/21 Altes Hafenamt mit
Wohnturm und Infopavillon

B.22 Virginia / Hotel 25hours

B.23/24/25 Projekte Südliches
Überseequartier

B.26 Science Center

Zentrale Hafencity

Central Hafencity

Hamburg Cruise Center Terminal 1

Standort Location Am Kibbelsteg **Architekten Architects** Renner Hainke Wirth Architekten, Hamburg **Bauherr Client** HafenCity Hamburg GmbH **Bauzeit Date built** 2003–04
Bruttogeschossfläche Gross floor area 1258 qm (sqm)

Das erste Cruise Center in der Hafencity
entstand in Folge strengerer Auflagen
für die Abfertigung an Kreuzfahrtterminals, die sich an den Spielregeln auf
Flughäfen orientieren. Es ist als temporäre Anlage konzipiert, bis das endgültige Terminal fertig ist. Die ursprüngliche
Lebenserwartung von etwa sechs Jahren ist schon lange erreicht, die Anlage
immer noch in Betrieb. Die Architekten
machten aus der Not eine Tugend und
beschlossen, das Provisorium als sichtbar kurzfristig angelegte Assemblage
aus Einheitscontainern zu bauen, die
mittels einfacher Holzfachwerkträger
ein gemeinsames Dach für die Abfertigung bekamen. Die gebrauchten
Container erhielten einen sinnfälligen
blauen Farbanstrich. Das mutige Hal-
lensystem als simpler Baukasten wurde
von anderen Hafenbehörden bis nach
Los Angeles nachgefragt. Mit dem Er-
satzbau und einem neuen Hotel wird
etwa 2015 begonnen.

Hafencity's first Cruise Center was designed to meet the requirements of
new passenger processing procedures
similar to those in effect at airports. Designed as a temporary facility pending
completion of the actual terminal. the
Center has already outlived its projected
six-year lifespan and is still in service.
Making a virtue out of necessity, the
architects conjured up a conspicuously
provisional design utilising an array
of used freight containers and a sail-
like roof supported by an open truss
framework. The blue colour scheme of
the weathered containers adds to their
charming simplicity. A daring design,
this simple modular system has since
been adopted by port authorities as far
away as Los Angeles. Commencement
of a replacement building and a new hotel is expected in 2015.

1

2

1 Containerarchitektur für die Kreuzfahrtschiffe – Foto aus den frühen Tagen der Hafencity Container architecture for cruise ships – photo taken in Hafencity's early days
2 Innenansicht Interior view

SAP Schulungs- und Bürogebäude
Training and Office Building

Standort Location Großer Grasbrook 17 **Architekten Architects** Spengler Wiescholek Architekten und Stadtplaner, Hamburg **Bauherr Client** HGA Objekte **Wettbewerb Competition** 2000 **Bauzeit Date built** 2001–03 **Bruttogeschossfläche Gross floor area** 12 500 qm (sqm)

SAP ist ein global arbeitendes Pionierunternehmen der Software-Entwicklung. Bereits im Jahr 2003 zog das Unternehmen in seine neue Geschäftsstelle mit Schulungszentrum, das erste Haus der Hafencity, ein. Architektonisch deutete das Haus schon an, wie die Hafencity heute in vielen Teilen aussieht: Das Einzelhaus passt sich der Matrix aus Block und Parzelle vorzüglich an. Außen eher zurückhaltend, überzeugt es mit seiner »Raum«-Kunst innen. Die zentrale, über alle Geschosse reichende, glasgedeckte Halle richtet sich konsequent zum Wasser aus. Die Halle ist Lobby, Schulungs- und Eventraum zugleich. Auch viele Büros ermöglichen den Blick bis zur historischen Speicherstadt und zum Grasbrookhafen. Im Umgang mit öffentlichen und halböffentlichen Räumen innerhalb eines Bürohauses war SAP Pionier. Viele (wie Unilever) folgten später diesem mutigen Konzept. 2013 zog als Nachmieter die Kühne Logistic University ein.

A pioneering software company with a global reach, SAP opened its new branch office and training centre in Hafencity as early as 2003, setting up camp in the first building to be completed. The building's architecture hinted at the shape of things to come in Hafencity: the alignment and scale of this block building is picture perfect. Its reserved exterior is misleading—inside a sleek interior design awaits. The glass-topped main hall spans the entire vertical length of the building and makes the most of its waterfront location. The hall is a lobby, training centre, and event location in one. As for the offices, many enjoy splendid views of the historical Speicherstadt and Grasbrookhafen. The design pioneered the integration of public and semi-public spaces within an office building—an approach that has since been adopted by numerous other companies, including Unilever. Since 2013 a new tenant—the Kühne Logistics University—delivers its services here.

1

2

1 Ansicht von Westen View from the west **2** Luftaufnahme in Richtung Altstadt Aerial view towards Hamburg's Altstadt

Kühne + Nagel Hauptquartier
Company Headquarters

Standort Location Großer Grasbrook 11–13 **Architekten Architects** Störmer Murphy and Partners, Hamburg **Bauherr Client** Kühne+Nagel (AC & Co.) KG **Bauzeit Date built** 2004–06 **Bruttogeschossfläche Gross floor area** 19450 qm (sqm)

Mit dem Ort verzahnen wollten die Architekten das elegant gegliederte Bürohaus, das in der Hafencity zur heiß ersehnten Kategorie der Unternehmens-Hauptquartiere gehört. »Mit dem Ort« heißt hier »mit dem Wasser«: Das Foyer im sechsgeschossigen »Flachbau« öffnet sich zum Grasbrookhafen. Dort soll eine Marina entstehen. Aus dem zwölfgeschossigen Turmbau erleben Mitarbeiter und Kunden einen Panoramablick über die Innen- und die Speicherstadt bis zur Elbphilharmonie und in den Hafen. Aber auch der Nahblick lohnt: Die Details der Fassade sind geschliffen, als wären sie von einem Industriedesigner entwickelt worden. Die Fassaden des Turms schwingen und laden aus wie ein Schiffskörper; nicht von außen zu sehen, aber gediegen: ein schön begrünter Innenhof.

The elegant form of this office building—a company headquarters, no less—is firmly rooted in its location, and in this case the location is all about the water. The lobby of the six-storey "flat-top" opens onto Grasbrookhafen, which is soon to be the site of a new marina. The twelve-storey tower block affords employees and clients panoramic views of the inner city and Speicherstadt and right across to the Elbphilharmonie. But sometimes a close-up view can be just as rewarding: the details on the façade are worthy of an accomplished industrial designer. The tower's façade swells and bulges like a ship's body; tucked away inside lies a verdant and oh-so-elegant courtyard.

1

2

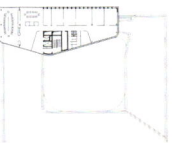

3

1+2 Blick auf den zwölfgeschossigen Turm und den flacheren Riegelbau, die einen Innenhof umspielen View of the twelve-storey tower and the lower block building framing an inner courtyard **3** Grundrisse 4–7. OG Floor plans, 4th–7th storeys

Commercial Center
Bürohaus Office Building

Standort Location Großer Grasbrook 9 **Architekten Architects** Baumschlager Eberle, Lochau/Österreich **Bauherr Client** DC Commercial GmbH & Co. KG, Hamburg **Wettbewerb Competition** 2005 **Bauzeit Date built** 2009–12 **Bruttogeschossfläche Gross floor area** 17800 qm (sqm)

B.04

Handwerklich sauber und nachhaltig: eine Architektur der eleganten Zurückhaltung, die mit ihren vielen präzisen Details Maßstäbe setzt; wegen seiner aufreizenden Unauffälligkeit vielleicht einer der stärksten architektonischen Beiträge. Außerdem belegt dieser Entwurf aus Voralberg die Spitze in allen ökologischen Belangen. Es ist eines der ersten neuen Kontorhäuser – zugeschnitten für viele Mieter und mit vielen kleinen Flächen –, das aufgrund der vernünftigen Konzeption und seines Klimakonzepts (z.B. Betonkerntemperierung, Wärmerückgewinnung, Sandwichfassade) schon vor der Fertigstellung das Umweltzertifikat in Gold der Hafencity erhielt. Die mehrschichtige Fassade ist ein innovativer Versuch, gläserne Architektur und Klimawandel zu vereinbaren. Ob sich solcher Aufwand lohnt, bleibt abzuwarten. Architektonisch ist die Außenwand eigentlich nur an den Ecken interessant, wo sie zeigt, wie sich die einzelnen Scheiben übereinanderschieben.

Clean, sustainable, solid: this is an elegantly reserved design with a wealth of details that will set new standards. Stylish and unobtrusive at once, the building is an architectural high ight on Großer Grasbrook. This masterful Austrian design is also ahead of its peers when it comes to sustainability. Built to service a large number of tenants, the Commercial Center was one of the first new business centres on site. Its intelligent design and climate control plan (concrete core temperature control, heat recovery, sandwich façades) won the building the Hafencity Golden Eco-Label long before it opened its doors. The Center's multi-layered façade is an innovative attempt to bring glass architecture into the age of climate change (and protection). Except for the over apping glazing on the corners, the building's exterior is all understatement and it remains to be seen whether the design will deliver the desired results.

1

2

3

1 An der südlichen Flanke des kleine Sandtorparks liegt mit aufwendiger, energetisch sinnvoller Glasfassade das Commercial Center. The Commercial Center, situated on the southern edge of the small Sandtorpark, with its elaborate, energetically optimised glass façade. **2** Architektonisch interessant: die Eckausbildung Architecturally interesting: corner design **3** Grundriss Regelgeschoss mit Innenhof Typical floor plan with inner courtyard

Katharinenschule in der Hafencity
School Building

Standort Location Am Dalmannkai 12 **Architekten Architects** Spengler Wiescholek
Architekten und Stadtplaner, Hamburg **Bauherr Client** Otto Wulff PPP Hafencity Schule
GmbH **Wettbewerb Competition** 2006 **Bauzeit Date built** 2006–09 **Bruttogeschoss-
fläche Gross floor area** 13300 qm (sqm)

Der allgemeine Wunsch »Zurück in die
City« bedeutet auch für Hamburg, wieder urbane Schulen, also Schulen mitten
in der Stadt zu bauen, die als Ganztags-
schule und darüber hinaus als Stadtteil-
zentrum funktionieren können. Architektonisch ist die Schule ein Raumwunder:
Eine Turnhalle wurde eingebaut, von
außen ist sie kaum wahrnehmbar. Hier
macht das Stapeln von Räumen Sinn,
denn der konstruktive Fußabdruck ist
schmal wie auch der ökologische. Dass
hier eine besonders liebevoll ausgesuch-
te Steinmischung und der nachwach-
sende Rohstoff Holz besonders gern
verwendet wurden, macht die Schule
auch stilistisch zum Sympathieträger.
Der Schulbau wird durch einen höheren
Bauriegel zur Straße abgeschirmt, dort
finden Wohnungen, eine Kita und andere Nutzungen Raum. Die Schule selbst
hat zwei »Gartenseiten«: zum intimen
Sandtorpark und – was anfangs heftig
umstritten war – auf dem Dach einen
Pausenhof mit kunterbunter Spielwelt.

Back to the city—back to school. In
Hamburg the inner city renaissance
has also seen the establishment of new
schools and dual-purpose educational
facilities. Moonlighting as a community
centre, this school is an architectural
wunderkind and a master of deception:
the new sports hall is practically invis-
ible. The architects opted for a multi-
storey complex, reducing the building's
spatial footprint to match its ecological
performance. Extensive wooden elements are complemented by a discern-
ing use of stonework, resulting in a
stylish finish; this is a design that is not
afraid to flaunt its eco-credentials A
block building shielding the school from
the road contains apartments and a kin-
dergarten along with other facilities. Pu-
pils enjoy access to two separate green
spaces: the adjoining Sandtorpark and
a somewhat controversial rooftop playground.

1

2

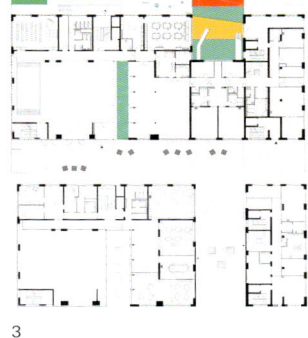

3

1+2 Der Platz ist begrenzt, daher entstand der Pausenhof auf dem Dach mit kunterbunter »fünfter Fassade«. Space is limited, so the playground area was constructed on the roof with a bright and quirky "fifth façade". **3** Grundrisse EG und 1. OG (links Schule, rechts Sondernutzungen) Floor plans, ground floor and 1st storey (on the left the school, on the right special uses such as daycare)

Sandtorpark
Public Park

Standort Location Sandtorpark **Architekten Architects** EMBT Arquitectes Associats, Barcelona **Bauherr Client** HafenCity Hamburg GmbH **Wettbewerb Competition** 2002 **Bauzeit Date built** 2010

Teil des umfassenden Freiraumkonzepts von EMBT ist auch der kleine Sandtorpark, eine grüne »Wiese« mitten im Quartier, zwischen hohen Häusern, der Schule und in der Nähe zu Restaurants und Läden. Das sind beste Voraussetzungen für den Business Lunch angloamerikanischer Prägung unter freiem Himmel – zumindest im Sommer. Es ist also ein kleiner »Central Park« entstanden, der große folgt demnächst weiter im Osten und heißt Lohsepark. Die zahlreichen Tritt- und Sitzstufen im Grün sind in einem Park nicht jedermanns Sache, aber sie erhöhen die, wie es im Planerdeutsch heißt, »Aufenthaltsqualität« stark, ebenso die Aussicht nach Westen ins Abendlicht und auf die Elbphilharmonie – das ist wohl eine der schönsten in der westlichen Hafencity. Noch als Zäune das junge Rasengrün schützten, begannen die Hafencity-Bewohner und -Besucher ihr neues Frei-Raum-Wohnzimmer liebevoll zu nutzen.

Situated at the heart of the quarter, Sandtorpark is integral to EMBT's comprehensive open space concept. Bordering the school, this intimate green space sits snugly among the quarter's taller buildings and is easily accessible from nearby restaurants and shops. This is Central Park en miniature—the ideal setting for an American-style outdoor business lunch in summer. Hafenc ty's Lohsepark, Hamburg's answer to The Big Apple's famous green lung, will soon follow further to the east. The flights of access and seating steps may not be to everyone's taste, but they create a pleasant atmosphere that entices visitors to linger and enjoy the stunning sunsets and views of the Elbphilharmonie afforded by the park's alignment. Hafencity's residents voted with their feet by flocking to their new green living room well before the fences around the young grass came down.

1

2

3

1–3 Dieser Park nimmt die Idee der New Yorker Pocket Parks auf, besonderes Merkmal: die bewegte Topografie der Rasenflächen. Inspired by New York's pocket parks, a special feature of this park is the undulating topography of the grassy areas.

Hofquartier
Residential Development

Standort Location Am Dalmannkai 6–10, Am Sandtorpark 8 **Architekten Architects** ASTOC Architects and Planners, Köln (örtliche Repräsentanz local representative: Kunst + Herbert, Hamburg); KBNK Architekten, Hamburg **Bauherr Client** HofQuartier GmbH & Co. KG (DS Bauconcept GmbH/Wernst 1. Beteiligungs GmbH) **Bauzeit Date built** 2009–11 **Bruttogeschossfläche der Häuser Gross floor area of buildings** A+B/G+H: 11 250 qm (sqm)

B.07/08

Auch dieses Projekt ist ein Angebot, die Hafencity zum attraktiven Standort des Wohnens zu machen: heller Stein und eine für die Baumasse (immerhin 68 Wohnungen) ordentliche und zum Teil kleinteilige Gliederung des Baukörpers. Die Fassade ist geprägt durch das zurückspringende Sockelgeschoss und den Wechsel von hellen Putz- und Glasflächen mit stark profilierten Rahmen in den Obergeschossen. Das Haus fügt sich selbstverständlich in die zugrunde gelegte Blockkonfiguration ein. So etwa steht es auf der Website der Architekten und zeigt ihr Bemühen, ordentliche Arbeit abzuliefern. In der Immobilienbeschreibung des Bauherrn herrschen Wendungen wie »exklusive Luxus-Wohnung über zwei Ebenen«, »moderne und sehr gute Raumaufteilung« oder »ruhige und doch zentrale Lage« vor. Fakten nicht für einen Architektur-, sondern für einen Immobilienführer, aber trotzdem aufschlussreich.

This project is guaranteed to enhance Hafencity's appeal as a residential location: housing a total of 68 apartments, its light stonework and soft, clear lines give it a gentle character. The building makes a strong visual impression with its set-back base, light plaster and glass surfaces, and eye-catching window frames on the upper levels. There's an effortless air to the design, belying the architects' studious endeavour to deliver a quality product—as detailed on their website. In the developer's real estate brochure, the building is praised for its "exclusive split-level luxury apartments," "modern and intelligent floor plan" and "peaceful but central location"— qualities that count on the property market.

1

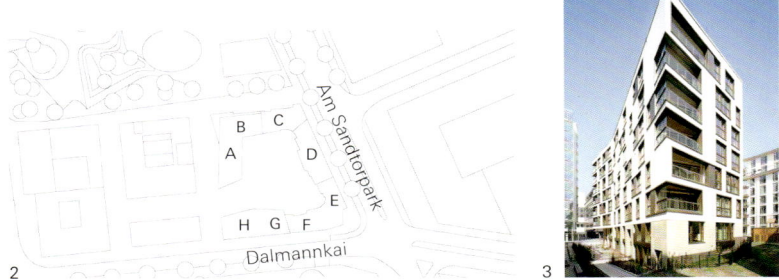

2

3

1 Hofquartier (ASTOC, Bauteile G + H): Guter Wohnungsbau hinter hellen Backsteinfassa-
den Hofquartier (ASTOC, buildings G + H): solid residential design behind light brickwork
façades 2 Lageplan (Hofquartier: KBNK Architekten (A+B), ASTOC Architects and Planners, Köln/Kunst+Herbert, Hamburg (G+H); Hafenliebe (C–F): Iris Neitmann Architektin,
vgl. S. 114–115) Site plan (Hofquartier: KBNK Architekten (A+B), ASTOC Architects and
Planners, Köln/Kunst+Herbert, Hamburg (G+H); Hafenliebe (C–F): Iris Neitmann Architektin (cf. pp. 114–115) 3 Bauteil KBNK Architekten Design by KBNK Architekten

Baugemeinschaft Hafenliebe
Mixed Use Development

Standort Location Sandtorpark **Architekten Architects** Architekturbüro Neitmann; unter Einbeziug eines Entwurfs für Haus C von incorporating a design for Building C by Schenk + Waiblinger Architekten, Hamburg **Bauherr Client** Baugemeinschaft Hafenliebe GbR, c/o Architekturbüro Neitmann mit and StadtLandFluss Entwicklungsgesellschaft mbH **Wettbewerb Competition** 2007 **Bauzeit Date built** 2009–11 **Bruttogeschossfläche Gross floor area** 7370 qm (sqm)

Vier Häuser, 54 Wohnungen und acht Gewerbeeinheiten: Es ist eines der Vorzeigeprojekte, was die Nutzerstruktur betrifft: Ein Projekt für Einzelhandel und Familienwohnen als Baugemeinschaft, Wohnen mitten in der Stadt – die Schule in Rufweite. Die Grundrissqualität geht mit üblichen Angeboten im Ausbau und Luxusmaterialien für Küche oder Böden in eine gute praktikable Richtung und lässt hybride Nutzungen nacheinander zu: Das heißt, hier ist Wohnen in verschiedenen Konstellationen (auch als Mehrgenerationswohnen) in Verbindung mit Arbeiten möglich. Solche Wohnhäuser haben naturgemäß viele Balkons – und in diesem Fall einen um ein Geschoss angehobenen Innenhof, der sich nach Süden und Westen öffnet. Dies und ein verspielter Umgang mit Hamburgs Material, dem Backstein, sorgen für eine Fassade, die bei vielen Besuchern und Bewohnern besser ankommt als der übliche Mix aus Stahl, Glas und Beton in der Nachbarschaft.

With four buildings, 54 apartments and eight commercial units this is one of Hafencity's architectural flagships. and combines retail and residential usage within a single ensemble, inviting families to settle in the heart of the city just a stone's throw away from the nearest school. The quality of the floor plans is matched by a selection of interior layout and flooring options, together with a range of luxury extras for kitchen areas. The practical design of the floor plans allows for hybrid use, including a variety of residential constellations (multi-generational living), telecommuting, and more. The building's numerous balconies and playful attitude to Hamburg's material of choice—brickwork—makes for a delightful façade that breaks with the uniform steel, glass and concrete of its neighbours. A raised interior courtyard, open to the south and the west, completes this urban idyll.

1

2

3

1 Gesamtübersicht: links Hofquartier (G + H), rechts Block Hafenliebe (F + E, vgl. Übersicht S. 113) Overview: Hofquartier (G + H) on the left, the Hafenliebe complex (F + E, cf. site plan on p. 113) on the right 2 Eckgebäude mit Läden (Erdgeschoss), Arztpraxen (2.+3. OG) und familienfreundlichen Wohnungen Corner building with shops (ground floor), doctors' offices (2nd and 3rd storeys) and family-friendly apartments 3 Schnitt mit dem höher gelegten Innenhof Sectional diagram with elevated inner courtyard

Hamburg-America-Center und Coffee Plaza

Standort Location Sandtorpark **Architekten Architects** Richard Meier & Partners Architects LLP, New York **Bauherr Client** Neumann Gruppe GmbH/DS-Bauconcept GmbH **Wettbewerb Competition** 2006 **Bauzeit Date built** 2008–10 **Bruttogeschoss-fläche Gross floor area** 27 100 qm (sqm)

Auf dem ehemaligen Betriebsstandort der Kaffeelagerei ist mit dem Hamburg-America-Center ein neuer Ort für US-Einrichtungen wie zum Beispiel den American-Business-Club entstanden. Er schließt die Baugruppe und den Park nach Nordosten ab. Architektonisch ist der ovale Hochbau, der das Ensemble und die Hafencity hier imposant überragt, das auffälligste Glied des Triumvirats. Hinter filigraner weißer Metallfassade mit mächtigen Glasfronten präsentiert das Architekturbüro hier jene Architektur, die Meier schon an seinen berühmten weißen Villen in den USA (und an der Hamburger Außenalster) perfektioniert hatte. Zumindest oben im Penthouse geht das Konzept auf. Diese »Hutkrempe« ist elegant. Die übrige Fassade allerdings ist nur präzise, und man hat sie schon gesehen. Mehr ist manchmal auch in der Moderne mehr. Eine weitere Hausscheibe an der Straße Am Sandtorpark mit grauen Metallfassaden hinter dem Hochhaus-

Located on a site formerly occupied by a coffee warehouse, the Hamburg America Center provides a much-needed hub for U.S. business ent ties and organisations such as the American Business Club, closing off the group and the park to the north-east. Towering above the ensemble and the wider Hafencity area, the oval-shaped highrise is the most conspicuous member of this threesome. With its delicate white metal façade and imposing glass surfaces, the building replicates the stunning architectural vision that Meier perfected both in his famous white villas in the USA and on Hamburg's Outer Alster. The concept is a success, at least as far as the penthouse is concerned, which adds an elegant "brim" to the upper level. The remainder of the façade is a work of precision, but one that is now all too familiar. In modern architecture, more is sometimes just that—more. Viewed from the west, the grey metal façade bordering Am Sandtorpark lends the

1

2

3

rundling verleiht diesem – von Westen gesehen – als Rückwand des Stadtraums perfekten Halt. Insgesamt zählen an dieser Stelle Parkqualitäten und Städtebau mehr als Fassadenaufgeregtheiten. Deswegen wird auch dieser grüne Stadtraum auf Dauer einer der besseren in der Hafencity sein.

curved highrise a powerful presence, making the Center a bulwark in the fast-flowing currents of urban space. Its untroubled façade reflects the planners' desire to shield the park and create a quiet zone, ensuring that this urban green space will rank among the best in Hafencity for a long time to come.

1 (Vorige Seite) Ein runder weißer Büroturm mit »Hutkrempe« krönt das Ensemble. (Previous page) A round white office tower with "brim" crowns the ensemble. **2** Zwei grau gehaltene Blöcke bilden das Rückgrat des Sandtorparks. Two grey blocks form the backbone of the Sandtorpark. **3** Blockansicht von Osten View from the east **4** Einen guten Überblick hat man vom Dachgarten des Hochhauses. A fantastic view can be enjoyed from the highrise's rooftop garden. **5** Ansichten Views **6+7** Grundrisse 2. OG Floor plans, 2nd storey

4

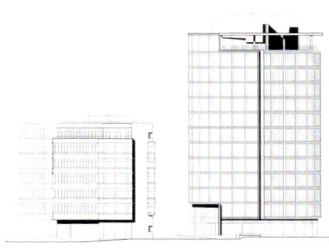

5

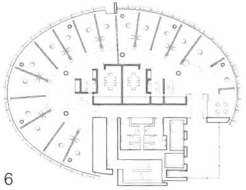

6

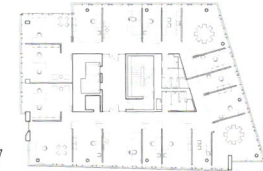

7

SKAI
Bürohaus Office Building

Standort Location Am Sandtorkai 50 **Architekten Architects** BLK2 Böge Lindner K2 Architekten, Hamburg **Bauherr Client** DWI Grundbesitz GmbH, Hamburg **Wettbewerb Competition** 2006 **Bauzeit Date built** 2007–09 **Bruttogeschossfläche Gross floor area** 19400 qm (sqm)

B.12

In direkter Nachbarschaft zur Speicherstadt und zu den bisherigen Neubauten am Sandtorkai antwortet der Entwurf mit einem ruhigen Baukörper in S-Form, der mit einem Einschnitt den Rhythmus der Einzelbauten am Sandtorkai aufnimmt und mit dem Bankgebäude ein Entree zur Hafencity bildet. Der Einschnitt zum Park nimmt die gegenüberliegende Öffnung an der Schule auf. So entsteht eine Sichtachse zur Katharinenkirche. In diesem Bereich bildet der Baukörper mit einer großzügigen Öffnung eine Verbindung von der tiefer gelegenen Straße zum Park. Am Sandtorkai wird durch die zweigeschossige Unterschneidung des Baukörpers eine Ausweitung des Straßenraums als Anlieferung und Vorfahrt gewonnen, während die zweigeschossige Auskragung am Platz den überdeckten Durchgang zur Hafencity darstellt. Die dunkelrote Aluminiumfassade passt sich selbstbewusst in die historische und in die neue Umgebung ein.

Bordering Speicherstadt and the more recent additions on Sandtorkai, the calm form of this S-shaped structure provides a succinct response to the rhythm of its neighbours. Together with the nearby bank building, Sandtorkai forms a powerful entrée to Hafencity. Situated adjacent to the park, the building's form guides visitors into its green depths, connecting the lower lying street with the green space and offering a clear line of sight through to St. Catherine's Church. On the corner of Am Sandtorkai the building's quadratic form is undercut across two storeys, creating an accessway for deliveries and visitors, while the overhanging storeys form a stylish sheltered entrance to Hafencity. The dark red aluminium façade is a self-conscious nod to the building's historical site.

1

2

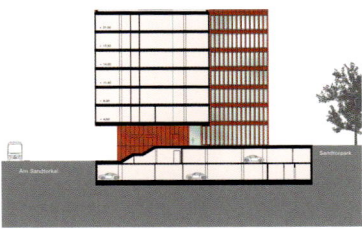

3

1+2 Sauber, kubistisch, rot: Fassade des Bürohauses zum Sandtorpark und zur Speicherstadt Clean, cubist, red: the façade of the office building facing Sandtorpark and Speicherstadt **3** Schnitt Cross section

Kibbelsteg-Brücken
Pedestrian bridges

Standort Location Kibbelsteg **Architekten Architects** gmp · von Gerkan, Marg und Partner, Hamburg in Planungsgemeinschaft mit in cooperation with WTM Engineers GmbH, Hamburg **Bauherr Client** GHS Gesellschaft für Hafen- und Standortentwicklung **Baudatum Date** built 2001–2002 **Länge Length** 220 Meter

B.13

Der erste Rammschlag für die Kibbelsteg-Brücken 2001 markierte den Baubeginn für die neue Infrastruktur der Hafencity. Fußgängern und Radfahrern ermöglichen die auf zwei Ebenen angelegten Brücken eine neue direkte Wegeverbindung zwischen der heutigen Hamburger Innenstadt, der Speicherstadt und der Hafencity. Bei Sturmflut gewährleisten die Brücken eine hochwassersichere Zufahrt für Feuerwehr, Polizei und Rettungsfahrzeuge und bildeten damit die Voraussetzung für den Ausbau der westlichen Hafencity. Figur und Nutzung dieses Brückenschlags zwischen Altstadt und Hafencity sind inzwischen so selbstverständlich geworden, dass man die Brücke an dieser Schnittstelle zwischen den fertiggestellten Neubauten und der alten Speicherstadt für uraltes Inventar hält. Ein besseres Kompliment kann man ihr nicht machen.

The first piles for Hafencity's Kibbelsteg Bridges were driven into the ground in 2001, marking the commencement of work on a significant infrastructural project. This two-level bridge links Hafencity with the inner city and the Speicherstadt development, providing pedestrians and cyclists with easy and direct access. The bridges form a flood-proof secure access route for emergency service vehicles and fulfilled a key requirement for the development of Hafencity's western sector. Since their opening, these bridges between the modern landscape of Hafencity and Hamburg's historical Altstadt have become so integral to life on the banks of the Elbe that it is hard to imagine the city without them. And what better compliment can one give?

1

2

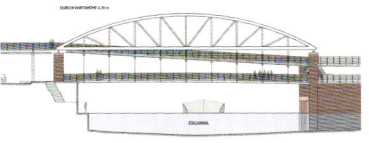

3

1 Die doppelstöckige Kibbelstegbrücke im Konzert anderer Brücken in der Speicherstadt
The two-storey Kibbelsteg Bridge in concert with other bridges in the Speicherstadt
warehouse district **2** Unterer Steg mit Blick auf St. Katharinen Lower bridge with view of
St. Catherine's **3** Schnitt Cross section

Das Herz der Hafencity: Das Überseequartier
Hafencity's Vibrant Heartland: Überseequartier

Mit dem Überseequartier (wie auch dem östlich anschließenden Elbtorquartier) ist so etwas wie die »City in der City« gemeint. Gern nennen es die Planer auch das »Herz« – dahinter steckt die Sehnsucht nach Leben für die Reißbrettstadt –, wobei der Begriff nicht korrekt ist, denn auch dieser Teil der Hafencity wurde am Computer generiert. Handelsstädte, im kleineren Maßstab auch die Marktplätze, entstehen an Kreuzungen von Handelswegen oder wichtigen Verbindungsstraßen. Das Überseequartier ist so ein magischer Punkt, es liegt zwischen der historischen Innenstadt und der Elbe, ebenso tangieren es die wesentlichen Ost-West-Verbindungen innerhalb der Hafencity. Ein archimedischer Punkt also. Wie baut man heute eine »Altstadt« oder Innenstadt? Sicher nicht wie ein Einkaufszentrum, wo unter Dächern dem Konsum gefrönt wird. Die Alternative hieß Einkaufen unter freiem Himmel – in Fußgängerstraßen und auf Plätzen. Der Autoverkehr endet in der darunterliegenden Parkgarage, während oben ein engmaschiges Wegenetz zum Flanieren entstand.

Like the nearby Elbtorquartier, the Überseequartier is Hafencity's "city within the city". Eager to see their creation come to life, planners like to refer to this quarter as the "heartland". Historically, trade centres and market towns sprang up at the intersection of important trade routes and alongside busy thoroughfares. Lying between the historical Altstadt and the River Elbe on Hafencity's central east-west axis, the Überseequartier is located at a truly Archimedean point. But how do you go about building what might eventually become a historical city centre? Certainly not in the same manner as a shopping centre, that post-modern temple of consumerism. The alternative: an open-air shopping experience with pedestrian zones and plenty of public spaces. Underground car parks provide discrete parking facilities while pedestrians stroll the quarter's numerous pathways above.

Der Überseeboulevard im nördlichen Überseequartier – mit Einkaufsgassen (fast) im Altstadtformat Überseeboulevard in the northern part of the Überseequartier – with side shopping streets (subtly) evocative of a historical city centre

Der Boulevard als Aorta des Lebens

Das Überseequartier und die ansässigen Einzelhändler hoffen auf dichte Besucherströme und entsprechende Kaufkraft. Der neue Überseeboulevard führt von Norden, von der City, mitten durch das Überseequartier. Er ist aber kein breiter Autostrip, sondern soll mit einem mäandrierenden Fluss verglichen werden. Alle Wege, Gassen und Plätze sind das präzise Resultat von Wahrnehmungen aus europäischen Städten, die uns immer wieder faszinieren: Brüche, Schwünge, Abwechslung, Einblicke,

The Boulevard: An Urban Artery

Überseequartier hopes to attract large numbers of visitors and the spending power to sustain a wide variety of retailers. The newly created Überseeboulevard runs southwards from the city straight through the heart of the quarter. Its similarity to a meandering river is intended—Überseequartier's pathways, lanes and public spaces replicate stylistic elements from countless European cities: sudden changes, organic curves, variety, intriguing details, cutaway views and wide open vistas. The boule-

Durchblicke, Geheimnisse. Der Boulevard weitet sich auf und wird wieder schmaler. Bisweilen gehen Querverbindungen ganz unterschiedlicher Art von ihm ab, solche, die durchstechen, oder solche, die auf Höfe und Plätze führen, Rampen, Treppen oder Terrassen verbinden verschiedene Ebenen – eine bewegte Stadt ist entstanden. Mithilfe von geschwungenen Laufwegen und Fassaden wurden überraschende Stadträume entworfen, die von der Kraft der überkommenen Stadt erzählen, wie wir sie vor allem aus dem Mittelalter kennen. Ausgedacht und gestaltet wurden sie – wie die übrigen Stadträume im Überseequartier und rund um den Magdeburger Hafen – von der Architektin Beth Galí und ihrem Büro BB + GG arquitectes aus Barcelona. Als Bodenbelag sieht die Katalanin auf der gesamten Fläche kolorierten Beton und Naturstein vor: Langeweile ist kein Gebot der Architektur des 21. Jahrhunderts.

Erwartet wurde die Antwort auf eine alte Frage: Kann man lebendige Städte planen? In den ersten Jahren wird sich das Konzept bewähren müssen, und sicher wird es einige Jahre dauern, bis der Boulevard wirklich lebt. Auch wäre es von den architektonisch aufwendigen Fassaden zu viel verlangt, allein zum Garanten der Urbanität zu werden – dazu bedarf es der Menschen, die hier arbeiten, flanieren, einkaufen, essen und trinken. Im rund 7,9 Hektar großen, sogenannten Herzen der Hafencity werden rund tausend Menschen wohnen und

vard appears to broaden and narrow at will. Here and there it intersects with a range of accessways, which guide visitors into courtyards, up and down ramps, along stairs and terraces to other levels—this is a dynamic city. Using gently curving walkways and building façades, the planners have succeeded in creating spaces that traditional models of urban development, especially the medieval. As with all of the public areas throughout the Überseequartier and around Magdeburger Hafen, these spaces are the work of Catalan architect Beth Galí and her Barcelona-based practice BB + GG arquitectes. The spaces are finished with a blend of coloured concrete and natural stone: banal features have no place in 21st-century architecture.

But the question remains: is it possible to plan a vibrant city? As so often, the proof of the pudding is in the eating and it will be several years before the boulevard begins to take off. Ultimately, whether or not the Überseequartier will emerge as a colourful urban space depends not on its spectacular architecture, but on the people who will come here to live, work, shop and socialise. Approximately one thousand people are expected to call Hafencity's 7.9 hectare "heartland" home, while a further 6-7,000 will come here to work, joined by up to 40,000 visitors every day. Of the projected 275,000 square metres of gross floor area, 60,000 square metres have been allocated for retailing and

rund 6000 bis 7000 Menschen arbeiten, darüber hinaus ist mit täglich 40000 Besuchern zu rechnen. 275000 Quadratmeter Bruttogeschossfläche gibt es, allein 60000 Quadratmeter stehen für Einzelhandel und Gastronomie zur Verfügung. Ein Schwerpunkt wird das Gelände rund um und im Alten Hafenamt als Ort für Gourmets und Genießer. Über 400 Wohnungen werden entstehen.

Und überall ist Wasser

Neben dem Boulevard ist die Osakaallee am Magdeburger Hafen die wichtigste Nord-Süd-Erschließung des Überseequartiers. Sie besitzt eine »städtische« und eine »ländliche« Seite, auf der Westseite umschließen Arkaden das Quartier, auf der anderen Alleeseite wird sie durch eine tiefer liegende Promenade am Wasser ergänzt – mehr Alternativen für die Aufenthaltsqualität einer Straße gibt es nicht. In den nächsten Jahren wird der südliche Teil des Überseequartiers realisiert – dann wird der Überseeboulevard Teil einer urbanen Aorta sein, die vom Rathaus bis an die Elbe reicht.

hospitality, much of it centred around Überseequartier's culinary bastion at the Alte Hafenamt building. Altogether, over 400 apartments will be built here.

Water, water everywhere …

Osakaallee on Magdeburger Hafen is Überseequartier's second most important north-south axis after the boulevard. The avenue has an urban and a "rural" face: arcades border the quarter on the western side, while to the east, a lower-lying promenade skirts the waterfront—what more could you wish for from an inner city avenue? The completion of Überseequartier's southern sector some time in the coming years will transform the Überseeboulevard into an urban artery that runs from the Rathaus right through to the Elbe.

Arabica, Ceylon und Java
Wohn- und Geschäftsgebäude Mixed Use Buildings

Standort Location Osakaallee 2–4, 6–8/Am Sandtorkai 2–4/Singapurstraße 1 **Architekten Architects** Arbeitsgemeinschaft Trojan Trojan + Partner und Dietz Joppien Architekten AG **Bauherr Client** Überseequartier Beteiligungs GmbH bestehend aus comprised of ING Real Estate Germany GmbH, Groß & Partner Grundstücksgesellschaft mbH, SNS Property Finance (vormals formerly Bouwfonds Property Finance) **Wettbewerb Competition** 2006 **Bauzeit Date built** 2007–2010 **Bruttogeschossfläche Gross floor area** Arabica: 11 250 qm (sqm); Java: 14 500 qm (sqm); Ceylon: 9750 qm (sqm)

Der nördlichste Teil des Überseequartiers wurde als erster Abschnitt bebaut und eröffnet. Bereits 2007 hatten hier die Arbeiten begonnen. Es ist ein Ort des Übergangs von der Speicherstadt zur neuen Hafencity. Die Architektur geht darauf ein, mittels eines fein gesponnenen und sehr schlanken Wohnturms im Ziegelkleid, der den gegenüberliegenden Speichern signalisiert: Schaut her, ich habe verstanden: Eure Kleidung ist auch meine (Arabica, im Nordosten des Quartiers). Der Block daneben (Java) ist ähnlich strukturiert und mit demselben Stein verkleidet. Er liegt an der Südseite des Sandtorkais und ist niedriger. Die Fensterbänder verraten, dass sich hier viele Büros befinden. Beim Dritten im Bunde – dem Wohnhaus Ceylon – haben die Lage und Ausrichtung zum Magdeburger Hafen für viele attraktive Wohnungen hinter einer Fassade gesorgt, die durch einen riesigen Einschnitt gekennzeichnet ist. Dieser macht das Haus durchlässig bis zum

Überseequartier's northernmost section was the first to be completed and opened to the public. Work began here as early as 2007, and the area forms a transition between the Speicherstadt and Hafencity developments. Its architecture reflects this role, and the calm brickwork exterior of the slender residential tower beckons to the nearby warehouses, extolling the virtues of their common heritage. (Arabica, located in Überseequartier's north-eastern corner). Clad in the same brickwork, the neighbouring block is similar in structure. Bordering on Am Sandtorkai, this office block is shorter in build, and its generous window strips promise plenty of light. Located adjacent to Magdeburger Hafen, the third structure in this ensemble features attractive waterfront apartments behind a red façade with a massive cutaway opening that connects the building with Überseeboulevard. The use of cutaway sections offsets the building's massive scale, while creating

1

2   3

1 Blick von Norden auf den markanten Turm Arabica, gefolgt vom Duplexwohngebäude Ceylon, rechts im Bild das Bürohaus Java am Sandtorkai View from the north of the distinctive Arabica Tower and Ceylon residential duplex building, on the right, the Java office building at Sandtorkai **2** Gegenblick Richtung Altstadt über den Überseeboulevard View in the opposite direction down Überseeboulevard towards the Altstadt **3** Grundriss 1.–6. OG Floor plan 1st–6th storeys

Überseeboulevard. Solche Lockerungs- und Durchdringungsübungen sind der Versuch, selbst bei der großen Körnung der Blocks für attraktive Ein- und Ausblicke sowie eine gute Belichtung auch im Inneren der Wohnanlage zu sorgen. Es ist ein Experiment, ob Wohnen im Herzen der City – so wie hier – in Hamburg genügend attraktiv sein kann.

Die Angebote sind verlockend: Latte Macchiato auf dem Boulevard – freie Sicht auf die Hafenbecken und die Elbe: Friedrichstraße und Ostsee zusammen – ganz frei nach Kurt Tucholsky! In den ersten Jahren nach der Fertigstellung tut sich das nördliche Überseequartier jedoch schwer, zum urbanen Bezirk zu werden. Die Wohnquartiere haben weniger Bezug zur Elbe als die ersten Blocks weiter im Westen, der Einzelhandel zögert bei der Anmietung. Der Versuch, mit verschwenkten Straßenkanten altstädtisches Milieu zu simulieren, ist weitgehend gescheitert. Der Versuch, modellhafte Strukturen zu entwickeln, wie ein Cityquartier mit hoher Verdichtung und gemischten Nutzungen aussehen kann, ist noch nicht schlüssig zu Ende gebracht. Im Süden des Überseequartiers wird es auch deswegen zu Veränderungen im Feinschliff der Planung kommen.

attractive views and flooding the residential block's interior courtyard with light. The building is an experiment in inner city residential living and brings the flair of Berlin's Friedrichstrasse to Hamburg's harbour precinct. Residents can enjoy a latte machiato on the boulevard, take in the sweeping views of the harbour and the Elbe, or stroll along the waterfront promenade – what more could you want?

This northernmost section of the Überseequartier has struggled to develop a truly urban character in its first years. The residential areas lack the proximity to the Elbe River enjoyed by the blocks further west and the uptake of retail floorspace has been sluggish. Attempts to imbue the site with historical flair through the application of curved street design have proven successful. As an attempt to establish model structures combining high-density planning with mixed-usage in an inner city location, this site lacks the necessary coherency. Planning for the southern sector of the Überseequartier will be refined to reflect lessons learnt here.

4

5

4 Java Ostansicht The Java complex, view from the east **5** In den Klinkerfassaden sind mehrere Geschossebenen zu großen Rahmenfeldern zusammengefasst. The storeys within the clinker brick façades are combined into large frames, fixed and movable elements thus melding into a kaleidoscopic frontal collage.

Pacamara
Wohngebäude Residential Building

Standort Location Singapurstraße, Tokyostraße, Am Kaffeelager **Architekten Architects** nps tchoban voss|Architektur und Städtebau **Bauherr Client** Überseequartier Beteiligungs GmbH **Wettbewerb Competition** 2006 **Bauzeit Date built** 2008–10 **Bruttogeschossfläche Gross floor area** 18500 qm (sqm)

Material und Duktus dieses Bauteils im nördlichen Überseequartier orientieren sich an den Bauten der Architekten Trojan + Trojan, die auch den städtebaulichen Wettbewerb gewonnen hatten. Zwei Gebäudekörper umschließen einen Wohnhof, der wie eine geschützte, halböffentliche Warft über dem Niveau des übrigen Überseequartiers liegt. Über mehrere Öffnungen wird eine Verbindung nach außen hergestellt: Ein Schlitz auf der westlichen Seite trennt beispielsweise den Körper vollständig und ermöglicht einen Zugang zum »Hofgarten« vom Straßenniveau aus. Helle Trennwände und -böden der Loggien sind kleine architektonische Aperçus, die die strengen Fassaden an der Westseite beleben. Zum Boulevard hin öffnet sich ein fünfgeschossiges Fenster über der Sockelzone und verschafft mit einem großen Balkon über dem Boulevard Ausblick und Verbindung.

With its characteristic style and choice of materials, this building in Überseequartier's northern sector has Trojan and Trojan (the winners of the urban planning competition) written all over it. Two elements enclose an elevated residential courtyard, shielding it from its surroundings while providing several points of access to this semi-public space. An incision in the western wing cuts through the building, connecting the courtyard with the adjacent road. The partition walls and floors of the loggias are decked out in light tones—an architectural aperçu which brings the western façade to life. A cutaway section spanning five storeys connects the courtyard with the outside world and affords residents views of the boulevard from a spacious balcony.

1

2　　　　　3

1 Den östlichen Abschluss des nördlichen Überseequartiers bildet zurzeit noch das Wohngebäude Pacamara. Hier sind ein Kinokomplex und ein Hotel geplant. The Pacamara residential building currently still marks the easternmost edge of the northern Überseequartier. A cinema complex and a hotel are in planning. **2+3** Blicke vom Überseeboulevard Views from Überseeboulevard

Büro- und Geschäftshaus Sumatra-Kontor
Office and Commercial Building

Standort Location Nördliches Überseequartier **Architekten Architects** EEA – Erick van Egeraat associated architects, Rotterdam **Bauherr Client** Überseequartier Beteiligungs GmbH bestehend aus comprised of ING Real Estate Germany GmbH, Groß & Partner Grundstücksgesellschaft mbH, SNS Property Finance (vormals formerly Bouwfonds Property Finance) **Wettbewerb Competition** 2003 **Bauzeit Date built** 2008–10 **Bruttogeschossfläche Gross floor area** 36500 qm (sqm)

»Das moderne, gemischt genutzte Sumatra-Kontor besticht durch seine für hanseatische Verhältnisse provokante Architekturlinie und wird mit seinem hohen Wiedererkennungswert das Überseequartier prägen.« So oder ähnlich wurde dieser größte Brocken im Quartier angekündigt. Tatsächlich ist er kantig, schräg, mit Brüchen – ein künstlicher Felsen im Hafengelände. Aber seine (zu) gewollten vertikalen Verwerfungen und das zurzeit noch auf Fernwirkung angelegte Streifenkleid wird nach und nach in der engen Blockrandwelt verschwinden. Und man ist geneigt hinzuzufügen: dankenswerterweise. Dieser erdfarbentürkise Konsum-Container kann knapp 5000 Quadratmeter Ladenfläche aufnehmen. Die Wohnungen befinden sich in einem eigenständigen Gebäudeteil an der Nord-Ost-Spitze an separaten Innenhöfen.

"Breaking with Hamburg's austere dress code, the Sumatra Building's provocative lines and unforgettable form make this mixed-use building a defining feature in Hamburg's Überseequartier". The building's construction was accompanied by much fanfare (as paraphrased above), and its jutting angular lines and fractured surface certainly paint a striking picture. But its overwrought vertical lines and striped façade are at their best when viewed from a distance and will soon be swallowed up as work on nearby buildings is concluded. And, one might add, perhaps that is all for the best. Dressed in earth tones and turquoise, this consumer block will eventually house approximately 5,000 square metres of retail space. Concentrated at the north-eastern corner of the complex, the building's residential apartments will enjoy access to separate courtyards.

1

2

3

1+2 Die erdfarbene Vorhangfassade, überdies noch merkwürdig verkrümmt, führte zu heftigen Diskussion: schön oder hässlich? The earth-coloured curtain wall, which is also oddly asymmetrical, sparked a heated debate in Hamburg as to its aesthetic merits – classy or trashy? **3** Blick auf das Sumatra-Kontor – über ein Grundstück, das später bebaut wird View of the Sumatra Building – overlooking a plot slated for later development

Altes Hafenamt
mit Wohnturm und Infopavillon
Altes Hafenamt, Residential Tower and Info Pavilion

Standort Location Osakaallee 14 **Architekten Architects** Bolles+Wilson, Münster **Bauherr Client** Überseequartier Beteiligungs GmbH bestehend aus comprised of ING Real Estate Germany GmbH, Groß & Partner Grundstücksgesellschaft mbH, SNS Property Finance (vormals formerly Bouwfonds Property Finance) **Wettbewerb Competition** 2006 **Bauzeit Date built** 2008 (1. Abschnitt / Pavillon 1st stage/Pavillon) **Bruttogeschossfläche Gross floor area** 5240 qm (sqm)

Rund um das denkmalgeschützte Alte Hafenamt entsteht das kulinarische und gastronomische Zentrum des Übersee- quartiers. Während im Alten Hafenamt selbst ein buntes, rein gastronomisches Angebot zu finden sein wird, sollte es auch eine Markthalle mit frischen Wa- ren geben. Das steht inzwischen infra- ge, stattdessen wird wohl ein Wochen- markt unter freiem Himmel eingerichtet werden. Im Info-Pavillon, der sich mit seiner Form vom üblichen rechten Win- kel verabschiedet hat, geben Modelle und Multimedia-Exponate Einblick in die Zukunft des hoffentlich bald quirli- gen Quartiers. Dabei sollte man auch auf die Innenarchitektur der verschie- denen Ebenen und das Design der Ausstellungsmöbel achten (Entwurf: 3deluxe, Wiesbaden). Das benachbarte Hotel 25hours erweitert sich mit einem Bordinghouse in den Turm.

The listed Altes Hafenamt (Port Authori- ty) building lies at the centre of Übersee- quartier's culinary heartland. With the Altes Hafenamt hosting a smorgasbord of culinary enterprises, the adjoining Markthalle was expected to embrace a variety of eateries and suppliers of fresh products. This concept has since been challenged and the establishment of an open-air weekly market seems likely in- stead. Models and multimedia exhibits on show at the eye-catching Info Pavil- ion offer visitors a glimpse of this vibrant district's future. The Pavilion's interior design and furnishings (design by 3de- luxe, Wiesbaden) go head to head with its angular exterior. The neighbouring hotel 25hours will expand into the tower with a boarding house.

1

2   3

1 Blick von der Osakaallee zum Überseequartier mit dem Infopavillon des Quartiers (rechts: Altes Hafenamt) Überseequartier with Info Pavilion, seen from Osakaallee (on the right: Altes Hafenamt) 2 Schnitt Pavillon Cross section of the Pavilion 3 Das geplante Ensemble aus Pavillon, Altem Hafenamt und Campanile The planned ensemble: Pavilion, Altes Hafenamt and Campanile

Virginia / Hotel 25hours
Hotel, Wohn- und Geschäftshaus Mixed Use Building

Standort Location Überseeallee 5 **Architekten Architects** BLK2 Böge Lindner K2 Architekten, Hamburg **Bauherr Client** Überseequartier Beteiligungs GmbH, Hamburg **Wettbewerb Competition** 2006 **Bauzeit Date built** 2008–11 **Bruttogeschossfläche Gross floor area** 23 730 qm (sqm)

B.22

Verglichen mit dem Nachbarn, dem Sumatra-Kontor, könnten die Gegensätze nicht stärker sein: ein Outfit mit einem hellen freundlichen Ziegelstein, auch wenn die vorgeschriebenen Dehnungsfugen manchmal zu sehr von der klaren Gliederung für Fenster oder Vorsprünge ablenken. Die städtebauliche Figur des Projekts war durch die Planungen des Überseequartiers vorgegeben. Der Entwurf interpretiert die Vorgaben, indem der Block oberhalb eines vollständig überbauten Erdgeschosses durch schmale Frakturen in den Eckbereichen geöffnet wird. Durch diese Öffnungen ergeben sich interessante Blickbeziehungen und räumliche Übergänge zwischen Innenhof und dem übrigen Überseequartier. Im Unterschied zur Straße sind, wie es in Hamburg üblich ist, die Wände im Hof zur besseren Reflektion des Lichts weiß, oder wie in diesem Fall mit hohem Glasanteil. Schon lange hat ein Hamburger Backsteinneubau nicht mehr eine solche Spannkraft entwickelt.

The contrast between Hotel Virginia and the neighbouring Sumatra Building could not be greater. While the mandatory expansion joints detract somewhat from the clear lines of Hotel Virginia's windows and protruding balconies, the building is dressed up to the nines in friendly light brickwork. Its form and scale were largely determined by the Überseequartier's urban planning concept. Making full use of the available space, the architects added a number of slender incisions to open the building above its massive base, creating interesting visual perspectives and connecting the building's inner courtyard with the rest of the quarter. The white walls in the courtyard are complemented by similarly coloured panels and plenty of glass on the building's exterior, ensuring that guests enjoy plenty of light. Hamburg has not seen a brick building sporting such an audacious design for many years.

1

2

3

1 Blick auf den gemischten Komplex Virginia (rechts vorne das alte Hafenamt, vgl. S. 137–138). Hier hat das 25hours Hotel Platz gefunden. View of the mixed-use Virginia complex (in front on the right, the Altes Hafenamt building, cf. pp. 137–138). The 25hours Hotel has taken up residence here. 2 Innenhof mit Wohnungen Inner courtyard with apartments 3 Grundriss Floor plan

Projekte Südliches Überseequartier
Southern Überseequartier Development Projects

Standort Location Südliches Überseequartier **Architekten Architects** Projekt Linnen: BDP, London; Projekt Silk: Léon Wohlhage Wernik, Berlin; Projekt Waterfront Towers: UN-Studios, Rotterdam **Bauherr Client** Überseequartier Beteiligungs GmbH, Hamburg **Bruttogeschossfläche Gross floor area** Linnen 40 520 qm (sqm), Silk 31 200 qm (sqm), Waterfront Towers 17 620 qm (sqm)

Während das nördliche Überseequartier bereits überwiegend realisiert und bezogen ist, wird mit dem Bauen im Süden des Quartiers jetzt erst begonnen. Dies wurde mit Arbeiten an der U-Bahn-Linie 4 begründet, deren Untergrundstationen zunächst im Rohbau gebaut werden mussten. Unter den Projekten fallen bereits in der Planung drei Projekte durch ihre kühnen Baukörper auf: Das Bürohaus Linnen variiert mit seiner hervorstrebenden Spitze wieder einmal erfolgreich das Dampfermotiv. Der Gebäudekomplex Silk auf den Überseeterrassen bietet auf drei Ebenen eine schöne neue Einkaufswelt, und die beiden tänzelnden Waterfront Towers weisen den Besuchern des Boulevards den Weg zum Wasser. Finanzierungsengpässe können leider für Verzögerung und auch Veränderungen der Planungen im südlichen Überseequartier führen.

While most of the buildings in the quarter's northern sector have now been completed, work is only just commencing to the south following the construction of several underground rail stations for Hamburg's subway. Three of these new projects are particularly notable for their striking forms: The Linnen building's jutting angular form is a highly evocative allusion to the ocean-going steamships of Hamburg's maritime past. On the Übersee Terraces, three storeys of the Silk building complex will be given over to retailing. Nearby, the capricious Waterfront Towers beckon visitors to the boulevard to join them at the water's edge. Unfortunately, funding shortfalls could cause delays and lead to changes in the plans for the southern sector of Überseequartier.

1

2

3

1 Visualisierung Projekt Linnen Visualisation of the Linnen building **2** Die Waterfront Towers sollen direkt am Elbstrom stehen. The Waterfront Towers will be situated right on the Elbe. **3** Der Komplex Silk soll Einzelhandel aufnehmen – auf drei Ebenen. The Silk building complex will be dedicated to retail outlets – over three levels.

Science Center

Standort Location New Orleans Straße **Architekten Architects** Rem Koolhaas mit and Office for Metropolitan Architecture (OMA), Rotterdam **Bruttogeschossfläche Gross floor area** 23 000 qm (sqm)

B.26

Es ist schon der zweite Entwurf von OMA, einem Büro des Rem Koolhaas, für ein Science Center – der erste war obsolet geworden, weil er in einer harmonischen Auseinandersetzung mit dem Cruise Center, in einem Spiel von konkaver und konvexer Form, von flach und hoch entworfen worden war, das projektierte Cruise Center jetzt aber weiter westlich geplant wird. Der gegenwärtige Entwurf für das Science Center sieht einen stehenden kantigen Ring aus Seecontainern vor, der direkt am Elbufer steht. Es ist Sinnbild für die Verbindung zwischen Hafen und Stadt und das Symbol eines Tors zur Wissenswelt. Das inhaltliche Konzept orientiert sich an einem Weltbaukasten: Zehn naturwissenschaftliche Schwerpunktthemen werden hier auf spannende Weise dargestellt und Kindern, Jugendlichen und Erwachsenen gleichermaßen verständlich gemacht. Realisierung und Baubeginn liegen noch im Planungsnebel.

This is the second science centre design prepared by Rem Koolhaas' OMA for Hafencity—featuring a visually captivating interaction of concave, convex, flat and vertical forms, plans for the first design were shelved when the site of the proposed Cruise Center was shifted westwards. The present design for the Science Center features an upright ring-shaped building of shipping containers positioned directly adjacent to the Elbe River. Symbolically, the Science Center opens towards the port and the city, forming a gateway to the world of knowledge. The Center's modular exhibition concept covers ten key topics, providing children, teens and adults alike with an exciting overview of the world of science. The planning process is ongoing and the building's future is as yet undecided.

Es sollte das zweite großartige architektonische Zeichen für die Zukunft der Hafencity werden: Aber mit der Realisierung wird man wohl warten müssen, bis die Elbphilharmonie vollendet worden ist – und das kann dauern. Touted as the second-largest architectural trademark of the future Hafencity, the realisation of the Science Center will have to wait until the Elbphilharmonie is completed – and that may take a while yet.

C.01/02 Spiegel-Verlag und
         Ericus-Contor
C.03/04/05 Germanischer Lloyd
C.06/07/08 Brücken-Ensemble
C.09 Internationales Maritimes
     Museum Hamburg
     im Kaispeicher B
C.10 Verwaltung Gebr. Heinemann
C.11 Hauptzollamt/Zollamt Hafencity
C.12 Ökumenisches Forum Brücke
C.13 Greenpeace-Zentrale
     und designxport
C.14 U-Bahn-Station Überseequartier
C.15 HafenCity Universität (HCU)
C.16 Baakenhafenbrücke
C.17 Aussichtsturm View Point

C.18 U-Bahn-Station HafenCity
     Universität
C.19 Automuseum Prototyp
C.20/21 Oberhafen-Kantine/
     neues Umspannwerk

Östliche
Hafencity

Eastern Hafencity

Der Neubau des Spiegel Verlags am Deichtor ist jetzt der imposante Auftakt der Hafencity. Er war als eine Art »Fenster« zur Stadt gedacht, die ursprünglich geplante Medienwand auf der zurückgesetzten Fassade wurde verworfen, nur der Rücksprung blieb.

The new Spiegel building at Deichtor now marks the towering entrance to Hafencity. Conceived of as a kind of "window" to the city, the originally planned media wall on the recessed façade was shelved, so that now only the cutout remains.

Von der Mitte ostwärts:
Dinge ändern sich rasch
From the Centre to the East: Plus Ça Change...

Inzwischen werden in der Hafencity die Gebiete östlich des Magdeburger Hafens bebaut: Sehr schnell bekommt die »östliche Mitte« ihre Konturen, und die Überschrift heißt hier »Wissenschaft und Bildung«. Mit der HafenCity Universität (HCU), der Kühne Logistics University, der Greenpeace-Zentrale und dem designxport hamburg entstehen weitere Bauten mit guten architektonischen und urbanen Konzepten, also in einer guten Platzierung zu den öffentlichen Räumen an Land und auf dem Wasser. Ergänzt wird der »Nutzungsmix« mit Angeboten für die Kreativbranche. Zwischen dem Magdeburger Hafen im Westen, dem Brooktorhafen im Norden und dem Lohsepark im Osten entsteht ein Viertel, das die urbanen Qualitäten eines kleinen Universitätscampus mit unmittelbarer Cityqualität (im Überseequartier) mischt.

Ob der gute Plan aufgeht, wird man bald wissen, weil die HafenCity Universität (eine spezielle Hochschule für alle Disziplinen des Bauens) jetzt ans Netz gegangen ist. Zwei Dinge sind aber

The sections of Hafencity east of Magdeburger Hafen are now under construction. The contours of this area are fast emerging and already the leitmotif is clear: "science and education". HafenCity University, the Kühne Logistics University, the Greenpeace head office and Hamburg designxport are realising high-quality architectural and urban design concepts that are well positioned in relation to the public spaces on land and water. This "mix of uses" is complemented by features attractive to creative professionals. Between the Magdeburger Hafen basin to the west, the Brooktorhafen to the north, and Lohsepark to the east, a quarter is emerging that blends the qualities of a small university campus with those of a bustling city centre (in the Überseequartier).

Now that the HafenCity University (a special university for all disciplines related to construction) has moved into its new building in Magdeburger Hafen, it will soon be seen whether this ambitious plan can work in reality. However,

schon deutlich geworden: Es wird langsamer vorangehen als im Westen, der architektonische Überraschungseffekt ist kleiner, auch wenn gerade auf insgesamt 30000 Quadratmetern Bruttogeschossfläche an der östlichen Uferpromenade des Magdeburger Hafens (Entwurf des Büros Bob Gysin + Partner BGP Architekten aus Zürich) eine anspruchsvolle Arkadenanlage als sogenannte Stadtloggia entsteht (vgl. S. 170–171).

Die östlichen Quartiere – der Masterplan wurde überarbeitet

Für die drei östlichen Quartiere Oberhafen, Baakenhafen und Elbbrücken wurde der Masterplan 2010 in Kooperation mit der »Behörde für Stadtentwicklung und Umwelt« und den Verfassern des ersten Masterplanentwurfs (Kees Christiaanse mit Astoc) überarbeitet (vgl. S. 26). Die Herausforderungen der urbanen Stadtentwicklung für die östliche Hafencity liegen auf der Hand: Räumlich sind die Quartiere nicht so kompakt und nicht so gut an die alte Innenstadt angebunden – weder mit direktem Blick auf die City noch auf die sich bereits entwickelnde Hafencity. Oberhafen und Baakenhafen sind überdies Gebiete, die sich über fast zwei Kilometer in die Länge ziehen. Am Baakenhafen und im Westteil des Quartiers Elbbrücken wird ein neuer Wohnstandort geplant. In den beiden Quartieren können knapp 3000

two things are already certain: work here will progress more slowly than in the largely completed western Hafencity, and the architectural surprise effect will be more modest, notwithstanding the creation of an ambitious waterfront arcade structure (the so-called "urban loggia", cf. pp. 170–171) measuring 30,000 square metres on the east bank of Magdeburger Hafen (design by Bob Gysin + Partner BGP Architects from Zurich).

The Eastern Quarters—the Master Plan Revised

The three eastern quarters of Oberhafen, Baakenhafen, and Elbbrücken necessitated a revision of the 2010 master plan (cf. p. 26) in consultation with Hamburg's Ministry of Urban Development and the Environment and the creators of the initial master plan (Kees Christiaanse together with Astoc). The challenges in terms of urban development in the eastern Hafencity are clear: these areas are neither as compact nor as well connected to the inner city as the eastern or central sections. It also lacks clear views of the city centre and the already completed sections of Hafencity. Moreover, Oberhafen and Baakenhafen are particularly elongated, stretching for over two kilometres. A new residential area is planned for Baakenhafen and the eastern section of the Elbbrücken quarter. Roughly 300 new apartments are likely to be built in both quarters, raising

neue Wohnungen entstehen, die Zahl der Wohnungen in der Hafencity insgesamt also von 5500 auf 8500 wachsen. Hamburg braucht dringend neue Wohnungen – hier werden sie in einem breiten Spektrum angeboten: Eigentumswohnungen, Baugruppenmodelle und – teilweise mit öffentlicher Förderung – familienfreundliche Mietwohnungen.

Der Masterplan aus dem Jahr 2000 erwies sich bisher als guter Ausgangspunkt für die weitere Planung und Realisierung. Allerdings wurden im Quartier Am Lohsepark grundlegende Anpassungen an den neuen Zentralpark notwendig und für den Ostteil sogar eine umfassende Revision. So hat die rigide Substitution der ostwestlich durch die östliche Hafencity verlaufenden Pfeilerbahnstrecke aus dem 19. Jahrhundert das alte Denkmal mit schützenswerten Stadtbahnbögen zerstört. Die neue Konstruktion ist ausschließlich ökonomischen Überlegungen geschuldet, obwohl es einen sehr eleganten Vorschlag des österreichisch-französischen Architekten Dietmar Feichtinger (1. Preis in einem Wettbewerb) gab. Anders als die nun realisierte Variante hätte sie den Bereich des Oberhafens nicht abgeriegelt, sondern dessen Entwicklung im Verbund mit anderen Gebieten der Hafencity Vorschub geleistet.

the total number of residential units in Hafencity from 5,500 to 8.500. Hamburg urgently needs new apartments, and those built here will cover a broad spectrum, including owner-occupied flats, cooperative models, and—in some cases publicly subsidised—family-friendly rental apartments.

The master plan from 2000 has so far provided a sound basis for ongoing planning and realisation. However, fundamental adjustments were called for in the Am Lohsepark quarter, and the eastern quarters also required thorough revision. The austere substitute for the distinctive arched railway viaduct from the nineteenth-century that ran through the east end of Hafencity involved the destruction of an historic monument. The new structure is exclusively a product of economic considerations, even though an extremely elegant and prize-winning proposal was submitted by the Austro-French architect Dietmar Feichtinger. Unlike the version that was chosen and has now been realised, Feichtinger's viaduct would not have sealed off the Oberhafen area, and would therefore have encouraged its integration with other parts of Hafencity.

Der ganz wilde Osten: Transformationsräume und die neue Kreativität

Nun aber würde der normale Entwicklungsprozess der Hafencity auf den Kopf gestellt, hieß es inzwischen auf der offiziellen Website der HafenCity GmbH zum Oberhafen. In dem Quartier wurde sichtbar die ehemalige Masterplanung grundsätzlich infrage gestellt und verändert. Statt hübscher Klötzchen-Ästhetik, wie sie im alten Modell im Kesselhaus zu sehen war und wie sie mit mächtiger (meist Blockrand-)Bebauung im Westen weitgehend realisiert wurde, wird jetzt auf Bestandssicherung der fast 400 Meter langen Bahnhallen und -schuppen gesetzt und »über eine graduelle Entwicklung nachgedacht«. Die Grundstücke werden nicht verkauft, sondern verbleiben dauerhaft im Eigentum des Sondervermögens Stadt und Hafen (HafenCity Hamburg GmbH). Sie bilden nun den Grundstock für das Kultur- und Kreativquartier Oberhafen – eine erstaunliche Karriere für eine alte Bahnfläche, die hochwassergefährdet ist und bis 2013 überwiegend für Logistikzwecke genutzt wurde. Zukünftig wird das Quartier Oberhafen Nukleus eines großen Kreativ- und Kulturquartiers sein.

The Wild Wild East: Transformative Spaces and New Creativity

The official Hafencity website claimed that the Oberhafen has turned on its head the original development process. It's already apparent that the development of this quarter involved fundamentally questioning and ultimately changing the master plan. In place of an aesthetic that favoured pretty little blocks, as could be seen in the 3D models on display in the Hafencity Info-Center, and as was realised in the voluminous developments (mostly based on closed-perimeter blocks) in Hafencity's west-end, the new approach involved retaining the almost 400-metre-long railway buildings and considering a gradual development. The lands here have not been sold, but will instead remain the long-term assets of the publicly owned HafenCity Hamburg GmbH. These lands form the core of a new cultural and creative quarter in the Oberhafen. This will give an astonishing new lease of life to this area, which is endangered by flooding and which was used until 2013 mostly for logistics. The Oberhafen quarter will become the nucleus of a major creative and cultural quarter.

Spiegel-Verlag und Ericus-Contor
Bürogebäude Office Buildings

Standort Location Brooktorkai/Ericusspitze **Architekten Architects** Henning Larsen Architects, Kopenhagen **Bauherr Client** Robert Vogel GmbH & Co. KG **Wettbewerb Competition** 2007 **Bauzeit Date built** 2008–11 **Nettogeschossfläche Floor area** 30 000 qm (sqm) Ericus-Contor 21 000 qm (sqm)

Es ist nicht verkehrt, an diesem wichtigen Zugang der Hafencity ein Haus wie ein hochgestelltes Schaufenster, also Architektur als Medium auszustellen – für den Spiegel-Verlag ist das eine willkommene gebaute Visitenkarte. Und stadträumlich bekommt der von der City aus blickende Betrachter Halt auf dem Screen. Die Fassaden des Spiegel-Komplexes (im großen Bauteil residiert der Verlag, im kleinen, dem Ericus-Contor, sind viele kleine Firmen ansässig), sind nicht so elegant und originell geworden wie erhofft. Das hat Gründe: Das ursprünglich vorgesehene »Medienfenster« als Megascreen ist im Zeitalter von iPhone und iPad obsolet geworden, und heute sind die ganz normalen Bürofassaden, auch wenn sie großenteils zurückgesetzt wurden und eine Art Screen simulieren sollen, nicht überzeugend. Die Fassade wirkt zu geschlossen und wegen des Sonnenschutzes zu überinstrumentiert. Dafür aber gewinnt das Projekt durch die großzügigen, öf-

It was not a bad idea to construct a building that resembles a vertical showcase at this important point of access to Hafencity. Here, the architecture is the medium and, moreover, for the client, Spiegel Publishing, an attractive calling card. Seen from the city the "screen" offers the viewer a sense of spatial composure. The façades of the Spiegel complex (the magazine publisher has its offices in the larger building, while the smaller volume, known as the Ericus-Contor, is home to numerous small companies) did not turn out as elegant and unique as originally intended. There is a reason for this: The original concept of a "media window" resembling a giant video screen has become obsolete in the age of the iPhone and iPad, and today these essentially run-of-the-mill office façades, though partially set back and intended to simulate a kind of screen, are no longer compelling. The façade appears too closed and slightly overwrought due to the

1

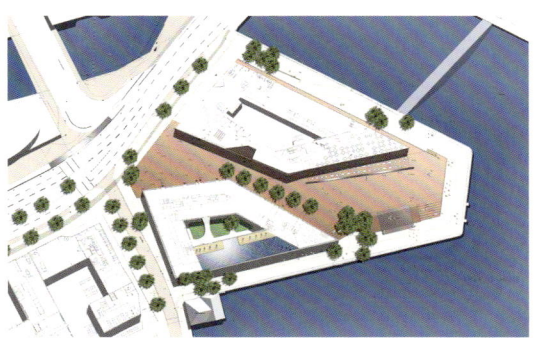

2

1 Imposanter Auftakt der Hafencity an der Ericusspitze/Deichtor: links Ericus-Contor, rechts Spiegel-Verlag Impressive entryway to Hafencity at Ericusspitze/Deichtor: Ericus-Contor (left) and Spiegel-Verlag (right) **2** Übersichtsplan Site plan

fentlichen Freibereiche, die zwischen den beiden Bauteilen und an den Kaimauern liegen. So wie das Unilever-Haus (vgl. S. 92–95) durch seine enge Verzahnung zwischen öffentlichem und privatem Raum überrascht, wird hier am östlichen Zugang zur Hafencity eine Art öffentlicher Glacis für alle entstehen. Auch die Vorbildfunktion für nachhaltiges Bauen wird deutlich: Der Komplex hat das Umweltzeichen der Hafencity in Gold erhalten. Nicht nur wegen der siebzig geothermischen Sonden, die in hundert Metern Tiefe den Wärmeaustausch herstellen, sondern auch weil der Gesamtprimärbedarf des Gebäudes auf weniger als hundert Kilowattstunden begrenzt wurde. Städtebaulich ist hier der Gegenpol zur am westlichen Ende gelegenen Elbphilharmonie entstanden: ein starkes östliches Eingangsportal und eine gute Ensemblewirkung mit dem gläsernen Deichtor-Center – in der Fernwirkung aufregend, so wie das eben ist, wenn Städte als großes Ereignis aus der Vogelperspektive im Stadtmodell geplant werden. Im gewaltigen Atrium ist eine beeindruckende Landschaft aus Rampen und Treppen entstanden, die die an den Außenwänden liegenden Büros verbindet.

sunscreens. Having said that, the project benefits greatly from the spacious public areas between the two buildings and along the quayside. Just as the Unilever building (cf. pp. 92–95) involves a surprising inter-meshing of private and public space, this project, at the eastern "gate" to Hafencity provides a kind of glacis that is open to all. It is also easy to see why this building is a model of sustainable architecture: It was awarded Hafencity's gold Ecolabel award for sustainability. Not just on account of the 70 geothermal heat exchange systems buried to a depth of 100 metres, but also because the building's total primary energy requirements have been capped at under 100 kW/h. In terms of the overall planning of Hafencity, this building is intended as the opposite number of the Elbphilharmonie: a strong eastern portal and a fitting complement to the neighbouring glass-and-steel Deichtor-Center. From a distance and from the air this ensemble fully lives up to the promise of an architect's model. The gigantic atrium presents a striking landscape of ramps and stairways which connect the offices lining the building's exterior.

3

4

5

3 Auch der Ausblick ist spektakulär, hier aus der Cafeteria mit Fragmenten der ehemaligen Spiegel-Kantine aus dem Altbau (Verner Panton, 1969). The view is likewise spectacular, here from the new cafeteria featuring legacy elements from the cafeteria in the old Spiegel building (Verner Panton, 1969). **4** Atrium mit Verbindungsrampen und -treppen Atrium with connecting ramps and stairs **5** Blick vom Atrium auf die Stadt View towards the city from the atrium

Germanischer Lloyd
Bürogebäude Office Building

Standort Location Brooktorkai 18 (und Nachbarn and neighbours) **Architekten Architects** gmp · von Gerkan, Marg und Partner, Hamburg; Störmer Murphy and Partners, Hamburg; Antonio Citterio Patricia Viel and Partners, Mailand **Bauherr Client** St Annen Platz GmbH & Co. KG c/o Quantum Immobilien AG **Wettbewerb Competition** 2005 **Bauzeit Date built** 2008–10; 2005–10 (Citterio) **Bruttogeschossfläche Gross floor area** 54000 qm (sqm); 16000 qm (sqm) (Citterio)

Klare Vorgaben für Baukörper und Materialien erzeugen eine deutliche Backsteinkante des lang gezogenen, knapp 200 Meter langen Baublocks, am Brooktorkai im Gegenspiel zur Speicherstadt. Allerdings gibt es gedeckte Freiräume und Atrien, und so entsteht auch der Eindruck eines mäandrierenden Baukörpers. Die sogenannte Hamburger Moderne des frühen 20. Jahrhunderts ist nicht weiß, sondern rot, aber sachlich. Mit dem Neubau der Zentrale des Germanischen Lloyds, die das Herzstück dieses Ensembles besetzt, haben mehrere Architekten bewiesen, dass dieser Ansatz auch im 21. Jahrhundert seine Berechtigung behält. Jeder Versuch, hier mit der Speicherstadt zusammen eine neue Hamburger Großstadtstraße zu schaffen und quasi in Fortführung des historischen Kontorhausviertels mit dessen kompromissloser Huldigung des dunkel gebrannten Klinkers zu bauen, kann nur in Hamburger Kleiderordnung eingehalten werden. Alles andere wäre

Thanks to clear guidelines on structural form and materials, this elongated 200-metre-long block on Brooktorkai reflects the angular, red-brick architecture of the Speicherstadt, which is located directly across the canal. However, this building also contains hidden atria and open spaces that convey the feeling of a meandering volume. The so-called Hamburg Modernist school of the early twentieth century is not white, but red, and down to earth With the new headquarters of Germanischer Lloyd, which is located at the heart of this ensemble, several architects have proven that this approach remains valid in the twenty-first century. Any attempt to create a new metropolitan boulevard in Hamburg—in this case involving the Speicherstadt—and essentially continuing the historical business district (the Kontorhausviertel) with its resolute homage to burnt clinker brick, can only be achieved by observing Hamburg's architectural dress code. Anything else

1

2

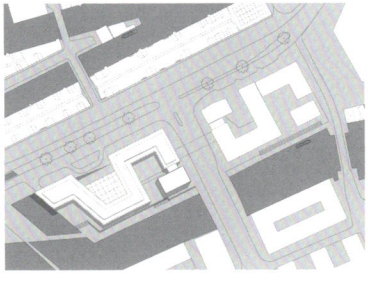

3

1 Übersicht über das Gesamtensemble von Norden, dem Brooktorkai The entire ensemble, seen from Brooktorkai in the north 2 Blick von unten durch ein Atriumsdach View of an atrium rooftop from below 3 Übersichtsplan Site plan

eine Fahrlässigkeit gegenüber der Hamburger Baukultur. So gelang der Beweis, dass mit hanseatischen Bildern die City an dieser Stelle richtig, d.h. konsequent, weitergebaut wurde. Die starke Rücksichtnahme auf die denkmalgeschützte Speicherstadt und das Kontorhausviertel könnte sich positiv auf die Entscheidung für ein UNESCO-Welterbe in Hamburg auswirken.

Die Architektur ist vieles: exakt, solide, traditionell. Eines ist sie trotzdem nicht: langweilig. Dafür sorgen die etwas andere Handschrift des Designarchitekten Antonio Citterio aus Mailand für einen Büro-/Wohnturm (Material: Naturstein) und der mutige Einsatz von Kupfer und Metall durch Jan Störmer für die beiden turmartigen Erhöhungen im Ensemble. Wermutstropfen: Die Eingangshalle des Hamburger Prestigeunternehmens Germanischer Lloyd ist belanglos, das haben die beteiligten Architekten von gmp zum Beispiel mit dem Zürich-Haus schon besser gemacht und mit mutigeren Beispielen bewiesen, dass sie es können!

would be an sign of disrespect towards Hamburg's architectural cu ture. By observing the code this building has furnished proof that the correct (i.e., consistent) way to develop the city is by adhering to Hanseatic tradition. The large degree of consideration given to the listed Speicherstadt and the Kontorhausviertel may have a positive influence on the decision in favour of UNESCO World Heritage Site status in Hamburg.

This architecture is manifold: exact, solid and traditional. Boring it is most certainly not. This is ensured by, among other elements, the marked signature of the Italian designer architect Antonio Citterio in a tower that unites office and residential use (material: natural stone) and the daring use of copper and other metals by Jan Störmer in the two tower-like elevations within this ensemble. The downside: the entrance hall to this building that houses one of Hamburg's most prestigious companies fa ls to impress. The architects involved from gmp have, in the past, provided ample proof that they can do a lot better, as can be seen in the Zurich Building!

4 Ansicht vom Fleet, Bauteil Germanischer Lloyd View of the Germanischer Lloyd building from the canal 5 Bauabschnitt von Antonio Citterio Building part designed by Antonio Citterio 6 Grundriss Bauteil Germanischer Lloyd Floor plan of the Germanischer Lloyd block

4

5

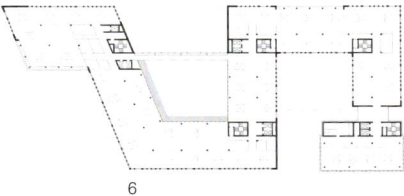

6

Brücken-Ensemble
Ensemble of Bridges

Museumspasserelle/Shanghaibrücke/St.-Annen-Fleet-Brücke **Standort Location** Nördliches Elbtorquartier **Architekten Architects** Dietmar Feichtinger Architectes, Paris, Ingenieure Engineers: WTM Engineers **Bauherr Client** HafenCity Hamburg GmbH **Wettbewerb Competition** 2004 **Bauzeit Date built** 2006–12

Die Shanghaibrücke verbindet die beiden Ufer des Brooktorhafens, über das Bauwerk führt die neue, hochwassersicher gelegene Shanghaiallee. Diese Brücke wirkt wie ein weiter Platz, der nur zufällig über dem Wasser liegt: Fast so breit wie lang, bietet sie neben dem Autoverkehr Fußgänger- und Radfahrerbereiche. Ihre Konstruktion versteckt sie komplett unter der Fahrbahn. Inzwischen sind zwei weitere Brückenschläge vornehmlich für Fußgänger von denselben Architekten gebaut worden: die Museumspasserelle als nördlicher Zugang zum Internationalen Maritimen Museum und die gänzlich neue St.-Annen-Fleetbrücke. Die Shanghaibrücke und ihre neuen Nachbarn über Wasser bilden eine »Familie« und sind Beispiele für die Konsequenz, in der Verpflichtung einer »Brückenstadt« zu stehen (Hamburg hat mehr Brücken als Venedig, Amsterdam und andere zusammen).

Shanghai Bridge straddles the Brooktorhafen, supporting one of Hafencity's most important lateral thoroughfares, Shanghaiallee. This bridge feels like a broad square that just happens to be built over water. Almost as wide as it is long, it accommodates pedestrians and cyclists as well as motorised traffic. The structural elements are all concealed beneath the roadway. The same architecture firm has since built two additional bridges—both principally for pedestrians—in Hafencity: Léon-Brücke which provide access to the IMM from the north, and the entirely new St.-Annen-Fleetbrücke. The Shanghaibrücke and its neighbouring bridges form a kind of "family" and exemplify a commitment to tradition in this city of bridges (Hamburg, after all, has more bridges than Venice and Amsterdam combined).

1

2

3

1 Geknickt: Léon-Brücke Dog leg: Léon-Brücke **2** Hochwassersicher und in der Wirkung wie ein Platz: Shanghaibrücke über dem Brooktorhafen Flood-proof and public plaza-like: the Shanghaibrücke spanning Brooktorhafen **3** Elegante Ansicht: St.-Annen-Fleet-Brücke Elegant perspective: St.-Annen-Fleet-Brücke

Internationales Maritimes Museum Hamburg im Kaispeicher B
Museum Building

Standort Location Koreastraße 1 **Architekten Architects** MRLV Architekten – Markovic Ronai Voss, Hamburg **Bauherr Client** Peter Tamm Sen. Stiftung **Bauzeit Date built** 2006–07 **Bruttogeschossfläche Gross floor area** 17 600 qm (sqm)

Das Internationale Maritime Museum Hamburg (IMH) ist eine Privatinstitution und fußt auf der Sammlung Peter Tamms. Hier hat es eine passende »Schatztruhe« gefunden, die in ihrem ursprünglichen, fast ruppigen Charme ohne modische Mätzchen die maritimen Kostbarkeiten aufbewahrt. Der Kaispeicher B gehört zu den ältesten Vertretern seiner Spezies (er stammt von 1888) und ist ein Eisen- und Holzskelettbau, umrissen von monolithischen Backsteinwänden und beschützt durch eine lebendige Dachlandschaft. Bis zum Umbau wurde er als Speicher genutzt und musste denkmalgerecht instand gesetzt werden. Die beiden versetzten Bauteile des Speichers entlang der Längsachse wurden miteinander verbunden und bilden durch großzügige Deckenausschnitte ein spannendes Raumkontinuum für die Ausstellungspräsentation mit edlen Holzfußböden, Sichtmauerwerk und kluger Tageslichtführung.

The Hamburg International Maritime Museum (IMH) is a private institution built around the collection of Peter Tamm. This building, with its authentic, almost rough charm, utterly devoid of modish gimmickry, is a fitting "treasure chest" for this collection of precious maritime objects. The old Kaispeicher B is one of Hamburg's oldest red-brick warehouses (it was built in 1888). Monolithic brick walls envelop a structural framework of iron and timber, and the ensemble is elegantly covered by a dashing roof-scape. It was in use as a warehouse right up to the time of conversion, and the redevelopment process was conducted in line with preservation criteria. The two sections that jut out of the building at both sides have been connected, and several large sections of the internal floors removed, producing a series of stimulating and expansive exhibition spaces that nonetheless form a continuum. This effect is heightened by wooden floors and clever use of natural light.

1

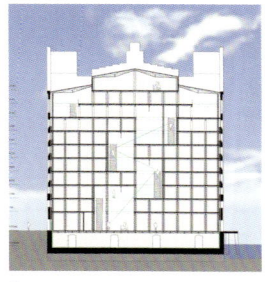

2   3

1 Gesamtansicht vom Kaispeicher B, daneben der Bau der Gebr. Heinemann (links im Bild: Germanischer Lloyd) Overall view of Kaispeicher B, next to it the Gebr. Heinemann building (pictured on the left: Germanischer Lloyd) 2 Querschnitt mit Atrien Cross section with atriums 3 Die alten Speicherböden wurden zum Teil geöffnet, so entstanden Atrien mit hohen Ausstellungsräumen. The floors of the old warehouse were partially opened up, creating atriums with high-ceilinged exhibition rooms.

Verwaltung Gebr. Heinemann
Company Headquarters

Standort Location Koreastraße 3 **Architekten Architects** Ulrich Arndt, Hamburg **Bauherr Client** Gebr. Heinemann, Hamburg **Bauzeit Date built** 2006–07 **Bruttogeschossfläche Gross floor area** 12 000 qm (sqm)

C.10

Der benachbarte Bauteil des IMH ist ein gutes Beispiel für den stetigen Weiterbau eines Speichers aus der Gründerzeit, der stark kriegszerstört war. Die ursprünglichen Bauteile stammen aus den Jahren 1877/78. Nach dem Krieg wurde nur wenig nachhaltig improvisiert und immer wieder weitergebaut. Der heute sogenannte Heinemannspeicher ist jetzt stark genug ausgebildet, um den nördlichen Kopf des Quartiers zu formulieren. Der Bau wirkt durch seine massive Backsteinaura seriös, auch wenn die kupfernen Treppengiebel aus den 1980er Jahren in den Dachzonen allenfalls als eine Applikation für alte Bautraditionen gelten können. Die Qualität des Hauses äußert sich klarer in der lockeren Lochfassade des jüngsten Anbauwerks mit seinen schräg gestellten Brüstungen.

The building next to the IMH is a good example of a late nineteenth-century warehouse that was heavily damaged in the War and added to incrementally over the years. The original structure dates from 1877/78, and, following the War, was hastily reconstructed. The section that is now referred to as the Heinemannspeicher is distinctive enough to form the northern masthead of Hafencity. Thanks to its brick solidity this building makes a serious impression, though the copper crow-stepped gables along the roof, which were only added in the 1980s can be regarded, at best, as a kind of lapel pin in support of older building traditions. The quality of the building is more clearly articulated in the punctuated façade and sloping balustrades of the most recent extension.

1

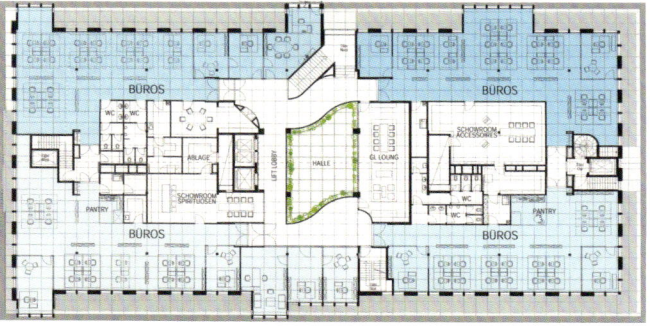

2

1 Das Bauwerk schließt direkt an den Kaispeicher B an (rechts). The building connects directly to the Kaispeicher B (right). 2 Grundriss 7. OG Floor plan of 7th storey

Hauptzollamt/Zollamt Hafencity
Central Customs Office

Standort Location Koreastraße 4 **Architekten Architects** Winking·Froh Architekten BDA, Berlin **Bauherr Client** Bundesanstalt für Immobilienaufgaben **Bauzeit Date built** 2010–11 **Bruttogeschossfläche Gross floor area** 10600 qm (sqm)

C.11

Das neue Hauptzollamt bildet den Abschluss des Blockrands an der Koreastraße/westliche Shanghaiallee. Die städtebaulich gewünschte Dominanz des benachbarten Kaispeicher-Ensembles bleibt unangetastet, denn dieser Baukörper wirkt zurückhaltend, obwohl er mit eigener Signatur entworfen wurde – natürlich in einer Fassade mit einem schmeichelnden roten Stein. Das kompakte neue Zollhaus zeichnet sich durch präzise ausformulierte Fenster- und Fassadenflächen aus und fügt sich auch durch die Klinker mit grünen Glasierungen in das Gestaltungskonzept dieses Quartiers der Hafencity und vor allem der historischen Speicherstadt ein. Das ist ein plausibler und richtiger Baustein an dieser Stelle.

The new Central Customs Office (Hauptzollamt) completes the block on Koreastrasse/Shanghaiallee. Although it makes its own distinct mark—naturally with a façade of flattering red stone—the overall impact of this building is restrained, and it does not interfere with the pre-eminence of the neighbouring Kaispeicher ensemble. The compact new customs building is distinguished by precisely defined windows and façades. Thanks to the use of clinker brick with a green glazing the façade matches the general appearance of this district, and more particularly the Speicherstadt. Overall, this building represents a plausible and appropriate architectural element at this location.

1

2

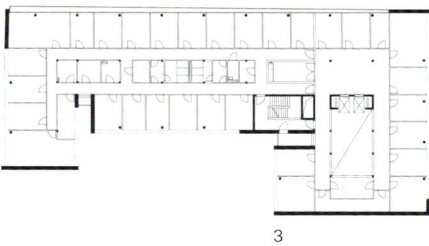

3

1 Zusammen mit den Nachbarbauten (Nidusloft, spine architects) bildet das Hauptzollamt eine starke Blockkante. Along with the adjacent buildings (Nidusloft by spine architects), the Central Customs Office (Hauptzollamt) forms a strong culminating point to the block. **2** Prägend für die Fassade sind die Einschnitte für die horizontalen Fensterbänder. Characteristic of the façade are the incisions for the horizontal bands of windows. **3** Grundriss Normalgeschoss Floor plan, full storey

Ökumenisches Forum Brücke
Ecumenical Forum

Standort Location Shanghaiallee 12 **Architekten Architects** Wandel, Hoefer, Lorch + Hirsch (Projektarchitekt Project architect Florian Götze), Saarbrücken **Bauherr Client** Grundstücksgesellschaft Shanghaiallee GbR **Wettbewerb Competition** 2009 **Bauzeit Date built** bis until 2012 **Bruttogeschossfläche Gross floor area** 4600 qm (sqm)

C.12

In einem einzigartigen Projekt haben sich 19 christliche Kirchen in Hamburg zu dem Verein »Brücke – Ökumenisches Forum Hafencity e.V.« zusammengeschlossen. Das öffentlich zugängliche Erdgeschoss des Forums dient als Begegnungsstätte, eine Kapelle bietet hier einen stillen Rückzugsort in dem zu erwartenden hektischen Großstadtbetrieb. Das neue Zentrum passt sich vom Material (Backstein) und der Form her in den Blockrand perfekt ein und ordnet sich unter. Mit wenigen gestalterischen Interventionen wird dem Gebäude sakrale Würde vermittelt: eine konkave Wölbung der Fassade, ein Kreuz und eine Glocke kennzeichnen den Ort der öffentlichen Kapelle. Das Kreuz leuchtet bei sonnigem Wetter in Hamburg gülden.

In a unique project, 19 Christian churches in Hamburg joined together to set up an association called Hafencity Ecumenical Forum, or simply, 'Brücke', meaning "bridge". The publicly accessible ground floor functions as a meeting place, while the chapel, also located at this level, offers a haven of stillness amidst the hectic bustle of the city. In terms of material (brick) and form the new centre adapts, even submits, to its surroundings. The centre acquires the dignity of a religious building through the slightest of interventions: concave hollows within the façade, a golden cross and a bell mark the location of the public chapel. The cross acts as a beacon on those occasions when the sun shines in Hamburg.

1

2

3

1+3 Die Fassade ist nicht starr, sondern wie eine textile Decke über das Haus geworfen, was interessante Licht- und Schattenelemente ergibt. The façade is not rigid, but thrown over the building like a textile blanket, allowing a fascinating interplay of light and shadow. **2** Innenansicht der Kapelle Interior view of the chapel

Greenpeace-Zentrale und designxport
Büros, Läden, Wohnungen Mixed Use Building

Standort Location Magdeburger Hafen **Architekten Architects** Bob Gysin + Partner
BGP Architekten ETH SIA BSA, Zürich **Bauherr Client** Baufeld Site 1–3: GOD Green
Office Development GmbH & Co. KG und GLD Green Living Development GmbH & Co.
KG; Baufeld Site 4: Grundstücksges. Hongkongstraße mbH & Co. KG **Wettbewerb
Competition** 2009 **Bauzeit Date built** bis until 2013 **Bruttogeschossfläche Gross floor
area** 55 000 qm gesamt (sqm total)

Neben dem designxport ist die Deutsch-
landzentrale der Umweltschutzorgani-
sation Greenpeace in das große Gebäude am Magdeburger Hafen eingezogen.
Das Ensemble wuchs durch seine Lage
am Magdeburger Hafen und eine beeindruckende, vorgelagerte Arkade von
170 Metern Länge zusammen. Die Idee
einer angestrebten »Stadtloggia«, hier
direkt zum Wasser orientiert, wurde
ansprechend umgesetzt. Auf zwei Ebenen – sowohl auf dem direkt am Wasser
gelegenen Promenadenniveau als auch
auf hochwassersicherem Warftniveau –
bieten die Gebäude großzügigen Raum
für Cafés, Geschäfte und Ausstellungen.
Die »Stadtloggia« ist ein zehn Meter tiefer und acht Meter hoher Arkadenraum
mit weiten Ausblicken über das Wasser.
Dieses Ensemble hat Charakter, und als
Vergleich drängen sich die beliebten
Alsterarkaden auf. Zum Komplex gehören auch Wohnungen.

This new structure on Magdeburger
Hafen accommodates both the designxport design centre and the offices of the
environmental NGO Greenpeace. The
ensemble is united by its adjacent location along the Magdeburger Hafen basin and by an impressive anterior arcade
spanning 170 metres. This is an attractive manifestation of the much-striven-
for idea of an "urban loggia", in this case
with a direct relationship to the water.
These twin buildings provide ample
space for cafés, business and exhibi-
tions at two levels—the promenade directly at water-level, and the higher level
at an elevation that is safe from flooding.
The "urban loggia" is a ten-metre-deep
and eight-metre-high arcade that offers
expansive views across the water. This
ensemble is brimming with character,
and naturally invites comparison with
the much-loved Alster Arcades.

1

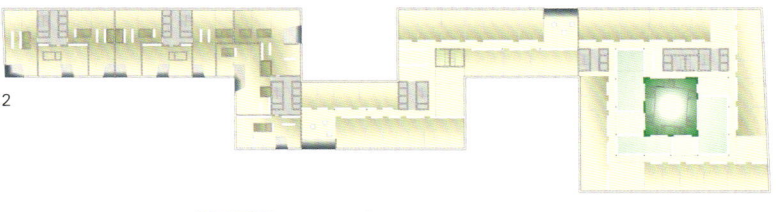

2

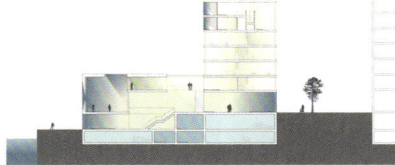

3

1 Ansicht von Westen aus dem Magdeburger Hafen; die vorgelagerte, über dem Wasser schwebende Promenade ist öffentlich. View of Magdeburger Hafen from the west. The anterior promenade suspended above the water is public. **2** Grundriss 3. OG Floor plan, 3rd storey **3** Querschnitt Cross section

U-Bahn-Station Überseequartier
Underground Railway Station

Standort Location Überseequartier **Architekten Architects** netzwerkarchitekten, Darmstadt **Bauherr Client** Hamburger Hochbahn AG **Wettbewerb Competition** 2005 **Baudatum Date built** 2012

Die U4 erhält zwei Haltestellen in der Hafencity: Überseequartier und Hafen-City Universität. Über den westlichen Zugang der Haltestelle Überseequartier (netzwerkarchitekten, Darmstadt) im Grasbrookpark erreicht man Strandkai und Dalmannkai, der östliche Zugang führt direkt zum Magdeburger Hafen. Das Spiel mit dem Wasser dominiert die Gestaltung der Haltestelle. In der inszenierten Unterwasserwelt leuchten die Wände in maritimem Blau, und an der Decke scheinen sich die Wellen des Meeres sanft zu bewegen.

Beide neuen Bahnhöfe (vgl. auch 180–181) verfügen für Hamburger U-Bahn-Stationen über sehr hohe Bahn-steighallen – sie waren kostengünstig möglich geworden, weil die Stationen im Tagebau erstellt werden konnten.

The U4, Hamburg's new underground rail line, will have two stations in Hafen-city: Überseequartier and HafenCity University. The Überseequartier station (netzwerkarchitekten, Darmstadt) has three entry/exit points: to the west at Grasbrook Park, in close proximity to Strandkai and Dalmannkai; to the east with direct access to Magdeburger Hafen. The dominant feature of this station is its playful approach to the theme of water. In this ersatz underwater world the walls emit a maritime blue glow, and the ceilings appear to roll in imitation of ocean waves.

The high ceilings above the plat-forms at both of these stations (see also pp. 180–181) are unusual for Hamburg's underground rail service – the open-cut construction of the stations reduced costs sufficiently to enable such gener-ous proportions.

1

2

3

1 Zugangsbereich Ost Eastern subway entrance **2** Systemschnitt Cross section
3 Bahnsteighalle: Farbgebung und Paneele stellen sich dem Thema Wasser. Platform hall: water-themed hues and panels.

HafenCity Universität (HCU)
University Building

Standort Location Überseeallee 16 **Architekten Architects** code unique architekten, Dresden **Bauherr Client** Freie und Hansestadt Hamburg, Behörde für Wissenschaft und Forschung **Wettbewerb Competition** 2006 **Bauzeit Date built** 2010–13 **Bruttogeschossfläche Gross floor area** 27 000 qm (sqm)

C.15

Die HCU ist eine innovative und gelungene Fortsetzung einer Kette von großartigen Gebäuden an der Südseite der Hafencity. Das Hauptgebäude setzt sich nach dem Entwurf von code unique architekten aus zwei flügelartigen Elementen zusammen. Viele Vorlesungssäle und Seminarräume erlauben einen direkten Ausblick auf die Elbe. Das Gebäude ergänzt mit seiner auffälligen Kontur bei der exponierten Lage am Wasser perfekt die neue Elbsilhouette der Stadt. Darüber hinaus beeindruckt auch dieser Bau mit seinen besonderen ökologischen Qualitäten; es wurde bereits nach dem Goldstandard des Umweltzeichens der Hafencity vorzertifiziert. Beide Teile des Baukörpers sind an einem städtischen Platz am Wasser entstanden. Offenheit wird hier zum Gestaltungsprinzip: Die HafenCity Universität ist Kommunikationszentrum, Kulturforum und Denkfabrik.

The HCU is a further link in a chain of successfully innovative buildings on the south side of Hafencity. Based on the competition-winning plans by code unique architekten, the main building of HafenCity University is a combination of two wing-like elements. Many of the lecture halls and seminar rooms enjoy direct views of the Elbe. With its striking form and prominent waterfront location, the building is the perfect complement to Hamburg's new riverside silhouette. But this building has much more than just looks to offer: even in the planning stage it was awarded Hafencity's gold Ecolabel for sustainability. Both sections of the building are arranged around an urban plaza. Openness is the key design principle here, reflecting the threefold brief of HafenCity University: as a communication centre, a cultural forum and a think tank.

1

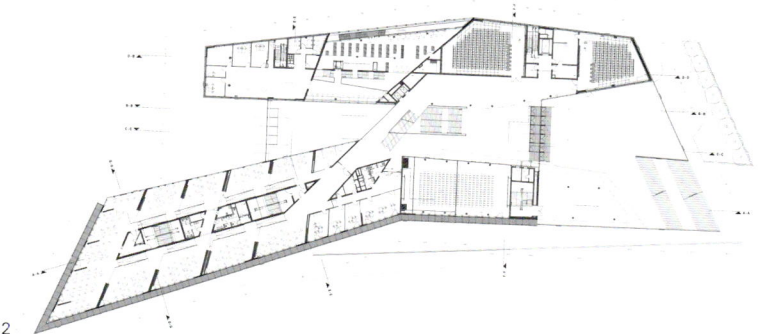

2

1 Der Universitätsbau öffnet sich zur Norderelbe. The HCU opens into the Northern Elbe.
2 Grundriss 1. OG Floor plan, 1st storey

Baakenhafenbrücke
Baakenhafen Bridge

Standort Location Überseeallee/Baakenallee **Architekten Architects** Wilkinson Eyre Architects, London **Bauherr Client** HafenCity Hamburg GmbH **Bauzeit Date built** bis until 2013

Den notwendigen Auftakt zum Quartier Baakenhafen bildet ein Brückenschlag. Die 130 Meter lange und 21 Meter breite Baakenhafenbrücke wird künftig den nördlichen Teil des Quartiers Baakenhafen mit seinem Südteil verbinden und markiert damit einen wichtigen Meilenstein für die zügige Entwicklung der östlichen Hafencity. Der erste Preis eines interdisziplinären Realisierungswettbewerbs hatte ein niedriges, ausdrucksstarkes Bauwerk zum Ergebnis, das insbesondere für Fußgänger die großartigen Blickbeziehungen über die Elbe und den Baakenhafen hervorragend inszeniert. Ein Hubelement ist beweglich, wenn Schiffe in den neuen Freizeithafen ein- oder aus ihm herausfahren.

Appropriately enough, the Baakenhafen quarter is accessed via a bridge. The 130-metre-long and 21-metre-wide Baakenhafen Bridge will connect the northern and southern sections of the Baakenhafen quarter, and represents an important milestone in the rapid development of the eastern Hafencity. The winner of the interdisciplinary competition is a low-set, highly expressive structure that makes the most of the excellent views of the Elbe and Baakenhafen basin, particularly for pedestrians. A section of the bridge is retractable to allow boats to enter and leave the new marina.

1

2

3

1–3 Die neue Verbindung zwischen den zentralen Bereichen der Hafencity und
dem Quartier Baakenhafen ist schwungvoll. Im oberen Bild rechts der translozierte
View Point (vgl. S. 178) The new connection between the central areas of the Hafencity and the Baakenhafen quarter is jaunty. The relocated View Point Tower can be
seen in the upper picture on the right (cf. p. 178)

Aussichtsturm
View Point

Standort Location Grandeswerderstraße (vorher formerly Am Kibbelsteg) **Architekten Architects** Renner Hainke Wirth Architekten, Hamburg **Bauherr Client** HafenCity Hamburg GmbH **Baudatum Date built** 2004

Die Red Box am Potsdamer Platz in Berlin, von der aus der dortige Baubetrieb der 1990er Jahre zu beobachten war, stand Pate für die Idee zum »View Point« in der Hafencity. Wie eine Giraffe streckt der orangefarbene Turm seine organisch geformte Aussichtsplattform in die Höhe, von der man das Wachsen der Stadt beobachten kann. Dabei steht der Farbklecks manchmal im Weg und muss umgesetzt werden. 2013 wurde der Aussichtsturm vom Kreuzfahrtterminal in die Nachbarschaft der Baakenhafenbrücke versetzt (vgl. S. 176): Von dort kann der Ausbau der östlichen Hafencity verfolgt werden.

Und am Ende des Wegs sollte der View Point unter Denkmalschutz gestellt werden – als ein gebauter Zeuge der gesamten Hafencity-Entwicklung.

Berlin's famous Red Box, which overlooked the massive construction site on Potsdamer Platz in the 1990s, was the inspiration for the Hafencity's View Point. The orange tower reaches skywards like a giraffe stretching to nibble at the highest branches, and is topped by an observation platform from which visitors can survey the surrounding development. This colourful addition to the landscape has been relocated several times to make way for new projects. In 2013 the View Point Tower was moved from the Cruise Center Terminal to the vicinity of the Baakenhafen Bridge (cf. p. 176). The expansion of the eastern Hafencity can now be followed from there.

A witness to Hafencity's prodigious evolution, View Point Tower is destined to live out its days as a listed structure.

1

2

3

1 Häufiger Gast in Hamburg: die Queen Mary 2 (Aufnahme vom alten Standort des Aussichtsturms) A frequent guest in Hamburg: the Queen Mary 2 (photo taken at one of the earlier locations of the View Point) **2** Bis 2013 blickte man vom View Point auf das Kreuzfahrtterminal und den Schatzinsel-Spielplatz (WPP Landschaftsarchitekten). Until 2013 the Cruise Center Terminal and the Treasure Island Playground (WPP Landscape Architects) could be seen from the View Point. **3** Frühe Aufnahme zu Beginn der Bauarbeiten in der Hafencity Early photo taken around the start of construction in Hafencity

U-Bahn-Station HafenCity Universität
Underground Railway Station

Standort Location HafenCity Universität (HCU) **Architekt Architect** C. Raupach, München; Licht: G. Pfarré/E. Döring; Design K. Stauss/J. Grillmeier **Bauherr Client** Hamburger Hochbahn AG **Wettbewerb Competition** 2005 **Baudatum Date built** 2012

Die Haltestelle HafenCity Universität liegt an der Versmannstraße süd-östlich des Lohseparks. Zwei Zugänge befinden sich direkt im Lohsepark, zwei weitere an der Versmannstraße. Die Gestaltung der vorläufigen Endhaltestelle nimmt das Thema des Hamburger Hafens als Containerumschlagplatz auf: Über dem Bahnsteig hängen kubische, an Schiffscontainer erinnernde Lichtbehälter, deren wechselndes farbiges Licht von den stahlverkleideten Wänden und der Decke reflektiert wird. In den nächsten Jahren wird man mit dem Ausstieg an der Station den Weiterbau der Hafencity im Osten direkt miterleben können, die U4 wird ebenfalls nach Osten verlängert – zumindestens bis zu den Elbbrücken. Später wird man vom östlichen Ausgang direkt das Oberhafenareal erreichen können.

HafenCity University station (Raupach Architekten, Munich) is situated along Versmannstrasse to the southeast of Lohsepark. Two of the entrances are located directly next to Lohsepark, with two others along Versmannstrasse. The design of this provisional terminus takes up the theme of Hamburg's importance as a container port: cubic lighting fixtures, their changing colours reflected by the steel-clad walls and ceilings, are suspended above the platforms, reminiscent in their form of colourful shipping containers. Commuters arriving at the station in the coming years will be well placed to observe the continued expansion of the Hafencity, with the eastward extension of the U4 taking the underground rail line at least as far as the Elbbrücken bridges. Later it will be possible to reach the Oberhafen area from the eastern exit.

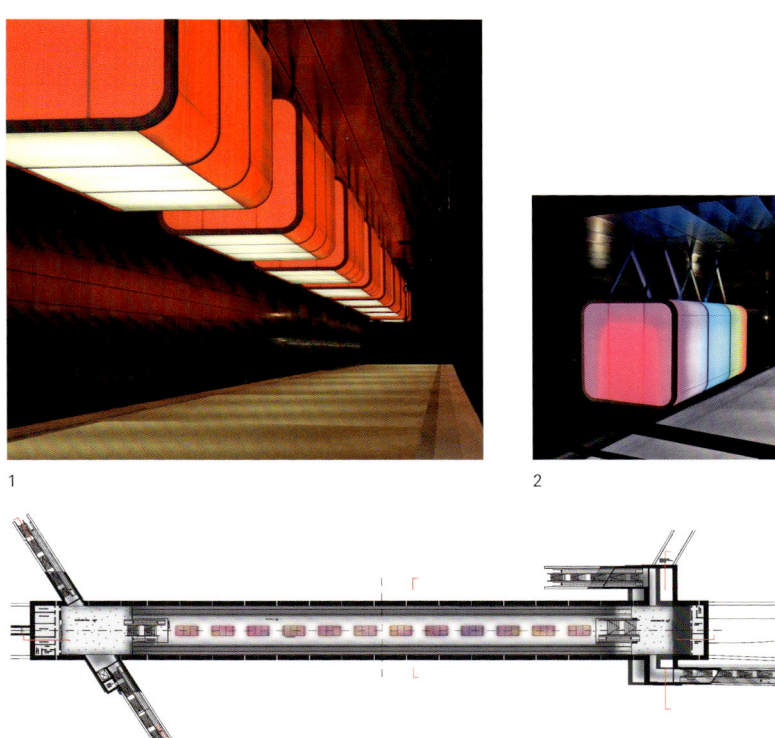

1+2 Die Gestaltung der Bahnsteighalle orientiert sich am Thema Hamburg und seinem Containerhafen. The platform design is inspired by the city and its role as a container port.
3 Haltestellengrundriss Station floor plan

Automuseum Prototyp
Automobile Museum

Standort Location Shanghaiallee 7 **Architekten Architects** Dinse Feest Zurl Architekten, Hamburg **Bauherr Client** Lohseplatz 1 Immobilien GmbH & Co. KG, Hamburg **Bauzeit Date built** 2007–08 **Bruttogeschossfläche Gross floor area** 2850 qm (sqm)

Historische Automobile stehen im Mittelpunkt der Sammlung Prototyp – Personen. Kraft. Wagen. Schwerpunkt der Sammlung ist die Marke Porsche, die mit mehreren seltenen Automodellen vertreten ist, viele davon Prototypen. Die ehemaligen Fabriketagen sind weiß gestrichen und teils mit weißem, hochglänzendem Kunstharzboden ausgelegt. Der Boden der Eventfläche im Erdgeschoss, die für Sonderausstellungen genutzt und für Events vermietet wird, besteht aus geschliffenem Asphalt. Den Architekten ist hier wieder gelungen, was sie vor etwa zwanzig Jahren in Ottensen mit den alten Zeisehallen begonnen hatten: ein Crossover zwischen alter Industriearchitekur und cooler Modernität, das die Strukturen schont, pflegt und neu definiert. Man nennt das inzwischen auch den Hamburger Weg der Denkmalpflege.

Historical automobiles are at the centre of the Prototyp Museum. The centrepiece of the collection is the Porsche brand, which is represented here by numerous rare cars, including numerous prototypes. The interior walls of this former factory building are painted white while many of the floors feature white, high-gloss synthetic resin. The floor of the event space on the ground level, which is used for special exhibitions and events, consists of polished asphalt. The architects have repeated a successful approach that they first used twenty years ago in Altona at the old Zeise propeller factory, combining industrial architecture and cool modernity in a way that protects, maintains and redefines existing structures. Already this approach is referred to as the "Hamburg method" of historic preservation.

1

2

3

1 Ansicht in Richtung Norden und City View towards the north and the city centre **2** Grundriss Automuseum Floor plan Prototyp Museum **3** Der Ausstellungsbereich: Weiße Böden, Wände und Decken bilden ein wunderbares Passepartout für die Edelkarossen. The exhibition space: white floors, walls and ceilings form a splendid backdrop for the luxury cars on display.

Oberhafen-Kantine / neues Umspannwerk
Restaurant and New Transformer Station

Standort Location Stockmeyerstraße **Architekten (Fassade) Architects (façade)** Heinle, Wischer & Partner **Bauherr Client** Vattenfall Europe **Bauzeit Date built** 2011–12

Am neuen Umspannwerk an der Stockmeyerstraße, direkt am Zugang zum Oberhafenquartier, zeigt sich die Sprunghaftigkeit von Zeit und Planung. Der recht ungehobelte Klotz hatte die Kubatur der ursprünglich geplanten Blockstruktur erhalten, passt nun aber nicht mehr hierher. Jetzt gibt der Bestand der alten Hallen den Maßstab an, da wirkt der Technikbau fremd, zu groß und zu technoid. Auch wenn es sich bei der Fassade um ein fein gesponnenes Wandgewebe handelt, das den Zweckbau adelt, wirft der Quader einen buchstäblichen Schatten auf die ursprünglich als Kantine für die Hafenarbeiter dienenden Gebäude des Kult-Restaurants »Oberhafen-Kantine«. Bei dem Bau mit dem versetzten Obergeschoss und der markanten Fensterform handelt es sich um eine Variante der expressionistischen Architektur – den Klinkerexpressionismus (Architekt: Willy Wegner, 1925). Im Dezember 2013 wurde der Bau durch eine Sturmflut stark beschädigt.

The new transformer station on Stockmeyerstrasse, right at the entrance to the Oberhafen Quarter, exemplifies the inconstancy of time and planning. This rather clumsy building doesn't really fit in here anymore. The problem is that it was designed to match the cubature of the original block plan. Now that the older buildings have been retained and act as a kind of benchmark, the transformer station appears too strange, too large and too technoid. In spite of its finely spun, fabric-like façade this functional building cannot shake off a certain blockish ungainliness. Moreover, it literally casts a shadow on the petite structure that houses the popular restaurant Oberhafen-Kantine (originally a dockers' canteen). This unusual little building with its offset upper floor and striking window openings actually exemplifies a particular variation of expressionist architecture: clinker brick Expressionism (Architect: Willy Wegner, 1925). The building was badly damaged in December 2013 by a storm flood.

1

2

3

1 Blick auf das neue Umspannwerk, gesehen von der Hafencity View of the new transformer station as seen from Hafencity 2 Oberhafen-Kantine im Sommer 2013 Historic Oberhafen-Kantine in summer 2013 3 Blick ins Obergeschoss Interior view of the upper floor

D.01 Steckelhörn 11
D.02 Katharinenhof
D.03 Neuer Dovenhof
D.04 Deichtor-Center
D.05 Speicherblock X
D.06 Umgestaltung der HHLA-Hauptverwaltung
D.07 Ehemaliges Freihafenamt
D.08 Speicherblock P
D.09 Kesselhaus
D.10 Hanseatic Trade Center I
D.11 Hanseatic Trade Center II

Speicherstadt und Hafenrand der Altstadt

Speicherstadt and Dockside Part of Altstadt

Die Speicherstadt als Teil des neu gegründeten Freihafens hatte
Ende des 19. Jahrhunderts ein historisches Stadtquartier mit
Ziegelhäusern verdrängt. Jetzt bildet sie das Verbindungsstück
zwischen Innenstadt und Hafencity und wird nach Aufgabe
des Freihafens neuen Nutzungen zugeführt (Aufnahme von 2007).

As part of the newly established free port, at the end of the 19th
century the Speicherstadt displaced a historic neighbourhood with
brick buildings. Now it links the old city centre and Hafencity, and
will be utilised in new ways once free port status is relinquished
(aerial photo taken in 2007).

Die Speicherstadt im Wandel der Zeit
The Speicherstadt Through the Ages

Am 29. Oktober 1888 wurde mit der Schlusssteinlegung ein gigantisches Unternehmen abgeschlossen, das im Kern nur sieben Jahre Bauzeit benötigte und für das mit dem Holländischen Brook ein ganzer Stadtteil abgebrochen werden musste: die Speicherstadt. Heute für alle Hiesigen und Fremden ein Ort, von dem man sagt: Ja, hier ist Hamburg! – Eine Hamburgensie, auf die sich möglicherweise bald der Weltruhm eines UNESCO-Welterbes begründen lässt. Mit Zinnen, Bögen und anderen Details ist die Speicherstadt eine zwar karge, aber geheimnisvolle und romantische hanseatische Herausforderung von Schloss Neuschwanstein, Kölner Dom oder des barocken Dresdens. Ihr rotes Gemäuer an dunklen Wassern wird in den Medien so häufig gezeigt wie der Michel oder die Binnenalster – nicht wegzudenken als Kulisse in jedem guten Kriminalfilm made in Hamburg.

Dabei war der Ursprung der Speicherstadt nur zentraler Teil eines Handels zwischen der Hansestadt und dem Deutschen Reich Ende des 19. Jahrhun-

On 29 October 1888 the keystone was fitted on an enormous architectural project that had taken just seven years to complete and for which an entire district— Holländischer Brook—was demolished: Hamburg's Speicherstadt or warehouse district. Today this is the place where locals and visitors alike are apt to exclaim (out loud or to themselves): "Yes, this is Hamburg!" It is a unique cityscape, and one that may soon bear the coveted title of UNESCO World Heritage site. With its parapets, arches and other beguiling details, the Speicherstadt is this Nordic merchant city's admittedly sparse, but undeniably mysterious and romantic, challenge to Neuschwanstein Castle, Cologne Cathedral and Baroque Dresden. The red-brick walls that melt into the dark canal waters are featured at least as often in the German media as Hamburg's other iconic landmarks, the Michel (St. Michael's Church) and the Inner Alster lake, and is an indispensable backdrop for any crime film made in Hamburg.

The origins of the Speicherstadt lie in a deal between the City of Hamburg

derts: Hamburg musste den Status als Freie Reichsstadt im neu gegründeten Deutschen Reich aufgeben, bekam dafür aber einen Freihafen, in dem alle Waren »auf der Durchreise« gelagert werden mussten, damit keine Zölle anfielen. Dafür wurden Speichergebäude errichtet, die einen für damalige Verhältnisse modernen Wirtschaftsverkehr zuließen: Wertvolle Waren wie Teppiche, Tabak oder Kaffee wurden hier über die Fleete in kleinen Hafenschuten angeliefert, zwischengelagert und über den Straßenweg zum Verkauf weitertransportiert. In Anlehnung an alte Hamburger Speicher entstand ein neuer, verdichteter, hoher Speichertypus in Reihenbauweise mit vielen Lager-»Böden« übereinander. Im Prinzip waren es Gewerbebauten, für die in Hamburg – wie für Siechenhäuser oder Gefängnisse – nur rohes, unverputztes Mauerwerk verwendet wurde.

Trotzdem verbergen sich die Lagerflächen hinter einer Architektur und einem Fassadenschmuck, der mitteilt, dass es um mehr als schlichte Nutzbauten geht, nämlich um »eine effektvolle Inszenierung zur Verherrlichung [von] Hamburgs wirtschaftlicher Kraft«, wie die Bauhistorikerin Karin Maak schrieb. Üppige und wehrhafte Gesten von Herrschaftshäusern und Palästen, Türme und Zinnen wurden den Speichern damals übergestülpt. Ausführender Architekt war Friedrich Andreas Meyer – ein Generalist, Ingenieur, Baumeister und Künstler zugleich. Ausgebildet wurde

and the central government of the German Reich in the late nineteenth century. When Hamburg became part of the newly founded German Empire in 1871, it had to forego its long-held independence as a "free city". In return it was granted a free port, within which goods could be stored for further transit and would not be subject to customs duties. The warehouses that were built to hold those goods supported what was at that time a highly efficient system of freight transportation: commodities such as carpets, tobacco, and coffee were delivered to the warehouses in small barges, stored temporarily and then transported onwards by road to market. The Speicherstadt featured a new type of warehouse building that drew on the forms of older Hamburg warehouses, but was higher and more compact, with the various storage levels stacked one above the other. Because these were commercial buildings, tradition demanded that only unplastered masonry be used.

These warehouses nonetheless convey, through their architecture and decorative façades, the message that they are more than mere functional structures; that they represent, in fact, in the words of the architectural historian Karin Maak, "a striking mise en scène that projected Hamburg's economic power." Architectural gestures borrowed from opulent mansions and palaces, and from fortified towers and battlements were incorporated into the new warehouses. The principal architect of the

er am Polytechnikum Hannover, wo die »Hannoversche Schule« unter Conrad Wilhelm Hase die große Renaissance des Mittelalters und seiner Ausdrucksformen einleitete und sich anschickte, das ganze Deutsche Reich zu erobern.

Mit den radikalen Veränderungen der Hafentechnik und des Seeverkehrs fiel spätestens nach dem Zweiten Weltkrieg die wirtschaftliche Grundlage für die Speicherstadt fort. Im Vergleich zur Logistik und Lagerung von Tabak oder Teppichen in modernen Gewerbegebieten war der Warentransport über die Fleete unwirtschaftlich geworden. Auch wenn immer noch viele Traditionsfirmen am Standort Speicherstadt verblieben, wurde eine generelle Umnutzung notwendig. Dies war aber mit großen Schwierigkeiten verbunden, da die niedrigen, sehr tiefen und daher schlecht belichteten Böden der Speicher sich nicht für Büros oder Wohnungen eigneten. Ein erster Versuch in den 1980er und 1990er Jahren, die Speicherstadt umzunutzen und zu modernisieren, scheiterte u.a. deshalb, weil vielleicht zu radikal gedacht wurde und man technisch noch nicht alle Möglichkeiten von heute besaß. Mittlerweile ist der hohe ideelle Wert der Speicherstadt, der einen hohen pflegerischen Aufwand rechtfertigt, Allgemeingut geworden. Inzwischen erfolgten aufwendige Umbauten für Büros und vor allem für Kultureinrichtungen. So hat beispielsweise eine der größten Modelleisenbahnen der Welt hier ihren Platz gefunden. Hinzu kommt

district was Friedrich Andreas Meyer, who was a generalist, an engineer, a master builder and artist all rolled into one. He trained at the Polytechnikum in Hanover, at a time when the "Hanover School" under Conrad Wilhelm Hase was promoting a renaissance of medieval styles of architecture throughout the German Reich.

Thanks to radical changes in port technology and shipping the economic basis for the Speicherstadt had ceased to exist by the end of the Second World War. The transport of goods such as tobacco and carpets via canal had become outmoded and inefficient compared to the logistics and storage possibilities of modern commercial zones. Though many established companies continued to trade from the Speicherstadt, it was clear that conversion to a new use was called for. This would not be easy to achieve, however, because the lofts of the Speicherstadt had low ceilings, were poorly lit and were therefore difficult to convert to offices or apartments. Initial attempts to redevelop and modernise the warehouses were made in the 1980s and 1990s, but mostly these failed, either because they were too ambitious or because the technical possibilities were more limited at that time. Since then the architectural and cultural value of the Speicherstadt became widely acknowledged, justifying the care and expense required for redevelopment and preservation. As a result, some of the warehouses were

Luftbild des Hafens und der Speicherstadt 1914 Aerial view of the harbour and the Speicherstadt in 1914

der ideale Standort: Die Speicherstadt ist jetzt das liebenswerte Bindeglied zwischen alter City und junger Hafencity – mit Aussicht auf die Mitgliedschaft im Weltkulturerbe.

successfully converted into offices or cultural venues, including the world's largest model railway. As we look to the future, the Speicherstadt is fast becoming the ideal Hamburg location, occupying the interstice between the old city centre and the new Hafencity. Its prospects of becoming a world heritage site don't hurt either.

Steckelhörn 11
Bürohaus Office Building

Standort Location Steckelhörn 11 **Architekten Architects** J. Mayer H. Architects, Berlin **Bauherr Client** Cogiton Projekt Altstadt GmbH, Hamburg **Bauzeit Date built** 2007–09 **Bruttogeschossfläche Gross floor area** 3954 qm (sqm)

Hamburg ist fruchtbares Terrain für den bekannten Berliner Architekten Jürgen Mayer H. Mit dem Bürohaus ADA 1 an der Außenalster leistete er einen gelungenen, aber provokanten Beitrag zum Bauen in der Backsteinstadt. Mit dem Bürohaus Steckelhörn 11 wird die Diskussion weitergeführt. Der Architekt kommentiert seinen Bau folgendermaßen: »Wie eine Flüssigkeit gleiten an der massiven Gebäudeform mit Keramikverkleidung vertikale Fensterbänder an den Fassaden herunter. Die Straßenfassade nimmt mit ihren abgerundeten Staffelgeschossen und der vertikalen Gliederung die Gestaltung und die Höhenentwicklung der Nachbargebäude auf. Die besondere Grundrissgeometrie lässt ein spannendes Gebäude entstehen!« Was das Hamburger Feedback anbelangt, fällt das Lob allerdings kleiner aus als bei ADA 1 (An der Alster 1) – vielleicht ist die Detaillierung der »Kaskade« doch ein bisschen zu grob und die Fassade hier in der Altstadt zu fremd?

Hamburg has been fruitful terrain for the well-known Berlin architect Jürgen Mayer H. His ADA 1 office block along the Outer Alster was an accomplished, albeit provocative, addition to Hamburg's architectural fabric. The new office building at Steckelhörn 11 takes up the debate where ADA 1 left off. In the words of the architect himself, "like a liquid, vertical window bands slither down the massive, ceramic-clad façade. The rounded contours of the mezzanine floors and the vertical articulation of the street-facing façade accommodate the height and design of the neighbouring building. The unusual geometry of the ground plan allows an exciting building to emerge". He garnered less praise in Hamburg for this building than for ADA 1 (An der Alster 1); perhaps the detailing of the "cascade" was a touch too crude, or this façade was considered a little too outlandish for the Altstadt?

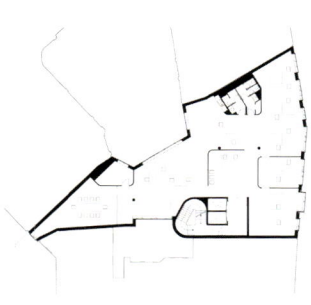

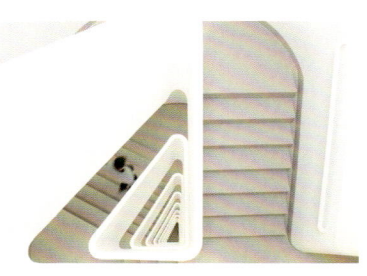

1 Grundriss 3. OG Floor plan, 3rd storey **2** Gesamtansicht von Südosten Overall view from the southeast **3** Treppendetail: Das asymmetrische Image wird innen wieder aufgenommen. Staircase detail: the asymmetrical image is taken up again in the interior design. **4** Eingangsbereich Entrance area

Katharinenhof
Büro- und Wohnhaus Mixed Use Building

Standort Location Zippelhaus 1–2 **Architekten Architects** Gössler & Schnittger, Hamburg **Bauherr Client** Philipp Holzmann AG **Baudatum Date built** 1993 **Bruttogeschossfläche Gross floor area** 3099 qm (sqm)

Nur rudimentär konnten die Zippelhäuser aus dem Jahr 1891, die direkt neben der Hauptkirche St. Katharinen standen, nach dem Krieg wieder aufgebaut werden. Bei einer notwendigen Sanierung wurde das Haus mit seiner schwerfällig wirkenden Neorenaissance-Relieffassade aufgestockt. Die Leichtigkeit großflächiger, bündig gesetzter Metallfenster klärt die Verhältnismäßigkeit zwischen Alt und Neu im Sinne einer harmonischen Gesamtheit zugunsten der Aufstockung. Eine überraschende Variante des guten alten »Weniger ist mehr«! Innen wird dieser Gegensatz radikaler ausgetragen: Der altehrwürdige gusseiserne Treppenaufgang wird beispielsweise durch eine rohe, industriell vorgefertigte Stahltreppe fortgesetzt. Einer der überzeugendsten Entwürfe des leider viel zu früh verstorbenen Architekten Daniel Gössler (1964–2003).

The Zippelhaus buildings, which were erected in 1891 next to the brick-Gothic St. Catherine's Church, one of the five churches that comprise Hamburg's famous skyline, were badly bomb-damaged in the Second World War and hurriedly restored afterwards. In its re-development in 1993, which was undertaken partly for structural reasons, the somewhat cumbersome neo-Renaissance relief façade was retained and extended. A light architectural touch in the form of flush-mounted metal windows articulates the relationship between the building's new and old elements, resulting in a harmonious whole that highlights the new features. The contrast between old and new is more pronounced in the interior. For example, the venerable cast-iron stair well continues into a raw, industrially pre-assembled steel staircase. This is one of the most impressive designs in the architectural legacy of Daniel Gössler (1964–2003), who died far too young.

1

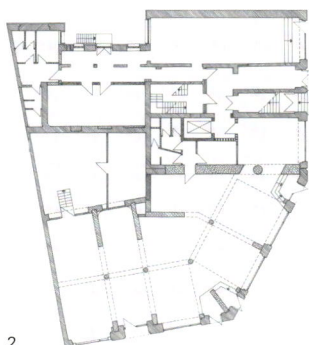

2

1 Blick von Süden (im Hintergrund die Hauptkirche St. Petri): eine vorbildliche Verwebung von alten und neuen Architekturen View from the south (in the background St. Peter's Church): a seamless amalgam of architecture old and new **2** Grundriss Floor plan

Neuer Dovenhof
Kontorhaus Office Building

Standort Location Brandstwiete 1 **Architekten Architects** Kleffel Köhnholdt Gundermann, Hamburg **Bauherr Client** Deutsche Grundbesitz Investmentgesellschaft mbH, Frankfurt **Wettbewerb Competition** 1988 **Bauzeit Date built** 1988–94 **Bruttogeschossfläche Gross floor area** 19 000 qm (sqm)

Der Neue Dovenhof (der ursprüngliche Dovenhof von Martin Haller stand dem jetzigen Gebäude gegenüber und wurde in den 1960er Jahren für die Doppel-Hochhäuser von Spiegel und IBM abgerissen) steht als Beispiel für eine ganze Reihe von prominenten neuen Kontorhäusern Hamburgs aus den 1990er Jahren, die sich jeweils durch einen überdachten Innenhof auszeichnen. Er ist ein janusköpfiger Spross des Kontorhaustyps. Dort, wo zehn Geschosse übereinander getürmt sind, wirkt er wie ein Solitär. Zur Willy-Brandt-Straße hin bildet der Bau eine schroffe Blockrandwand, als wolle er nachträglich ganz allein das ursprünglich zerrissene Straßenbild der Ost-West-Magistrale heilen. Blau-rote Steine, Messingkandelaber und keramikverkleidete Säulen bezeugen ihre Reverenz an die expressionistischen Nachbarn im Kontorhausviertel. Innen wird das Glasatrium von vier martialischen Aufzugstürmen aus rohem Beton flankiert.

The new Dovenhof building (the original Dovenhof, designed by Martin Haller and located directly opposite, was demolished in the 1960s to make way for the twin towers of Spiegel magazine and IBM) is typical of a series of prominent new office buildings that was constructed in Hamburg during the 1990s. The defining feature of this building is a glass-roofed interior courtyard. This is a Janus-headed scion of traditional Kontorhaus architecture. At its centre, with a ten-storey-high tower, this building has a solitary appearance. The façade facing Willy-Brandt-Strasse is a steep wall that encloses a perimeter block. In retrospect it seems as though this building was a solo attempt to put right the disjointed streetscape of Ost-West-Strasse. Bluish red bricks, a brass candelabra, and ceramic-clad columns testify to a reverence for the Expressionist architecture of the neighbouring Kontorhausviertel. Inside, the atrium is flanked by four stern elevator shafts.

1

2

1+2 Der Neue Dovenhof kurz nach der Fertigstellung The Neuer Dovenhof building shortly after completion

Deichtor-Center
Bürohaus Office Building

Standort Location Oberbaumbrücke 1 / Willy-Brandt-Straße 1 **Architekten Architects** BRT Architekten LLP Bothe Richter Teherani, Hamburg **Bauherr Client** Becken Investitionen + Vermögensverwaltung, Hamburg **Wettbewerb Competition** 2000 **Bauzeit Date built** 2000–02 **Bruttogeschossfläche Gross floor area** 24 000 qm (sqm)

D.04

BRT Architekten nahmen hier einst selbst Quartier und schmückten ihr Büro in den Innenhöfen mit Bar und Strandkörben. Was gebaut wurde, sollte nicht nur Architektur, sondern Lebensausdruck einer neuen Generation von Dienstleistungsberufen sein. Die Architektur selbst macht keine wesentlichen Aussagen über die Weiterentwicklung des Typus' Kontorhaus. Die Größe (BRI: 140 000 Kubikmeter) ist hier zu tolerieren, weil das Kontorhausviertel mit seinen großvolumigen Bauwerken gegenüberliegt. Die Spitze, die sofort den Vergleich zum Chilehaus nahelegt, ist für Architekturfotografen bedeutend, für Passanten hingegen nicht beeindruckend. Auch die Proportionen der riesigen Glaswände sind handwerklich bewältigt. Auf dreieckigem Grundriss werden die Büroetagen im Zickzack geführt, auch hier sind wieder imposante Innenhöfe zu sehen. Das Haus markiert vis-à-vis dem neuen Spiegel-Gebäude jetzt den östlichen Eingang der Hafencity am Deichtor.

BRT Architects decided to take up quarters next to the Speicherstadt, and even decorated the interior courtyards of their building with a bar and beach chairs. The idea was to create a building that expressed not only architectural values, but would also represent the new generation of service professions. In purely architectural terms this structure contributes nothing particularly novel. Such an immense volume (140,000 cubic metres) is tolerable at this location because it matches the scale of the nearby Kontorhausviertel, Hamburg's historical business district. The acute corners, which immediately invite comparison with Fritz Höger's iconic Chilehaus, while meaningful for architects, are likely to go largely unnoticed by most passers-by. The proportions of the immense glass walls are relativised by craftsmanlike touches. Located vis-à-vis the new Spiegel building, the Deichtor-Center now marks the eastern entrance to the Hafencity.

1

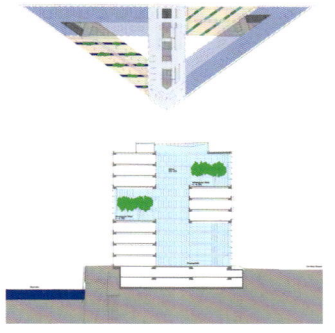

2

3

1 Gesamtansicht von Süden Overall view from the south 2 Schemagrundriss und -schnitt
Schematic plan and cross section 3 Ansicht von Norden View from the north

Speicherblock X
Bürohaus Office Building

Standort Location Brooktorkai 1–2 **Architekten Architects** gmp · von Gerkan, Marg und Partner, Hamburg **Bauherr Client** Quantum Immobilien AG **Bauzeit Date built** 2001–02 **Bruttogeschossfläche Gross floor area** 5200 qm (sqm)

Eine Baulücke am Brooktorkai 1 und 2 wurde nach fast einem Jahrhundert mit einem neuen Kontorgebäude geschlossen. Statt eines ursprünglich geplanten Doppelturmgiebels mit Zwischenfassade im Stil der übrigen Speicherstadt wurde das Speicherstadtmotiv modern umgesetzt – allerdings auch in Backstein, mit stehenden Fensterformaten und Risaliten. In diesem Gebäude steckt jetzt ein bisschen die Sachlichkeit des Architekten Werner Kallmorgen, der in der Nachkriegszeit in der Speicherstadt nicht nur den Kaispeicher A gebaut hatte. Das repräsentative Treppenhaus des Neubaus dient zugleich als kleiner verglaster Lichthof und bietet einen schönen Ausblick auf den Deichtormarkt. Die Geschosse können getrennt vermietet und zusätzlich jeweils mittig geteilt werden.

This new office building filled a gap site at Brooktorkai 1 and 2 that had been empty for almost a century. Instead of building twin gable towers with a façade in between as originally planned, the architects opted for a more modern interpretation of the Speicherstadt motif that nonetheless retained key elements such as vertical window forms and projections. It contains a touch of functionalism reminiscent of Werner Kallmorgen, who was extensively involved in rebuilding the Speicherstadt after the War, and was responsible, among other things, for Kaispeicher A, recently reincarnated as the plinth of the Elbphilharmonie building. The grand stairway of this building also functions as a small light well and offers excellent views of Deichtormarkt. Each floor of the building may be leased separately, and divided if so required down the middle.

1

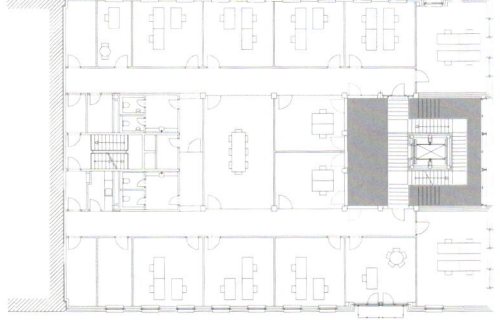

2   3

1 Ansicht aus Richtung Deichtor: gelungene Ergänzung der Speicherstadt mit modernen
Stilmitteln View towards Deichtor: fitting complement to the Speicherstadt with modern
style elements **2** Bürogrundriss Regelgeschoss office floor plan, full storey **3** Treppenhaus
als verglaster Lichthof Stairwell as glazed atrium

Umgestaltung der HHLA-Hauptverwaltung
Bürohaus Office Building

Standort Location Bei St. Annen 1 **Architekten Architects** gmp · von Gerkan, Marg und Partner, Hamburg **Bauherr Client** HHLA Hamburger Hafen- und Lagerhaus AG **Bauzeit Date built** 2000–02 **Bruttogeschossfläche Gross floor area** 10 770 qm (sqm)

Das Neorenaissance-Gebäude Bei St. Annen 1 galt immer als »Rathaus der Speicherstadt«. Mit hellrotem Verblendmauerwerk, dekorativen Gliederungen aus Sandstein und den verzierten Giebeln und Türmen war und ist es das Gesicht in der Masse. Die angrenzenden Speicher Holländischer Brook 4–6 wurden seit Jahren als Erweiterungen für Bürozwecke genutzt. Der nun alle verbindende Zentralraum zwischen Verwaltungs- und Speicherbau konnte beeindruckend in eine haushohe Halle umgewandelt, gläsern überdacht und mit einem Glaslift ausgestattet werden. Das Holzskelett der Speicher, glasierte Klinker, Schiefer, Kupfer, polierte Granitsäulen, Terrakottakacheln, Gusseisensäulen und der Stuck des Speicher-Rathauses – alles zusammen ist ein wahrer Steinbruch der Baugeschichte. Durch das neue Glasatrium wird alles zu einem neuen harmonischen Ganzen vereint.

The neo-Renaissance building at Bei St. Annen 1 has long been regarded as the pre-eminent structure within the Speicherstadt. If the Speicherstadt was truly a municipality in its own right, this would be its town hall. With its light-red facing masonry, decorative sandstone features, and ornate gables and towers, this building stands out from the crowd. The neighbouring warehouses at Holländischer Brook 4–6 were in use for many years as an office extension. The central space between the office and warehouse sections has now been converted into an enormous atrium that extends right from the ground floor, is covered by a glass roof, and also features an attractive glass elevator. The timber framework, glazed clinker brick, slate, copper, polished granite columns, terracotta tiles, cast-iron pillars and stuccoed ceilings make this stately warehouse building a veritable archive of architectural history. The new glass-covered atrium succeeds brilliantly in binding the entire ensemble together.

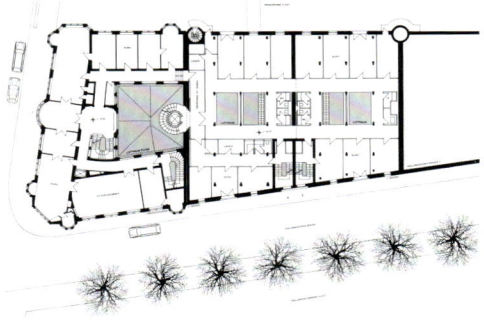

1

2

3

4

1 Das »Rathaus der Speicherstadt« The "city hall" of the Speicherstadt **2** Interieur als Verbindung zwischen Alt und Neu Interior as interstice between old and new
3 Die haushohe Halle ist oben verglast. The vaulted ceiling of the hall is glazed on top.
4 Grundriss mit Büros Floor plan with offices

Ehemaliges Freihafenamt
Kontorhaus Office Building

Standort Location Bei St. Annen 2 **Architekten Architects** SKA Sybille Kramer Architekten, Hamburg, mit and Christoph Konerding **Bauherr Client** Hamburger Hafen und Logistik AG (HHLA) **Bauzeit Date built** 2011–13 **Bruttogeschossfläche Gross floor area** 4700 qm (sqm)

Das Freihafenamt war einer der ersten Nachkriegsbauten in der Speicherstadt. Werner Kallmorgen baute es bis 1954 neu auf dem Grundstück des zerstörten Ostteils des Speicherblocks R. In einer zeitgenössischen Würdigung hieß es, er stelle die nachbarschaftliche Beziehung nicht durch Anpassung, sondern durch Kontrast wieder her. Kallmorgen setzte bei allen seinen Bauten in der Speicherstadt moderne klare Formen gegen den vorherrschenden Historismus.

Nach dem Abbau der Zollzäune wurde grundlegend saniert, und es gab einen neuen Mieter, eine Werbeagentur. Der Innenhof ist nun verglast – aus Brandschutzgründen, aber auch, um ein »Abstürzen« der Besucher zu verhindern. Kallmorgens gläserne Kassettendecke ist verschwunden (ein Lichtband erinnert an ihre Position). Dafür blickt man heute vom alten schwarz-weiß gefliesten Boden sieben Geschosse in die Höhe. Zudem wurde einer der letzten originalen Pater Noster in Hamburg erhalten.

The Freihafenamt (Free Port Authority) was one of the first post-war buildings in the Speicherstadt. Werner Kallmorgen built it in 1954 on the property of the destroyed eastern part of Speicherblock R. According to a contemporary appraisal, he restored the neighbourly relationship nit by means of adaptation, by creating contrast. With all of his buildings in the Speicherstadt, Kallmorgen confronted the prevailing historicism with clear, modern forms.

There was a thorough renovation after the customs fences were dismantled, and a new tenant was found, an advertising agency. The inner courtyard is now glazed (for fire protection reasons), but also to prevent visitors from "plummeting down". Kallmorgen's coffered glass ceiling has disappeared (a light band marks its position). Instead, it is now possible to look up from the black-and-white tiled floor to a height of seven storeys. Furthermore, one of the last remaining original paternosters in Hamburg is held here.

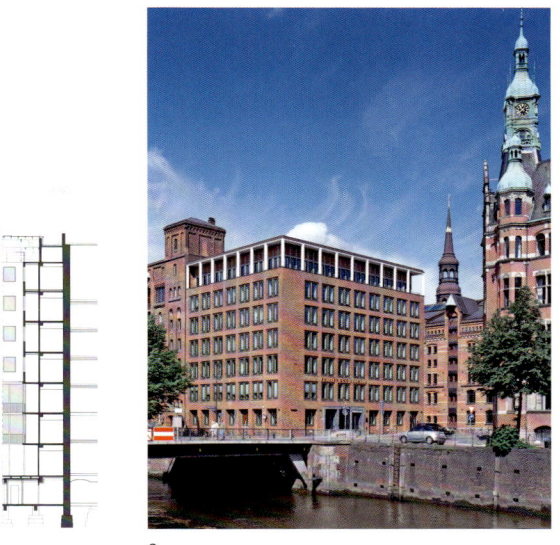

1

2

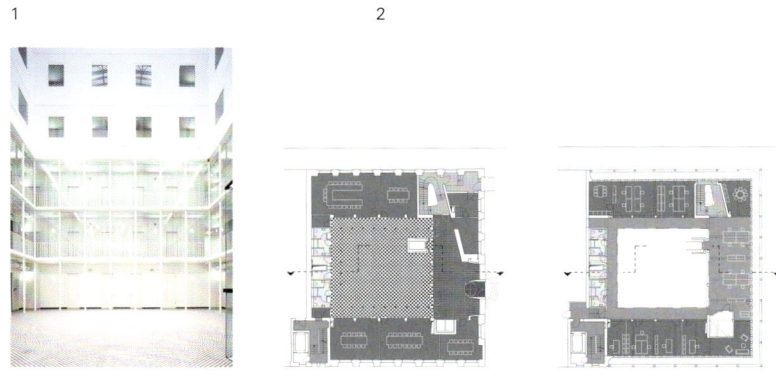

3

4

5

1 Schnitt Cross section **2** Blick übers Wasser auf das ehemalige Freihafenamt, rechts im Bild: St. Annen View across the water to the former Freihafenamt; right: St. Annen Church **3** Überglastes Atrium Glazed atrium **4+5** Grundrisse Floor plans

Speicherblock P
Umbau Bürohaus Office Building (Redevelopment)

Standort Location Neuer Wandrahm 1–4 **Architekten Architects** Hamburger Hafen und Logistik AG (HHLA) in Kooperation mit in cooperation with Kramer Biwer Mau Architekten, Hamburg **Bauherr Client** Hamburger Hafen und Logisitk AG (HHLA) **Bauzeit Date built** 2006 **Bruttogeschossfläche Gross floor area** 23 000 qm (sqm)

Man könnte es eine prototypische Maßnahme nennen, wie hier aus einer denkmalgeschützten Speicherstruktur moderne Büroräume wurden. Die neuen Zutaten sind vor allem drei eingefügte Lichthöfe, die das Problem der mangelhaften Belichtung durch große Raumtiefen mindern. Bedenkt man, dass hier zwischen Denkmalschutz und Brandschutz vermittelt werden, nach außen der alte Auftritt bewahrt und ein Umgang mit den eigentlich zu geringen Raumhöhen gefunden werden musste, ist die Lösung überraschend frisch und modern – wenn auch innen manchmal fast brachial. Der Umbau dieses Speicherblocks war ein Meilenstein für die Umwidmung der Speicherstadt und der gelungene Nachweis dafür, wie neues Leben in die Speichergemäuer einziehen kann.

One could call this a prototypical approach; the creation of new office spaces within a listed historical warehouse. The new ingredients consist principally of three added light wells, which break up the original spaces and mitigate the problem of insufficient lighting. Considering that the architects were walking a fine line between monument protection and fire prevention, that they were obliged to retain the external appearance, and had to find a way to deal with the low floor height, this solution is surprisingly fresh and modern, though occasionally almost brutishly forceful. The conversion of this warehouse block was a milestone in the redevelopment of the Speicherstadt, and successfully demonstrated that it was possible to breathe new life into these old brick walls.

1 Gesamtansicht Overall view **2** Neue Lichthöfe erhellen die alten Speicherböden. New light wells illuminate the old warehouse floors. **3** Perspektivschnitt durch einen Lichthof Sectional view of a glass-roofed inner court **4** Grundriss Floor plan

1

2

3

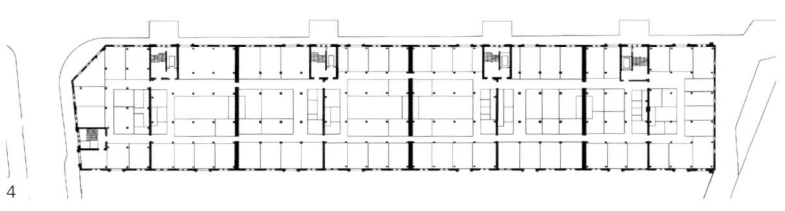

4

Kesselhaus
Infocenter der Hafencity Hafencity Information Centre

Standort Location Am Sandtorkai 30 **Architekten Architects** gmp · von Gerkan, Marg und Partner, Hamburg **Bauherr Client** Hamburger Hafen und Logistik AG (HHLA) **Bauzeit Date built** 2000–01 **Bruttogeschossfläche Gross floor area** 1335 qm (sqm)

Der historische Backsteinbau von 1886/ 87 war einst die Energiezentrale der Speicherstadt – im übertragenen Sinn ist er es in seiner Funktion als Info-Haus für die Aufbauphase der Hafencity heute wieder. Schon von Weitem ist das neue Infocenter an den beiden Drahtkorb-Türmen zu erkennen, die an die echten Schornsteine des ehemaligen Elektrizitätswerks erinnern. Das Kesselhaus wurde von 1886 bis 1888 durch Franz Andreas Meyer errichtet, der als »Spiritus Rector« der Speicherstadt gilt. Heute ist der Innenraum ein Multifunktionsraum mit Terrasse, einem großen Hafencity-Modell (32 Quadratmeter), mit Fotos und Multimedia-Installationen. Hier finden auch viele Workshops und Vorträge statt: ein Hotspot für die Hamburger Architekturszene. In einem der ehemaligen Schornstein-Stümpfe – dem nun sogenannten »Leuchtturm« – ist ein kleiner Ausstellungsraum entstanden.

This historical brick boiler house, which dates from 1886/87, was once the energy centre of the Speicherstadt. Figuratively speaking, it has re-assumed this role, as the information centre for the initial phase of the Hafencity development. Even from a distance the Kesselhaus stands out due to its twin "wire basket" towers, which references the original chimneys of this early power plant. The Kesselhaus was built between 1886 and 1888 by Franz Andreas Meyer, who was the guiding light behind the Speicherstadt. The building's interior is now a multi-functional space with a terrace, a large-scale (32 square metres) 3D model of the Hafencity, and numerous photographs and multimedia installations. This is also a venue for workshops and lectures—a hotspot in Hamburg's architecture scene. One of the chimney "stumps", referred to as the "lighthouse", now houses an intimate exhibition space.

1

2

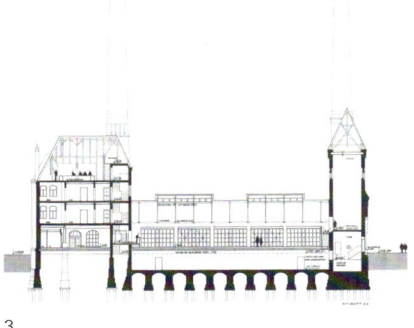

3

1 Blick auf das große Stadtmodell der Hafencity View of the large-scale 3D model of Hafencity **2** Kesselhaus mit Drahtkorbinstallationen, die an die ehemaligen geziegelten Schornsteine erinnern The Kesselhaus with wire basket installations representing a nod to the former brick chimneys **3** Längsschnitt Longitudinal section

Hanseatic Trade Center I
Erweiterung Extension of the Speicherstadt

Standort Location Am Sandtorkai, Kehrwieder **Architekten Architects** gmp · von Gerkan, Marg und Partner, Hamburg **Bauherr Client** HTC KG **Bauzeit Date built** 1997–99 **Bruttogeschossfläche Gross floor area** 45400 qm (sqm)

Als die Architekten von gmp die kriegs-zerstörten Teile der Speicherstadt im Westen wiederaufbauen sollten, machten sie dort weiter, wo sie mit ihrem Zürichhaus in der Altstadt aufgehört hatten, und bauten im Jahre 1999 auf einer Länge von 208 Metern eine Staffel von Kontorhäusern mit verglasten Atrien. Die Außenwände sind als klassische Mauerwerksfassaden passend zur Ziegelfarbe der Speicherstadt ausgebildet. Vom heutigen Standpunkt aus kann man sich mit den kantigen Baublöcken anfreunden, weil sie im Osten von der verspielten Speicherstadt auf feinsinnige Weise konterkariert werden und in ihrer Harmlosigkeit den Neubauten der Hafencity im Süden als ruhiger Hintergrund dienen. Zum Ensemble gehört ein Restaurant-Pavillon auf der historischen Kai-Bastion. Der zweigeschossige Pavillon mit einer Länge von 44 Metern öffnet sich vollverglast zum Binnenhafen und zur Stadt.

When the architects from gmp received the tender for the westward extension of the Speicherstadt, they continued where they had left off with the Zurich building (offices of the Zurich Insurance Group) in the Altstadt, and constructed a 208-metre-long series of office buildings with glass-roofed atriums. The external walls were designed as a classical masonry façade, and even the colour of the brick matches the appearance of the Speicherstadt. From a contemporary perspective it's easy to see the appeal of these angular buildings, which provide a sensitive counterpoint to the more playful traditional architecture of the Speicherstadt, and moreover they now serve as a calming backdrop to the bolder new interventions at the southern end of the Hafencity. The ensemble includes a restaurant pavilion located on the historical bastion. The two-storey-high, 44-metres-long pavilion faces the river port and the city through a fully glazed façade.

1

2

3

1+2 In der für sie typisch kantigen, modernen Weise bauten gmp an dieser Stelle die historische Speicherstadt weiter. gmp extended the historic Speicherstadt employing their trademark angular, modern style. **3** Grundriss Floor plan

Hanseatic Trade Center II

Standort **Location** Am Sandtorkai 74–77 **Architekten Architects** Kleffel Köhnholdt Gundermann, Hamburg **Bauherr Client** HTC GmbH & Co. Grundbesitz KG, Hamburg **Wettbewerb Competition** 1990 **Bauzeit Date built** 1991–96 **Bruttogeschossfläche Gross floor area** 22 400 qm (sqm)

Die Bebauung im Bereich der Kehrwiederspitze nördlich der Elbphilharmonie erscheint aus heutiger Sicht wenig spektakulär. Zu Beginn der 1990er Jahre hatte man nämlich auf alle Experimente verzichtet und die mutigen Entwürfe des deutsch/britischen Duos Alsop & Störmer oder des Römers Massimiliano Fuksas verworfen. Der entstandene runde Turm (Nägele, Hofmann, Tiedemann u. Partner/Frankfurt, nicht abgebildet) beherbergt Büros und verdient kaum eine Würdigung in einem Architekturführer, ebenso wie die Bebauung an der anderen Seite des Sandstorkais: Was dort gebaut wurde, ist sachlich und aus Ziegel (Kohn Pedersen Fox, New York), aber trivial. Optisch herausragender, aber vielleicht nicht allen hohen Ansprüchen des extravaganten Orts der Kehrwiederspitze gerecht geworden, ist die gebogene Hochhausscheibe mit spitzer Nase und elliptischem Dachhut.

From a contemporary perspective, the buildings located to the north of the Elbphilharmonie on Kehrwiederspitze seem decidedly unspectacular. This may be because in the early 1990s there was not yet much appetite for daring experiments in Hamburg. Consequently, the bold designs submitted by the Anglo-German duo Alsop & Störmer and the Italian architect Massimiliano Fuksas were overruled. The centrepiece of the ensemble, a round office tower by Nägele, Hofmann, Tiedemann u. Partner, Frankfurt (not shown), is hardly worth mentioning in an architectural guide to Hamburg. The same is true of the building on the opposite bank of Sandtorkai, a functional yet essentially trivial brick structure by Kohn Pedersen Fox from New York. A more outstanding visual component of the ensemble is the sharply contoured block at the westernmost edge, with its pointed nose and elliptical crown.

1

2

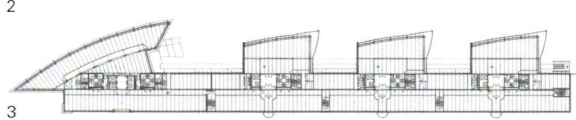

3

1 Ansicht Hanseatic Trade Center, Bauteil Kleffel Köhnholdt Gundermann View of the Hanseatic Trade Center, designed by Kleffel Köhnholdt Gundermann **2** Gegenblick von der Stromseite (im Vordergrund Bauteile von Kohn Pedersen Fox) Opposite view as seen from the river (building parts in the foreground: Kohn Pedersen Fox) **3** Grundriss Floor plan

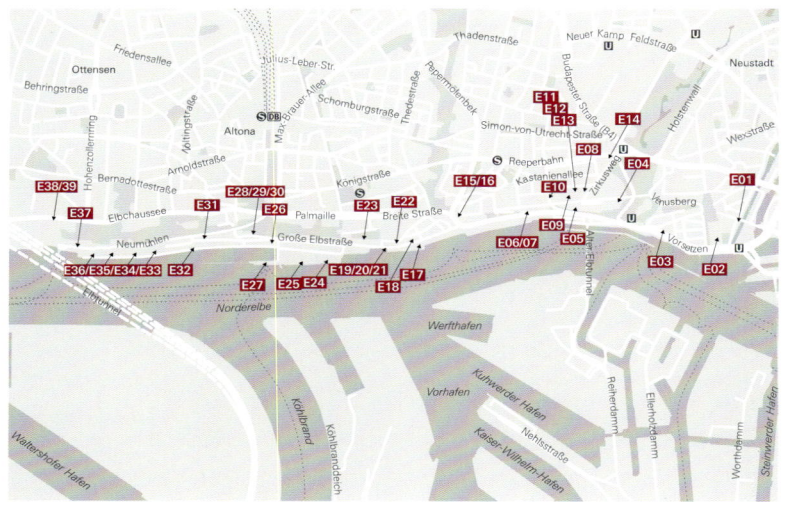

Perlenkette: Von der Alster bis Övelgönne

The "String of Pearls": from the Alster to Övelgönne

Seit den 1980er Jahren wächst Hamburg wieder an seinen Strom heran, viele alte Hafengrundstücke wurden mit sogenannten »Perlen« der Baukunst besetzt, hier vom Westen, von Neumühlen (vorn das alte, umgebaute Kühlhaus) her gesehen: Hamburgs neue »Perlenkette«.

Since the 1980s Hamburg has been regaining its former glory, with many old harbour sites becoming "pearls" of architecture, viewed here from Neumühlen (in the foreground the old converted icehouse) in the west: the "Perlenkette", or "string of pearls".

Die »Perlenkette« – Wo der Umbau der Waterfront begann

The "String of Pearls"—Where the Waterfront Project began

Hamburgs Oberbaudirektor von 1981 bis 1998, Egbert Kossak, trug die Verantwortung für eine strategisch-kreative Leistung, die im wahrsten Sinne des Wortes die Richtung in der Stadtentwicklung für die nächsten Jahrzehnte, wenn nicht Jahrhunderte vorgegeben hat: die strikte Förderung einer Rückwendung Hamburgs an den Elbstrom. Nach dem Zweiten Weltkrieg hatte sich die Hansestadt kommod rund um die Alster eingerichtet, konnte aber bis dato ihren eigentlichen Kern an der Elbe nur unvollkommen wiederherstellen. Kriegszerstörungen und eine radikal geführte Auto-Magistrale mit dem programmatischen Namen Ost-West-Straße (heute Willy-Brandt- und Ludwig-Erhard-Straße) unterbrachen das alte Kontinuum der Bürgerstadt, die sich natürlich zum Hafen orientiert hatte. Inzwischen waren letzte Lücken geschlossen worden. Hafenviertel wie in der Neustadt und die Landungsbrücken erfreuten sich zunehmender Beliebtheit, vor allem bei Touristen. Egbert Kossak erfand für seinen Plan

Egbert Kossak, Hamburg's Director of Urban Development from 1981 to 1998, was responsible for a strategic and creative decision that set the agenda for Hamburg's urban development during the following decades, if not centuries: the return to the Elbe. After the Second World War Hamburg realigned around the Alster Lake, and failed, until recently, to re-establish its true centre of gravity along the Elbe. War damage and a radically intersecting thoroughfare (prosaically titled Ost-West-Strasse and more recently renamed—in sections—Willy-Brandt-Strasse and Ludwig-Erhard-Strasse) severed the old continuum of the trading city that naturally faced towards the port. By the time Kossak came along the last remaining gaps had been filled. Dockland areas such as the Neustadt and the Landungsbrücken jetties were enjoying increasing popularity, particularly among tourists. Kossak came up with a fitting "brand" for his plan. He wanted to enhance the many deserted dockland sites with fine architecture, and pictured a string

eine »Marke«. Er wollte die vielen nun freigewordenen Hafengrundstücke mit feinen Architekturen aufwerten und sah viele gläserne Bauten vor, die nun die Backsteinstadt ergänzen sollten, und wollte so eine »Perlenkette« auffädeln. Viele Wettbewerbe ließ er ausschreiben und lenkte das Interesse internationaler Architekten auf Hamburg, was bis dato nicht üblich gewesen war.

Inzwischen sind in über zwanzigjähriger Bautätigkeit die meisten Pläne zwischen Neumühlen und Deichtor realisiert worden. Es beginnt spektakulär im Westen. Sind bei der Fahrt mit den praktischen HADAG-Elbfähren stromaufwärts eben noch die ehemaligen Fischerdörfer Blankenese und Övelgönne zu sehen, fast dörflich oder mit wunderschönen Elbchaussee-Villen im Geesthang, folgt plötzlich der kräftige Auftakt der »Perlenkette« ganz steinern mit der Rekonstruktion eines ehemaligen Kühlhauses, das durch eine Kuppel aufgesteckt wurde und heute als Seniorenheim genutzt wird. Es folgen Glaskuben in Neumühlen, die als Polderbauten bekannt wurden, Um- und Erweiterungsbauten im Fischereihafen sowie das alte England-Fährterminal, das nun durch eine neue »schräge« Schönheit eines Kreuzfahrtterminals ergänzt wird. Hier ist inzwischen kaum mehr ein Grundstück frei – moderne Bauwelten treffen auf Strukturen des Fischmarkts und einen Straßenstrich.

Westlich des Altonaer Fischmarkts wurde in den 1990er Jahren damit be-

of glass buildings along the Elbe that would enliven the red brick city. Thus the idea of the "Perlenkette", or "string of pearls", was born. Kossak invited numerous competitive tenders and broke the mould by attracting international architects to Hamburg.

Following more than twenty years of intensive construction most of the plans that were developed for the north bank of the Elbe from Neumühlen to Deichtor have been realised. It all began in the west, with a spectacular new landmark. If one takes one of the passenger ferries upriver passing the former fishing villages of Blankenese and Övelgönne, the view along the north bank alternates between rusticity and opulence; then, suddenly, one is confronted with the stony opening "bead" of the "Perlenkette". This reconstructed and refurbished coldstorage tower has been crowned with a glass dome and now functions as a retirement home. Following this, we encounter the glass cubes at Neumühlen, then the converted and extended buildings at the old fishing port in Altona, and the old England-Ferry terminal, to which the boldly designed new cruise ferry terminal has been added. There's hardly an empty lot remaining along this stretch of the north bank—modern architecture side by side with fish warehouses and even a miniature red-light district.

The area immediately to the west of the famous Fischmarkt saw the first moves—in the 1990s—to redevelop disused warehouses and an old malt

gonnen, die ehemaligen Speicher und eine Mälzerei umzunutzen. Dabei konnten die wuchtigen Industriefassaden erhalten, aber durch Aufstockungen und Zubauten ergänzt werden. Der Bereich rund um das Stilwerk wurde im Zusammenhang mit dem »kultigen« und international bekannten sonntäglichen Fischmarkt der erste gelungene urbane Umnutzungsversuch am Hafenrand. 1984 wurde die ehemalige Fischauktionshalle rekonstruiert und ist heute ein beliebtes Veranstaltungszentrum, auch wenn sie bisweilen nasse Füße bekommt. Der Abschnitt in St. Pauli setzt die »zwei Etagen« des Altonaer Geländes mit seinem »Balkon« fort. Die untere Zeile der damals umkämpften Hafenstraße wurde in den 1990er Jahren durch öffentlichen Wohnungsbau ergänzt. Spektakulärer sind die erst in letzter Zeit errichteten Zacken einer neuen Stadtkrone auf St. Pauli, dem Bavaria-Brauviertel, in der Beletage dieses Waterfront-Abschnitts. Dank der Hochhäuser changiert er zwischen spektakulär und lästig. Hamburg baut keine Hochhäuser in der City, es sei denn, der Investor will es so ...

Weiter östlich glänzen die Blechfassaden des neuen Verlagshauses von Gruner + Jahr, einer der wertvollsten Perlen der Kette. Etwa dort, in Höhe der U-Bahn-Station Baumwall, wurden am Herrengraben und weiter im Norden auf der Fleetinsel weitere Baulücken geschlossen, wodurch ein erster gelungener Link zwischen Elbe, City und Alster

house. The massive industrial façades were retained, with new sections, floors and extensions added. It was in this area around the Stilwerk designer arcade and world-renowned Sunday-morning fish market that the first successful attempt at urban harbour redevelopment took place. In 1984 the old fish auction hall was reconstructed and is now a popular event location, despite its occasional predilection to flooding. The St. Pauli section of the waterfront continues the "two-tier" approach to the waterfront development, exemplified at the panoramic "Altonaer Balkon" or "Altona's balcony". In the 1990s—at a time when Hafenstrasse was still the scene of notorious battles between police and left-wing squatters—several public housing projects were built here. The more spectacular architectural additions came later with the recent zigzag development on the site of the old Bavaria Brewery. With its commanding views of the port and city this area, known as the Hafenkrone or "harbour crown", is the piano nobile of St. Pauli's waterfront. Thanks to the new high-rise buildings the Hafenkrone is alternately spectacular and irksome. Traditionally Hamburg doesn't allow high-rise buildings near the centre, unless, it would seem, the investors insist.

Further upstream we encounter the shimmering sheet metal façades of the new offices of publishers Gruner + Jahr, one of the most precious "pearls" on the string. In that vicinity, north of Baum-

entstand, unter anderem über die ge-
fürchtete Barriere der Ost-West-Straße
hinweg. Ein zweiter Verbindungsweg
führt jetzt von der Binnenalster über die
neue Europa-Passage weiter zum Dom-
platz bis zur Hafencity. Ohne die »Perlenkette« wären die Planungen für eine
Hafencity gar nicht möglich gewesen.
Geografisch erreicht die »Perlenkette«
ihr Ende am Deichtorplatz.

wall metro station, several other gap
sites have been filled, and in the process
a link has finally been established between the Elbe, the city centre and the
Alster, including a clear route along Herrengraben, crossing the dreaded barrier
of Ost-West-Strasse, and leading to the
Fleetinsel. A second connecting route
now runs from the Inner Alster through
the new Europa-Passage, across Dom-
platz and through to the Hafencity.
Without the "Perlenkette", which ends
at Deichtorplatz, the Hafencity would
never have been possible.

Aztekenkontor
Büros und Geschäfte Office and Commercial Building

Standort Location Schaarsteinwegsbrücke 2 **Architekten Architects** Hakki Akyol und and Philipp Kamps in at Akyol Gullotta Kamps, Hamburg **Bauherr Client** Norddeutsche Grundvermögen Bau- und Entwicklungsgesellschaft mbH & Co. KG **Bauzeit Date built** 1910/2006 **Bruttogeschossfläche Gross floor area** 3741 qm (sqm)

E.01

Das Kontorhaus steht zwar in der zweiten Reihe, doch die kecke Aufstockung, wie eine Mütze aufgezogen, erzeugt Aufmerksamkeit – bis zum Zollkanal. Unmittelbar am Herrengrabenfleet gelegen, wurde das Gebäude 1910 als moderne Stahlskelettkonstruktion mit massiven Außenwandpfeilern erstellt. 1943 wurden große Teile durch den Krieg zerstört. Im Zuge der Aufstockung und Sanierung konnten alte Proportionen wiedergewonnen werden. Die Architektur der Aufstockung ist einerseits eine Reverenz an den historischen Ursprung und andererseits durch die Wahl von Materialien und Details eng mit unserer Zeit verbunden. Die neuen Geschosse wurden mit einer Metallfassade verkleidet und durch vorgehängte, umlaufende horizontale Lamellen zusammengefasst. Die horizontale Lamellenstruktur gewährleistet einen optimalen Sonnenschutz. Innen strahlt das Kontorhaus heute wieder die typische hanseatische Haltung aus: zurückhaltende Würde ohne Pomp.

Though it is located a block back from the harbour-front, thanks to the bold addition of two new storeys, nestled on top like a cap, this office building catches the eye all the way from the Zollkanal. This steel skeleton structure with massive external pilasters was originally built overlooking Herrengrabenfleet canal in 1910 and was badly bomb-damaged in 1943. The recent refurbishment and floor extension allowed the Aztekenkontor to regain some of its former glory. The added storeys defer in form to the historical origins of the building, yet in material and detail they are very contemporary. The new storeys have been given a metal façade in the form of non-bearing peripheral slats that completely surround the upper stores in a horizontal direction. This orientation also ensures that the slats provide optimal solar protection. On the inside the Aztekenkontor once again exudes typical Hanseatic poise: understated elegance and an absence of pomp.

1

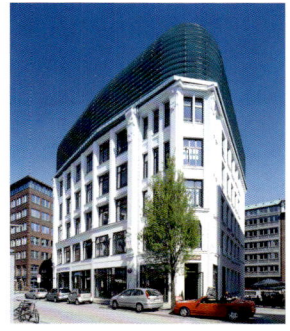

2   3

1+2 Gesamtansicht vom Fleet und vom Eingang Overall view from the canal and from
the entrance 3 Ausblick durch die Verkleidung der Aufstockung View through the lamella
cladding of the additional storey

Gruner + Jahr
Verlagsgebäude Press Building

Standort Location Am Baumwall 11 **Architekten Architects** Steidle & Partner, München; Kiessler & Partner, Hamburg; Schweger & Partner, Hamburg **Bauherr Client** Gruner + Jahr AG & Co. KG **Wettbewerb Competition** 1983/84 **Bauzeit Date built** 1987–90 **Bruttogeschossfläche Gross floor area** 88 000 qm (sqm)

Mehr als zwanzig Jahre alt ist dieses Beispiel spezieller Hamburger Verlagsbaukunst. Irritiert wurde die Stadt nur kurz, als der Pachtvertrag auslief. Man könne sich natürlich auch preiswerter an der Peripherie niederlassen, hieß es bei Gruner + Jahr. Konnte man nicht: Dieser Verlag gehört hierher, direkt an den Hafen, mit dem »Blickkontakt« zur Welt. Das Gebäude wurde maßgeschneidert, was bedeutete »transparent, demokratisch und licht – eine Medienwerkstatt; weder Verlagsmaschine, noch feierliche Selbstinszenierung eines Medienkonzerns: eine Stadt mit Straßen und Plätzen«. – Soweit die damaligen Ziele der Verlagsleitung für ihren Neubau. Die bayerischen Architekten verwendeten viel Metall, vor allem Zink, und ließen schmale schlanke Profile für Fenster und Sonnenschutz an die Fassaden montieren, als ginge es um ein Kreuzfahrtschiff. Doch ganz hanseatisch steckten sie die gespreizten und mit Zink verkleideten Betonstützen in Backsteinpantoffeln. Eine Verbeugung

More than twenty years after its completion, the headquarters of the publishing giant Gruner + Jahr remains one of the finest buildings of its kind. The city experienced just a brief moment of discomfort when the lease ran out on this site. The more fiscally conscious voices at Gruner + Jahr argued that it would be much cheaper to build new offices on the periphery. Perhaps so, but this publishing house is a natural denizen of the waterfront where it can maintain direct "eye contact" to the outside world. The building was custom built for Gruner + Jahr, meaning it was specifically designed, in the words of senior management, to be "transparent, democratic and light—a media workshop; neither a publishing apparatus nor an act of solemn self-promotion by a media corporation: a town with streets and squares." The Munich-based architects used a great deal of metal, particularly zinc, designed slender openings for windows, and mounted sunshades

1

1 Blick vom Michel Richtung Hafen; Gruner + Jahr verstand sein Hauptquartier nicht als Verwaltungsgebäude, sondern als Verlags-»Stadt« in einer Grünachse am Hafen View from St. Michael's Church towards the harbour; Gruner + Jahr did not want its headquarters to be an administrative building, but instead a publishing "town" at the centre of a green harbourfront hub
2 Übersichtsplan Site plan

2

vor der Backsteinstadt? »Ein Verlagshaus ist kein Bürohaus«, sagt der Architekt Uwe Kiessler. Deswegen hatte er zusammen mit Otto Steidle (1943–2004) eine Stadt entworfen. Geradezu penibel orientiert sich der Neubau an den strukturellen Merkmalen einer schachbrettartig gebauten Stadt. Vier Flurstraßen laufen in dem nur fünfgeschossigen Gebäude-Ensemble (Ausnahme: ein runder Turm) im rechten Winkel auf die Elbe zu. Daran angeschlossen liegen die Einzelbüros. Zwischen zwei Büroachsen wurden kleine, karg begrünte Innenhöfe angelegt. Nach zwanzig Jahren sind weitere Bauteile hinzugekommen: Der Park nebenan und zu Füßen des Michels funktioniert prima – wie in London oder New York als Lunchgarten. Das Prinzip der »Verlagsstadt« bewies so manche Schwäche wie etwa zu lange Strecken, aber eines überzeugt umso klarer, je mehr das Bauwerk in die Jahre kommt: Es altert in Ehren und setzt Patina an, so wie drüben im Hafen alte Kräne, Docks oder Helgen. Kleiner Tipp am (Hafen-)Rand: Die giebelständigen Langhäuser des Verlags interpretieren ein sehr altes Hamburger Hausmotiv gelungen neu.

on the façades, as though this were a cruise ship. And yet, fully in keeping with Hamburg's Hanseatic traditions, they dressed the supporting zinc-clad concrete columns in red-brick slippers. Can we interpret this as a discreet homage to Hamburg's architectural traditions? "A publishing house is not an office building," according to architect Uwe Kiessler. That is why, together with Otto Steidle, he designed a building based closely on the structural characteristics of a grid-patterned town. Four corridors run perpendicular to the Elbe through the five-storey ensemble. This linearity is broken only by a circular tower. The individual offices are all accessed via the corridors. Small, sparsely landscaped interior courtyards are positioned between two of the axes. Over the years more buildings and sections have been added, and the neighbouring park at the foot of the iconic St. Michael's Church (affectionately known to locals as "der Michel") is the perfect spot to enjoy lunch al fresco, just like in London or New York. The concept of a "publishing town" revealed certain limitations, such as the long walking distances between different sections of the complex. Having said that, this is a structure that is ageing gracefully, gaining a natural patina just like the nearby cranes and docks. The design of the Gruner + Jahr complex, with its gable ends facing the harbour, also masterfully reinterprets a very old architectural motif in Hamburg.

3

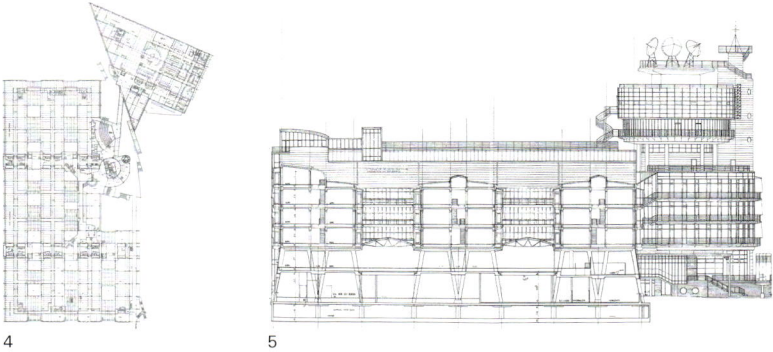

4   5

3 »Rückansicht« mit dem Turm vom Park "Rear view" with park tower **4+5** Grundriss und Schnitt Floor plan and cross section

Johannisbollwerk
Büro- und Wohnhaus Mixed Use Building

Standort Location Johannisbollwerk 16 **Architekten Architects** APB Architekten, Hamburg **Bauherr Client** Johannisbollwerk GbR **Bauzeit Date built** 1991–93 **Bruttogeschossfläche Gross floor area** 6070 qm (sqm)

Die schmale (als nicht bebaubar geltende) Baulücke zwischen Johannisbollwerk und Dietmar-Koel-Straße bot durch die Tiefe und Spitzwinkligkeit des Grundstücks ambivalente Bebauungsmöglichkeiten. An der Hafenseite wird das Haus – vergleichbar mit einem Passepartout – geschickt von typischen Putzfassaden aus der Gründerzeit gehalten und eingerahmt. Dort dominiert eine akkurate Stahlfassade in einer dunklen, kräftigen Pfosten- und Riegelkonstruktion mit vielen quadratischen Fenstern. Im Obergeschoss deuten präzise gesetzte Gauben und Loggien an, dass man hier auch wohnen kann. Der schluchtartige Eingangsschlitz in Rot geht im Erdgeschoss innen in einen schmalen Lichthof über. Das schafft Licht und Durchblick auch für die rückwärtige Hauszeile bis zum Hafen. Die »Rück«-Seite nimmt mit weißer Lochfassade die Maßhaltigkeit der alten Wohnhäuser in der Dietmar-Koel-Straße auf.

The gap site between Johannisbollwerk and Dietmar-Koel-Strasse, considered by many as unsuitable for development, offered ambivalent architectural possibilities due to its narrowness, depth and acute angles. The side of the building facing the harbour is deftly contained and framed by typical nineteenth-century rendered façades, which act as a kind of passe-partout. The dominant feature here is a finely executed steel façade in a darkly powerful post and beam construction with numerous quadratic windows. The precisely placed dormer windows and loggias on the upper floor indicate that this building is also for living in. The chasm-like entrance through a red slit on the ground floor leads the visitor into a narrow light well, which ensures that sufficient natural light suffuses the angular building. The "rear" of the building, with its white punctuated façade, echoes the dimensional stability of the old residential buildings on Dietmar-Koel-Strasse.

1

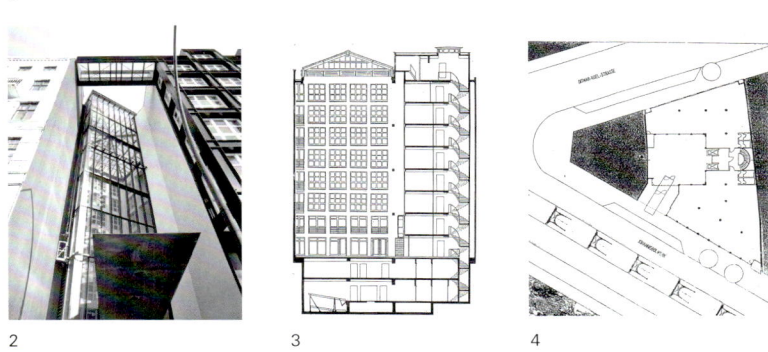

2   3   4

1 Gesamtansicht mit Hochbahnviadukt Overall view with elevated public transport bridge **2** Eingang im Hauseinschnitt Narrow entranceway to the building **3** Schnitt Sectional diagram **4** Übersicht Site plan

Hotel Hafen Hamburg – Classic & Residenz
Hotel Building

Standort Location Seewartenstraße 9 **Architekten Architects** Kleffel Köhnholdt, Hamburg (1. Erweiterung 1st addition 1985); meyer fleckenstein architekten stadtplaner, Hamburg (2.+3. Erweiterung 2nd and 3rd addition 1992–99) **Bauherr Client** Giesela und Wilhelm Bartels **Bauzeit Date built** 1985–99 **Bruttogeschossfläche der Erweiterungen Gross floor area of the additions** 1000 qm (sqm) Hotelzimmergeschoss (hotel room floor) / 1000 qm (sqm) Konferenz- und Saalgeschoss (conference and event floor)

Eine Assemblage des Aufstiegs und Wandels von St. Pauli: Ein ehemaliges Seemanns- und Schwesternheim avancierte zum Hotel und wurde noch munter erweitert und überlagert. Zuerst entstand ein dickleibiger Turm in postmoderner Aldo-Rossi-Manier (Kleffel & Köhnholdt, 1985). Dieser wird von einem schwingenden, klassisch modernen Riegel und einem flachen aufgesetzten Zylinder umformt und herausgefordert. Aluminiumblech, Beton und Glas, so scheint es, wollen dem archetypischen Turm mit seinem Backsteinkleid mitteilen, dass die schwebende, horizontal gegliederte Architektur die bessere ist. Das Ensemble wurde 1999 noch durch eine beeindruckende Glastonne aufgestockt.

This ensemble epitomises perhaps better than any other the recent process of transformation in St. Pauli: a former seaman's hostel and the nurses' residence from the neighbouring hospital were converted into a hotel, then in several stages new sections and layers were added. The first addition was a portly tower in post-modern Aldo Rossi style (Kleffel & Köhnholdt, 1985). This is both complemented and defied by a curved, classically modern oblong block with a flat, cylindrical extension above. It's as though the aluminium sheeting, concrete and glass elements were responding to the archetypical lower section of the tower with its brick mantel, sending the message that horizontally oriented architecture is the superior form. This ensemble was crowned in 1999 with an impressive half-barrel in glass.

1

2

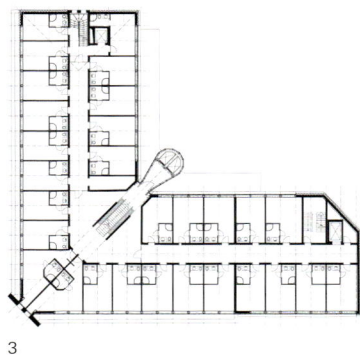

3

1 Das Hotel Hafen Hamburg besteht aus vielen Bauabschnitten, herausragend dabei ist der Turm aus postmodernen Zeiten. The Hotel Hafen Hamburg building has seen many additions since its erection, the most conspicuous being the postmodern tower. **2** Hofansicht View of the courtyard **3** Grundriss mit Hotelzimmern Floor plan with hotel rooms

Erweiterung des Bernhard-Nocht-Instituts für Tropenmedizin

Extension Building of the Bernhard Nocht Institute for Tropical Medicine

Standort Location Bernhard-Nocht-Straße 74 **Architekten Architects** kister scheithauer gross architekten und stadtplaner, Köln **Bauherr Client** Freie und Hansestadt Hamburg, vertreten durch die Behörde für Stadtentwicklung und Umwelt Ministry for Urban Development and Environment on behalf of the City of Hamburg **Bauzeit Date built** 2004–09 **Bruttogeschossfläche Gross floor area** 6185 qm (sqm)

Der Anbau birgt Speziallabore mit höchstem Sicherheitsanspruch und -standard (S2- bis BSL4-Labore) – im Volksmund auch »Virenbunker« genannt. Dieser Hochsicherheitstrakt ist mit zwei Geschossen in den Geesthang eingegraben und gibt sich auch formal sehr zugeknöpft. Doch ist er ein Ziegelmonolith, der der Backsteinstadt und deren hohen Ansprüchen gerecht wird. Immerhin steht er neben Fritz Schumachers altem Institutsgebäude, ohne vor Achtung in die Knie zu gehen, und gibt stattdessen eine Figur mit Grandezza ab. Der Neubau hat recht galant am Hang Platz genommen und zeigt, wie man das Thema Waterfront auffällig ausreizen kann, ohne unnötig in die Höhe gehen zu müssen. Kleine Spielerei am Rande: In der durch horizontale Fensterbänder gestalteten Fassade fallen vorn an der westlichen Schmalwand drei Kastenfenster auf, die um die Ecke gezogen werden – Fenster mit »Augenaufschlag« in der ansonsten ernsthaften Fassade.

This extension block houses highly specialised laboratories, popularly known as the "virus bunker", and therefore requires maximum security. Two entire storeys are buried within the slope that runs down to the Elbe. The initial impression is formal and reserved. Yet this monolith is a worthy addition to Hamburg's architectural fabric. It has the confidence to stand next to Fritz Schumacher's institute building without making any apologies. Rather, it exudes its own particular grandeur It cuts a strangely gallant figure on the slope, and demonstrates that even relative low-rise buildings can push the boundaries of waterfront development. An amusing margin note: the pattern of horizontal ribbon windows that dominates the main façade is interrupted along the sloping western edge by three box-type windows that turn the corner. This playful "wink" breaks the building's otherwise serious mien.

E.05

1

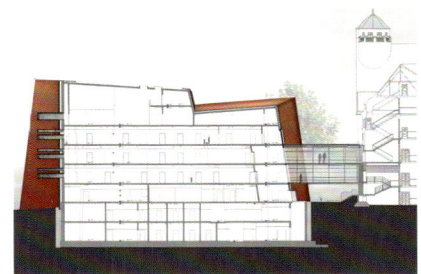

2

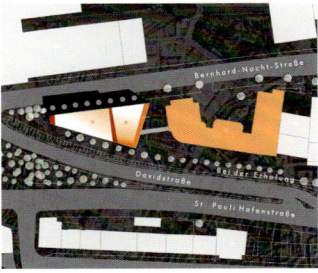

3

1 Überzeugende Lösung: die Erweiterung des Bernhard-Nocht-Instituts an den historischen Fritz-Schumacher-Bau Convincing solution: the extension of the Bernhard Nocht
Institute adjacent to the historic Fritz Schumacher building **2** Längsschnitt mit Übergang
zum Altbau Longitudinal section with passageway to old building **3** Lageplan Site plan

Wohnen an der Hafenstraße
Residential Development on Hafenstrasse

Standort Location Hafenstraße 104/Bernhard-Nocht-Straße 46–48 **Architekten Architects** Architekten-Contor Schäfer Agather Scheel, Hamburg **Bauzeit Date built** 1997

Die Hafenstraße war jahrzehntelang das Symbol der Auflehnung gegen hanseatisches Establishment, die Hausbesetzungen wurden per TV in die deutschen Wohnzimmer übertragen. Das alles ist Vergangenheit. Die Gegenwart sind Neubauten, die zwar nicht nach einem ursprünglich geplanten Entwurf von Zaha Hadid, sondern durch Hamburger Architekten entstanden sind, aber sie passen sich sicherlich besser ein. Die Häuser sind so weiß wie diejenigen auf einer ägäischen Insel. Wie dort ergibt das Ensemble eine gegliederte, fein eingestellte Hangbebauung aus Wohnungen, Balkonen und Dachterrassen. Zum Projekt gehört auch die benachbarte Schulerweiterung Friedrichstraße (E.07 nicht abgebildet, Architekten: Welm, Seifert, Möller).

For decades the name Hafenstrasse was a byword for rebellion against the establishment. Images of the buildings, which were occupied by left-wing radicals, were viewed in living rooms throughout Germany. But that's all history now. These days we have new residential developments on Hafenstrasse—not based on designs by Zaha Hadid as originally planned, but by Hamburg architects, with the result that they fit in all the better. In terms of colour scheme (all white) and form, these buildings are reminiscent of Greek villages. The result is a delicately constructed architectural ensemble, consisting of apartments, balconies and roof terraces. This project also included an extension to the neighbouring school on Friedrichstrasse (E.07 not shown, Architects: Welm, Seifert, Möller).

1

2

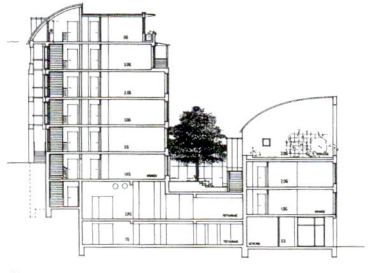

3

1 Ansicht von der Elbe View from the Elbe **2** Obere Straßenansicht Bernhard-Nocht-Straße (im Schnitt links) Street view of upper Bernhard-Nocht-Strasse (left side of cross section) **3** Schnitt Cross section

Astraturm
Bürohaus Office Building

Standort Location Zirkusweg 2 **Architekten Architects** KSP Jürgen Engel Architekten, Frankfurt am Main **Bauherr Client** DWI-Grundbesitz **Wettbewerb Competition** 2004 **Bauzeit Date built** 2006–07 **Bruttogeschossfläche Gross floor area** 13 285 qm (sqm)

E.08

Die moderne Lade- und Lagerhalle der St.-Pauli-Brauerei (1992, Architekten Silcher uund Werner) war trotz ihrer 12 000 Quadratmeter Nutzfläche ein moderater, sensibler Eingriff in ein Umfeld mit kleinteiliger Wohnbebauung. Bei so viel architektonischem Feinsinn ist es bedauernswert, dass diese Halle einem neuen Quartier auf dem ehemaligen Bavariabrauerei-Gelände weichen musste – mehr noch: Die ehemalige Gewerbenutzung diente als Begründung dafür, dass hier ein viel zu großer Anteil von Büros entstanden ist – dem Flächennutzungsplanrecht war das geschuldet. Nicht nur die alte Halle verschwand, auch das im übertragenen Sinn wie ein Pilsglas gestaltete Astra-Hochhaus. Der dicke Beton-»Stiel« des alten Hochhauses war für Aufstockungen und Ausbauten nicht geeignet, das neue Haus ist nicht mehr so originell, auch wenn es im Dachgeschoss eine Art Veranda erhielt: Hier wurde der Begriff von der Hafenkrone sehr wörtlich genommen.

The modern warehouse complex at the Astra Brewery in St. Pauli (built in 1992 by Silcher and Werner Architects) was, despite its size (12,000 square metres of floor space), a moderate and sensitive intervention in an area largely defined by small-scale residential buildings. In light of such architectural discretion, it is a shame that it fell victim to a new development on the site of the old brewery. Even worse: because the original development was commercial, Hamburg's land use and planning laws allowed the new development to devote far too much space to offices. Not only did the old warehouse complex disappear, so too did the old Astra Tower with its iconic Pils-glass form (like an oversized wine glass). It was demolished because the thick concrete "stem" supporting the tower did not easily allow for extension or addition of new floors. The new tower is not as original. It seems someone may have taken the idea of the Hafenkrone a little too literally.

1

2

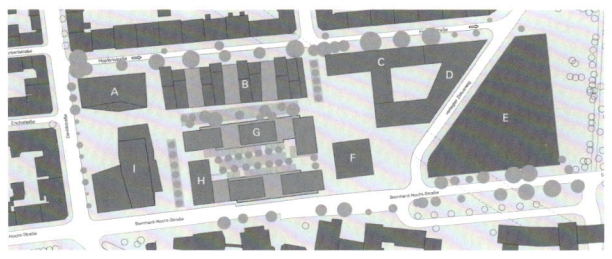

3

1 Der Astraturm als Kontrapunkt zum kleinteiligen Gefüge auf St. Pauli The Astra Tower as a counterpoint to small-scale development in St. Pauli **2** Turm mit Neubauten in der Nacht Tower and new buildings at night **3** Lageplan Site plan: **A** Brauhaus Brewery (David Chipperfield Architects), **B+C** Wohnhäuser Baugenossenschaft Bergedorf-Bille Residential Buildings (**B** pfp architekten, **C** Störmer Murphy and Partners), **D** Bavaria Office (Axthelm Architekten), **E** Atlantic Haus (Herzog + Partner / gmp), **F** Astraturm Astra Tower (KSP Jürgen Engel Architekten), **G** Brauquartier Hanse Bau Genossenschaft (Steidle + Partner), **H** Hollandhaus (Coido Architects), **I** Empire Riverside Hotel (David Chipperfield Architects)

Atlantic Haus
Bürohaus Office Building

Standort Location Bernhard-Nocht-Straße 113 **Architekten Architects** Herzog + Partner Architekten BDA, München (Entwurf Design); gmp · von Gerkan, Marg und Partner, Hamburg (Ausführung Execution) **Bauherr Client** Korund GmbH – Quantum Immobilien AG u. HSH Real Estate AG **Bauzeit Date built** 2005–07 **Bruttogeschossfläche Gross floor area** 34 000 qm (sqm)

Auch das zweite Hochhaus ist eine eher schlechte Replik gängiger Turmbau-Muster (vielleicht in einer Übernahme von Renzo Pianos Debis-Haus am Potsdamer Platz in Berlin). Aber weder eine solche Geistesverwandtschaft noch die recht klar gegliederten Fassaden mit dem alles überragenden, sehr schlanken Treppen- und Aufzugsturm rechtfertigen das hohe Haus an dieser Stelle – hier oben am Geestrand, an der Waterfront, konkurrieren solche hohen Häuser immer mit den Hauptkirchentürmen und der gewachsenen Stadtkrone und beschädigen sie. Allenfalls in einer Funktion als Wohnturm wäre dieses Projekt städtebaulich zu rechtfertigen. Der Turm und zwei achtgeschossige Flügelbauten, die ihn einrahmen, sprengen an dieser Stelle die gebaute Kleinteiligkeit von St. Pauli. Schade, denn architektonisch zeigt das Hochhaus mit seiner sichtbaren, gekreuzten Tragkonstruktion hinter der Glaswand Ansätze einer prägnanten Fassadenausbildung.

The second high-rise on the former brewery site is a rather poor specimen of contemporary tower construction, that appears to borrow from Renzo Piano's Debis Building at Potsdamer Platz in Berlin. But neither this, nor the clearly structured façades and the distinctive, slender tower that accommodates stairwells and elevator shafts, can justify the construction of such a tall building at this location. At the top of the slope that directly overlooks the port, tall buildings such as this inevitably compete with and ultimately impair Hamburg's church-steeple skyline. From an urban development perspective, the only acceptable structure of such dimensions at this point would be residential. The tower and the twin eight-storey wings on either side represent a serious interference with the architectural dimensions of St. Pauli. It's unfortunate, because the Haus, with its visible cross-wise supporting structure behind a wall of glass, demonstrates a succinct and effective façade design.

1

2   3

1 Blick auf die neue Stadtkrone St.Paulis auf dem Geestrand mit den beiden Turmhäusern Astra (links) und Atlantic (rechts). Nicht allen Hamburgern gefällt diese starke Veränderung. View of the new "crown" of St. Pauli with the Astra Tower (left) and Atlantic Haus (right) high-rise pair. Not everyone in Hamburg approves of this major change to the skyline. **2** Schnitt Cross section **3** Lage des Projekts im neuen Brauquartier Site of the project in the new Brauquartier

Empire Riverside Hotel und Brauhaus
Mixed Use Building

Standort Location Bernhard-Nocht-Straße 97 **Architekten Architects** David Chipperfield Architects, Berlin **Bauherr Client** Empire Riverside GmbH & Co. KG **Bauzeit Date built** 2002–07 **Bruttogeschossfläche Gross floor area** Hotel 21 000 qm (sqm), Brauhaus 5500 qm (sqm)

E.10

Das Hotel mit 328 Zimmern im 21-geschossigen Turm, der L-förmige Sockel und das direkt anschließende Büro- und Geschäftsgebäude »Brauhaus« bilden zusammen mit den benachbarten Hochhäusern und dem Turm der St.-Michaelis-Kirche nach dem Willen der Bauherren Hamburgs neue »Hafenkrone« – eine von vielen ungeliebte Bekrönung, denn das neue Viertel wirkt für die gewachsene Struktur des traditionellen Rotlicht- und Amüsierviertels wie ein Dolch im Leib. Architekturenthusiasten werden allerdings durch die sensible Fassadenarbeit des Architekten entschädigt, der in Berlin mit dem Neuen Museum auf der Museumsinsel einen außergewöhnlichen Erfolg feierte. »Die homogene Schicht der feingliedrigen Fassade fasst das skulpturale Gebäude-Ensemble zu einer Einheit zusammen und betont die Vertikale«, so der Architektenkommentar. Will heißen: Der Komplex ändert seine Kontur und Form je nach Perspektive und Position des Betrachters.

With 328 rooms in a 21-storey tower on an L-shaped base, this hotel forms Hamburg's new "Hafenkrone" skyline together with the directly adjacent »Brauhaus« commercial building, the neighbouring towers and the steeple of St. Michael's Church. This "crown" has found as many detractors as admirers. The problem for many is that the new quarter appears like an attempt to eliminate the centuries-old structure of this red-light and nightlife district. Architecture enthusiasts, however, will appreciate the sensitive façade design by the same architect who enjoyed such extraordinary success with the Neues Museum in Berlin. According to the architect's own notes, "The glass-bronze façade is structured with a post-beam construction, which emphasises the vertical. It covers the buildings as a homogeneous layer, unifying the different volumes". This structure changes its contours and format depending on the viewer's perspective and position.

1

2

3

1 Dem gut gestalteten Hotel-Hochhaus gönnt man den herausragenden Auftritt. Even detractors must admit the high-rise hotel is well-designed and striking. **2** Blick von der Elbe auf die neue Waterfront von St. Pauli View of the new St. Pauli waterfront from the Elbe **3** Eingang und Fassade Entrance and façade

Baugenossenschaft Bergedorf-Bille I
Wohnhäuser Cooperative Residential Buildings

Standort Location Brauquartier/Bernhard-Nocht-Straße (Hopfenstraße 15–21) **Architekten Architects** Prof. Jörg Friedrich, PFP Architekten BDA, Hamburg **Bauherr Client** Baugenossenschaft Bergedorf-Bille eG **Wettbewerb Competition** 2002 **Bauzeit Date built** 2008 **Bruttogeschossfläche Gross floor area** 15300 qm (sqm)

Auch die Wohnhäuser im Quartier verdienen ein ambivalentes Urteil. Trotz einer teilweise bestechenden Qualität – wie in diesem Fall der spannenden, lebhaften Haus- und Freiraumkomposition – bleiben sie im Quartier dennoch fremd. Man kann weder den sinnvollen Grundrissen noch den geschickt angelegten Balkonen und Terrassen irgendeinen kompositorischen oder funktionalen Fehler nachweisen. Aber man kann durchaus darüber nachdenken, ob diese Wohnungen, die als innerstädtische Alternativen zu den alten Quartieren in Eimsbüttel oder Eppendorf für eine bestimmte Klientel geplant waren, dort hingehören, wo die Grenze für das Flaschenbierverbot in St. Pauli liegt und sich häufig Berge von Glasscherben auftürmen. Stadtsoziologisch betrachtet, wird es noch Zeit brauchen, bis diese Wohnqualität von Loft- oder Penthouse-Wohnungen und das wilde St. Pauli kompatibel sind.

Even the residential buildings within this quarter deserve an ambivalent appraisal. Though delightfully attractive in many regards—this is a lively and exciting blend of architecture and open space—they remain alien to this quarter. It's impossible to fault either the sensible floor plans or the cleverly positioned balconies and terraces in terms of composition or function. However, it is worth considering whether these apartments, which were conceived for a certain clientèle as a more urban alternative to the fashionable districts of Eimsbüttel or Eppendorf, actually belong at a place where the street-party zone of St. Pauli begins and piles of broken glass often litter the streets. In terms of urban sociology, it will certainly take some time before the residential opulence of lofts and penthouse apartments is compatible with the street life of St. Pauli.

1

2

3

1+2 Die Wohnanlange ist vorbildlich strukturiert und gegliedert, zudem mit Dachterrassen und üppigen Balkons ausgestattet. The residential complex is exquisitely structured and organised, plus features rooftop terraces and generous balconies. 3 Schnitt Cross section

Wohnblock im Brauquartier
"Brauquartier" Residential Block

Standort Location Bernhard-Nocht-Straße **Architekten Architects** steidle architekten, München **Bauherr Client** Hansa Baugenossenschaft, Hamburg **Wettbewerb Competition** 2002 **Bauzeit Date built** 2004–07 **Bruttogeschossfläche Gross floor area** 17 100 qm (sqm)

Südlich der vier »Stadthäuser« von Jörg Friedrich liegt, getrennt durch den zentralen Quartiersboulevard, der sich diesen Namen noch verdienen muss, ein Wohnhof, dessen zwei gegenüberliegende Zeilen von einem Architekten stammen, der für seinen feinfühligen menschlichen Wohnbau bekannt geworden ist. Es sind gute Grundrisse für etwa 120 frei finanzierte Wohnungen entstanden, besser vielleicht als in der Hafencity. Angeboten werden Maisonette-Typen, die Erdgeschoss-Wohnungen besitzen kleine Gärtchen, und wenn man mit den Bewohnern ins Gespräch kommt, verraten sie, dass sie früher zu teuer im Eimsbütteler Altbau gewohnt haben und diese Nähe zur Stadt jetzt im Neubau genießen. Das anschließende Bürohaus stammt von Coido Architects, Hamburg / Rotterdam.

To the south of the four "townhouses" designed by Jörg Friedrich, separated by the quarter's central boulevard (which is not yet worthy of that name), is a courtyard with two facing rows of apartments by an architect with a reputation for designing sensitive residential buildings on a human scale. He drew up plans for around 120 privately financed apartments at a standard better, perhaps, than in the Hafencity. These are all maisonette-type apartments, with miniature gardens attached to those on the ground floor. When you talk to the residents you quickly discover that they used to live in over-priced late-nineteenth-century buildings in Eimsbüttel, and now enjoy the proximity to the city. The adjacent office building is designed by Coido Architects, Hamburg / Rotterdam.

1

2

3

1 Ansicht des Wohnblocks in Richtung Empire Riverside Hotel View of the residential block looking towards the Empire Riverside Hotel 2 Innenhof mit dem Astraturm im Hintergrund Inner courtyard with the Astra Tower in the background 3 Grundriss Erdgeschoss Floor plan, ground level

Baugenossenschaft Bergedorf-Bille II
Wohnhäuser Cooperative Residential Buildings

Standort Location Hopfenstraße **Architekten Architects** Störmer Murphy and Partners, Hamburg (Entwurf Design), Neumann + Partner Architekten, Hamburg (Ausführung Execution) **Bauherr Client** Baugenossenschaft Bergedorf-Bille **Wettbewerb Competition** 2007 **Bauzeit Date built** 2008 **Bruttogeschossfläche Gross floor area** 4540 qm (sqm)

Der östlichste Wohnblock schließt an die Bürobauten an; dort an dem kleinen Quartiersplatz gibt es auch einen Supermarkt. Der lang gestreckte Baukörper ist durch Betonfertigplatten im Erdgeschoss und weißen Putz in den Obergeschossen geprägt. Aus einer dreistöckigen Basis entwickeln sich vier Turmhäuser an der Seite zur Hopfenstraße und wirken für St. Pauli fast wie das Bollwerk einer »gated community«. Letztendlich sind dies städtebauliche Vorgaben des Quartiersabschlusses, und der Übergang zum Maßstab der Bürohäuser ist gut gelöst. Die Wohnungsgrundrisse sind solide, und das ist gut so, weil der Eigentümer, eine Baugenossenschaft, für eine Klientel steht, die weder Loftcharakter noch Marmorküchen braucht bzw. bezahlen will ...

The eastern apartment block is connected to the office buildings. There's also a small supermarket on the square. This elongated structure features off-white clinker brick. Four low-rise apartment towers sit atop a three-storey base along Hopfenstrasse. At first glance this looks like the bulwark of a gated community. In fact, this building is the result of an urban planning deal for this quarter, and the transition to the scale of the office buildings is well executed. The layout of the apartments is sensible, and that's just as well, because the owner, a cooperative building society, represents a clientèle that doesn't require or can't afford loft apartments or marble kitchens.

1

2

3

1 Der Wohnblock der Baugenossenschaft vom Quartiersplatz gesehen The apartment block as seen from Quartiersplatz **2+3** Ansicht von Norden / Altbaubestand St.Pauli View from the north

Tanzende Türme

Hotel und Bürohaus Hotel and Office Building

Standort Location Reeperbahn 1 **Architekten Architects** BRT Architekten LLP Bothe Richter Teherani, Hamburg **Bauherr Client** Projekt Elbpark GmbH & Co. KG, Strabag Real Estate GmbH **Wettbewerb Competition** 2003 **Bauzeit Date built** 2009–11 **Bruttogeschossfläche Gross floor area** 64 000 qm (sqm)

»Der eigenen Fantasie sind keine Grenzen gesetzt. Die Türme müssen genauso locker und schräg sein wie St. Pauli auch« – so in etwa lautete die Vorgabe. Die Architekten entschieden sich fürs Schräge, das aus der Mitte kippt: 770 Stützen der »Tanzenden Türme« neigen sich bis zu 7,5 Prozent zur Seite. Beide Türme verfügen über in zwei Richtungen schräg gestellte Außenstützen in Fertigteilbauweise, die im sechsten und 17. Obergeschoss ihre Richtung ändern. Die Grundrisse verschieben sich, bleiben jedoch deckungsgleich. Die Fassaden überspielen die Schrägen durch doppelgeschossigen Blechrahmen. Das gesamte Ensemble, zu dem am Fuß des Hochhauspaars auch ein Hotel mit 215 Zimmern und der wiedererstandene Kult-Musikclub »Mojo« gehören, polarisiert in Hamburg. Denn Emotionen zu bauen gelingt kaum, wenn man einen streng kalkulierten Kostenrahmen einhalten muss.

How does one plan and build architecture for an environment that is downright dilapidated, subversive, aged and even seedy in the daytime? With boundless imagination and a design that matches St. Pauli in its off-the-cuff and off-beat spirit. The architects developed a decidedly skewed solution to the challenge: the 770 pillars of the "Dancing Towers" tilt sideways at angles of up to 7.5 per cent. Both towers are equipped with chamfered external supports made of prefabricated components that change direction on the sixth and seventeenth storeys. This feature dislocates the floor plans, which remain congruent however. The sloping surfaces of the façade are concealed within through the use of double-shell sheet steel frames. The entire ensemble—including a hotel with 215 rooms at the foot of the towers and the latest iteration of cult nightclub "Mojo"— has polarised opinion in Hamburg. Structures that speak to our emotions are seldom created without breaking the bank.

E.14

1

2

3

1 Ansicht von der Reeperbahn View from the Reeperbahn **2** Ansicht vom Millerntor View from Millerntor **3** Übersichtsplan (oben in der Zeichnung Reeperbahn) Site plan (with the Reeperbahn at the top of the drawing)

Hinter der Waterfront: Eine City für das 21. Jahrhundert entsteht

Behind the Waterfront: The Emergence of a Twenty-first-century City

Was steckt hinter der Waterfront? Und welche Pläne hat Hamburg heute für seinen historischen Innenstadtbereich innerhalb der Wallanlagen entwickelt? Seit Beginn des 19. Jahrhunderts sind diese verschwunden und aufgelassen. Die hinzugewonnenen Flächen wurden für neue Straßenringe nach Wiener Muster und später für großartige Grünanlagen genutzt, die seit den 1930er Jahren auch als Gartenschauen dienten. Um die Jahrhundertwende zum 20. Jahrhundert wurde auf einem Teil des Terrains eine Eisenbahn-Verbindungsbahn zwischen Hamburg und Altona gebaut, das heißt, die alten Kopfbahnhöfe wurden miteinander verbunden. Bis heute sind diese Wallreste und damit die alte mittelalterliche Größe der Hafenstadt sichtbar geblieben – im Süden wird sie vom Norderelbe-Strom begrenzt. Da dort schon immer das Wasser schützte, waren Wehranlagen nicht notwendig.

Mehrere Katastrophen haben für einen jeweils grundlegend veränderten Wiederaufbau gesorgt: Der mittelalter-

What lies behind the waterfront—what plans does the city of Hamburg have for the historical inner city within the old city walls? These fortifications were gradually abandoned or removed from the early nineteenth century onwards. The space that was opened up as a result was first used to build major ring roads, based on the example of Vienna, and later for beautiful parks and green areas. At the turn of the twentieth century a railway line was constructed on a section of the terrain, connecting the two terminal stations at Hamburg and Altona (at that time separate cities). To this day some remains of the fortifications that marked Hamburg's medieval city limits to the north, east and west can still be seen. Hamburg's southern boundary was marked at that time by the Elbe.

Hamburg's architectural character has been greatly influenced by disasters and the ensuing reconstruction. The medieval city that was dominated by typical North-German timber-framed buildings was largely destroyed during

liche Charakter einer norddeutschen Fachwerkstadt ging größtenteils 1842 durch den Großen Brand verloren. Ende des 19. Jahrhunderts mussten nach verheerenden Cholera-Epidemien aus hygienischen Gründen viele der engen und verwinkelten Gängeviertel abgerissen werden – so entstand Platz für die moderne City einer Großstadt, zum Beispiel für das Kontorhausviertel mit dem berühmten Chilehaus.

Eine schöne Stadt, aber abends ohne Menschen

Trotz weiterer Zerstörungen im Zweiten Weltkrieg war die Hamburger Innenstadt in den letzten fünfzig bis sechzig Jahren im Wiederaufbau insgesamt zu einer wunderbaren und schönen geworden, die allerdings lange Zeit zur Vereinsamung verurteilt schien. Eine starke architektonische Mischung machte sie aus, die die Kraft der mittelalterlichen Backsteinkirchen und einiger musealer Fachwerkareale mit all den eklektizistischen Bauerinnerungen aus der Zeit nach dem Großen Brand 1842 für Börse, Rathaus und vieles mehr, also mit Baukunst aus dem Neobarock und der Neorenaissance vereinte. Dazu kam die Reformarchitektur der frühen Moderne, der Backsteinexpressionismus und einige harmlose, aber perfekte Wiederaufbauten der Nachkriegszeit. In den 1980er Jahren entstand ein stattliches System von Passagen im Rückraum des prominenten Uferboulevards Jungfern-

the Great Fire of 1842. Then, at the end of the nineteenth century, following several devastating cholera epidemics, many of Hamburg's densely populated working-class neighbourhoods of narrow and winding lanes were torn down. This created a lot of new space for modern development, such as the Kontorhausviertel with the famous Chilehaus.

A beautiful city devoid of nightlife

Following wide-scale destruction in the Second World War, Hamburg's inner city has received even more beauty treatment over the last fifty to sixty years, and it shows. However, for much of this time it has been a belle without a ball. It is defined by a strong architectural mix, which unites the strength of the medieval brick churches and several old streets of timber-framed houses with the eclectic vestiges of the period following the Great Fire of 1842—neo-Baroque and neo-Renaissance structures such as the Börse and Rathaus. To this was added the reform architecture of the early modern period, Brick Expressionism, and numerous harmlessly perfect reconstructions of the post-War period. The 1980s saw the emergence of a handsome complex of shopping arcades in the area to the rear of Hamburg's most prominent boulevard, Jungfernstieg. The Rathaus square was spruced up and has since functioned as

stieg an der Binnenalster. Der Rathaus-markt wurde prächtig ausstaffiert und funktionierte von nun an als »gute Stube« der Stadt für so manches Stadtfest, wie auch später der Innenhof zwischen Börse und Rathaus mit Steinplatten und Brunnen fein gemacht wurde, als läge er mitten in Florenz.

Imponierend, hanseatisch, touris-tisch – doch leider wohnten zu wenige Leute im inneren Wallgebiet, allenfalls gab es außerhalb der nördlichen Neu-stadt noch Hausmeisterwohnungen. Spätestens nach dem damaligen La-denschluss von 18.30 Uhr und dem Fei-erabend der vielen Büroangestellten fiel die Stadt in einen allabendlichen Schön-heitsschlaf. Die urbane Hamburger Kraft bewies sich anderswo: in St. Pauli, Ottensen, Eppendorf oder Winterhude.

Mittlerweile haben sich die Din-ge zum Guten geändert – die Laden-schlusszeiten sind nun weniger restrik-tiv, und inzwischen eilen die Menschen sogar sonntags in die Stadtmitte. Die City wird sommertags in vielen Teilen zu einem großen Straßencafé. Die so-genannte Aufenthaltsattraktivität wurde an den Fleeten und Plätzen gesteigert, viele Hotels und leider auch neue Bü-robauten sind entstanden. Die Innen-stadt wurde nachverdichtet, das heißt, wo immer es ging, wurde aufgestockt. Es entstanden elegante »Hüte« für alte Baukörper. Wo das nicht funktionierte, wurde und wird rück- und neugebaut, allerdings um den Preis der Gefahr, dass die City ihren eigenen Maßstab, die Kör-

a kind of front parlour for the city, the scene of occasional festivals and exhibi-tions. The courtyard between the Börse and the Rathaus, with its cobblestones and fountain, has been given a similarly Florentine makeover.

Impressive, Hanseatic and touris--friendly—and yet there were still far too few people living within the old city walls. At most, there were a few janitors' apartments to the north of Neustadt. Every evening once the shops had closed (at the legally mandated time of 6.30 pm) and the many office workers had gone home, the city centre fell back into its beauty sleep. Hamburg's urban vitality lay elsewhere: in St. Pauli, Ot-tensen, Eppendorf and Winterhude.

Since then things have taken a turn for the better. The shop closing times are no longer as restrictive, and people now flock to the city centre even on Sun-days. On a summer's day many parts of the city centre now resemble one great street café. Much has been done to tempt people to linger by the canals and squares, many new hotels have opened, and unfortunately numerous new office buildings as well. The city centre has been "densified"; in other words, new storeys have been added to as many buildings as possible. As a result many older buildings now sport elegant new "headwear". In cases where this wasn't possible, buildings have been stripped back or new structures erected, though this has endangered somewhat Ham-burg's unique scale, natural grain and

nung und den Charakter verlieren könnte. Man kann die Baukräne und Gerüste kaum zählen, die dort in diesen Jahren aufgestellt werden.

Seit 2010 gibt es ein neues, offizielles Hamburger Innenstadtkonzept. Konsolidierung heißt das Stichwort: Es gibt Ansätze, die City als Wohn- und Lebensstandort zu verbessern (zum Beispiel die neuen Wallhöfe in der Nähe des Millerntors oder das Brauquartier auf St. Pauli, das aber streng genommen nicht zur Innenstadt gehört). Die Hamburger Innenstadt wurde ein immer wichtigerer Baustein des wachsenden Tourismus für Hamburg. Das führte zum Ausbau des luxuriösen Einzelhandels (Alsterhaus, Europa-Passage, Neuer Wall) oder zur qualitativen Verbesserung der zahlreichen Kultureinrichtungen wie den großen staatlichen Museer oder der Staatsoper, die größtenteils auf der Linie des alten Wallrings liegen, aber auch der Kunstmeile zwischen der »Galerie der Moderne« und dem Deichtor-Center. Genau dort (vgl. S. 200–201) wird diese Meile sich in die Hafencity hinein weiter verlängern: Die City richtet sich auf die neue Hafencity aus. Wege und Achsen in Nord- und Südrichtung werden gestärkt und ausgebaut. Das Schlüsselmotiv heißt: zurück an die Elbe!

character. The cranes and scaffolds that have gone up in the last few years are too numerous to count.

And most recently, since 2010, Hamburg has its own official development plan for the inner city. The catchword is consolidation. Already attempts have been made to improve the inner city's qualities as a residential area (for example, the new Wallhöfe complex near the old Millerntor gate, or the apartment complexes on the site of the old Bavaria brewery in St. Pauli. though strictly speaking the latter isn't part of the inner city). The inner city is of major importance for Hamburg's growing tourism trade. This has led to the development and expansion of luxury retail complexes (Alsterhaus, Europa-Passage, Neuer Wall) and the revamping of numerous cultural institutions (such as the major public museums or the State Opera House), most of which are located along the route of the old walls. The same applies to the art district between the Gallery of Contemporary Art at the Kunsthalle and the Deichtor-Center. This is set to expand from Deichtor (cf. pp. 200–201) into the Hafencity. If one takes a closer look at the new inner city development plan it becomes clear that the old inner city is now turning towards the new Hafencity. Return to the River Elbe!

Dock 47 und Pinnasberg 45
Bürohäuser Office Buildings

Standort Location Pinnasberg 45/47 **Architekten Architects** Spengler Wiescholek Architekten und Stadtplaner, Hamburg **Bauherr Client** Grundstücksgesellschaft Pinnasberg 47, Grundstücksgesellschaft Pinnasberg 45 GmbH & Co. KG **Wettbewerb Competition** 2001 **Bauzeit Date built** 2001–04/05 **Bruttogeschossfläche Gross Floor area** 4300 qm (sqm)/2100 qm (sqm)

Das östliche Ende der großartigen Achse Elbchaussee/Palmaille bildet eine respektvolle Kurve nach rechts zum Wasser der Elbe am Fischmarkt. Diese Lage hat den Häusern in Anspielung auf die großen Docks gegenüber und die Hausnummer 47 den Namen eingebracht. Die Architekten hat dies ermutigt, ein wenig Gas zu geben und das Bürohaus in kräftigem Rot und asymmetrischer Linie zu entwickeln. Es sind nur wenige Grad (vier Prozent), die das Gebäude aus dem Lot gekommen ist. Aber in Hamburg wird Mut nicht immer belohnt – vor allem die Farbe im Kontext zur weißen Palmaille wird kritisiert. Im Innern ist das Haus funktional gegliedert und geschossweise in je zwei Einheiten teilbar. Eine Besonderheit ist das der geneigten Außenwand parallel folgende Treppenhaus, das auf diese Weise Seh- und Gehgewohnheiten konterkariert. Das schwarze Nachbarhaus Nr. 45 stammt von denselben Architekten.

Perhaps Hamburg's most elegant thoroughfare, the almost 10-kilometre waterfront drive along the Elbchaussee and Palmaille, graciously curves to the right to face the Elbe at Fischmarkt. The name of the building at the corner is a combined reference to the Blohm + Voss dry docks opposite, and to the street number 47. The location inspired the architects to boldly experiment with this intensely colourful and brilliantly asymmetrical building. The defining vertical line is just a few degrees (four per cent) out of plumb. But audacity is not always rewarded in Hamburg, and the red façade, which contrasts so starkly with the white townhouses of Palmaille, was the subject of particular criticism. Inside, the building is functionally organised and may be roughly divided into two levels. An unusual feature is a staircase that runs parallel to the incline of the outer wall. The black neighbouring building at no. 45 was designed by the same architects.

E.15/16

1

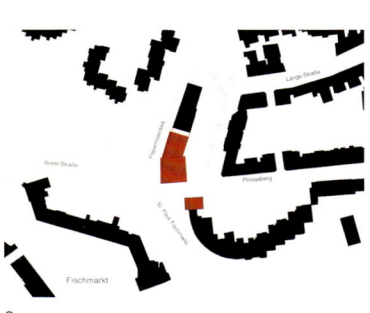

2

3

1 Blick von Westen über St.Pauli auf die Landungsbrücken und die City im Hintergrund, in der Bildmitte Dock 47. View from the west over St. Pauli and Landungsbrücken, with the city centre in the background and Dock 47 in the centre **2** Übersicht Overview **3** Fassadenansicht View of the façade

Stadtlagerhaus
Former Municipal Warehouse

Standort Location Große Elbstraße 27 **Architekten Architects** Störmer Murphy and Partners, Hamburg **Bauherr Client** Garbe-Bau-Technik GmbH **Bauzeit Date built** 1998–2001 **Bruttogeschossfläche Gross floor area** 10300 qm (sqm)

E.17

In direkter Elbuferlage am Hamburger Fischmarkt umfasst das ehemalige Stadtlagerhaus (davor eine Industriemühle) den Umbau zweier denkmalgeschützter Speichergebäude. Die vierstöckige, fast gläserne Aufstockung mit 28 Wohnungen stärkt die Kubatur des ersten Teils. Die Wohnetagen sind als Klima- und Akustikpuffer mit einer Doppelfassade ausgestattet, deren Fenster bei Bedarf geöffnet werden können. Zusammen mit dem spitzen Satteldach des anderen Bauteils entstand eine städtebauliche Landmarke, welche die Große Elbstraße rund um Stilwerk und Holzhafen dominiert. In den unteren Geschossen haben Büros und ein Restaurant ihre neue Heimat gefunden. Die Verbreiterung der Kaimauer und das Restaurant im Erdgeschoss kündigen den Auftakt des Elbwanderwegs nach Westen an. Aufgrund der Lage im hochwassergefährdeten Bereich ist das Gebäude über eine Stahlbrücke an das »Festland« angeschlossen.

Right on the banks of the Elbe at Hamburg's Fischmarkt, this project in the former municipal warehouse (Stadtlagerhaus) involved the redevelopment of two listed historical buildings. The four-storey upward extension, which is almost fully glazed and incorporates 28 new apartments, strengthens the original cubature of the building. The residential floors have been given a double-skin façade, which provides both a climatic and an acoustic buffer, yet windows can be opened if needed. This, together with the pointed saddle roof of the second building creates an architectural landmark that now dominates the area around the Stilwerk shopping arcade and the old timber port on Grosse Elbstrasse. The lower floors of the former grain mill now contain offices and a restaurant. A widening of the quay wall and the restaurant on the ground floor mark the starting point of the Elbe hiking trail that continues for 23 kilometres to the west.

1

2

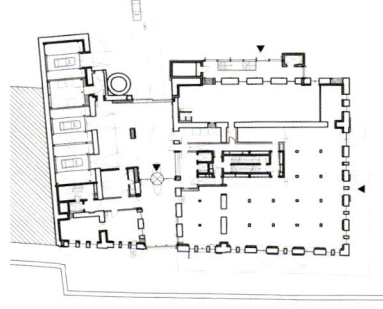

3

1 Ansicht vom Strom (Stadtlagerhaus rechts im Bild) mit Nachbarbauten View from the river (former municipal warehouse on the right) with adjacent buildings **2** Ansicht von der Landseite View from land **3** Grundriss Floor plan

Stilwerk
Läden und Geschäftshaus Commercial Building

Standort Location Große Elbstraße 68 **Architekten Architects** Lange Vogler & Partner; Rolf Heide **Bauherr Client** Garbe KG **Bauzeit Date built** 1993–96 **Bruttogeschossfläche Gross floor area** 11 000 qm (sqm)

E.18

Neben dem Stadtlagerhaus spielt in diesem alten Gewerbe- und Industrie-ensemble eine ehemalige Mälzerei die Hauptrolle, deren Metamorphose zu einem Design-Kaufhaus symbolisch für die Veränderungen Hamburgs unten am Elbstrom ist. Außen in all seiner Back-steinwucht mit altem Kamin weiterhin fühl- und spürbar, spielen sich die we-sentlichen Eingriffe und Veränderungen innen ab. Dort fand das »Stilwerk«, ein Zusammenschluss von Design- und Möbelgeschäften, Platz auf mehreren Galerien, die um einen Lichthof geführt werden. Der Designer und Innenarchi-tekt Rolf Heide hat hier in einer puris-tisch zu nennenden Grundstimmung in Weiß und Grau ein gut funktionierendes Passepartout für all das teilweise schril-le Design geschaffen, das verkauft wer-den will. Beeindruckend ist der kathe-dralenhafte Innenraum des Atriums.

Next to the Stadtlagerhaus, a former malt house plays the lead role in an ensemble of redeveloped commercial and industrial buildings. Their metamor-phosis into a designer mall is symbolic of the changes that have taken place at Hamburg's waterfront. From the outside one can still feel the elementary force of this brick colossus, while the most important interventions and changes take place on the inside. This is home to Stilwerk, a multi-storey conglomera-tion of design and furniture stores, with galleries arranged around a central light well. The designer and interior architect Rolf Heide created a general mood here in white and grey that can best be de-scribed as purist. This provides an ex-cellent frame for the sometimes brash design creations that are on sale here. Particularly impressive is the atrium's cathedral-like interior.

1

2

3

1 Luftfoto aus Richtung Elbe: Eine alte Mälzerei wurde zum Möbelkaufhaus. Aerial photo taken over the river: a former malt house was converted into a design and furniture showcase. 2 Blick ins Atrium A look inside the atrium 3 Brücke zur Evakuierung bei Hochwasser Flood evacuation bridge

Holzhafen
Büro und Wohnen Mixed Use Building

Standort Location Große Elbstraße 57–63 **Architekten Architects** ASTOC Architects and Planners, Köln, in Zusammenarbeit mit in cooperation with Kees Christiaanse, Rotterdam, örtliche Repräsentanz local representative: Kunst+Herbert, Hamburg **Bauherr Client** B&L Gruppe, Hamburg **Wettbewerb Competition** 1994 **Bauzeit Date built** 2000–03 (Bürogebäude Ost Eastern office building), 2009–11 (Bürogebäude West, Wohnhochhaus Western office building, residential tower) **Bruttogeschossfläche Gross floor area** Bürogebäude Ost 16000 qm (sqm, eastern office building), Bürogebäude West 15300 qm (sqm, western office building), Wohnhochhaus 9000 qm (sqm, residential tower)

In den 1990er Jahren war das Projekt heftig umkämpft. Im Rückblick und angesichts der Erfahrung, wie schnell sich Hamburg mit der Hafencity verändert, wirkt die damalige Kritik heute überzogen. Vor allem die GAL-Fraktion der Bezirksversammlung Altona hatte mit Haken und Ösen gekämpft, um dieses Bauwerk zu verhindern, weil doch nur wieder ein Bürohaus die Sicht der ursprünglichen Elbuferbewohner zerstören würde. Das Ergebnis lehrt jedoch, dass eine entsprechende auf den Ort ausgerichtete Architektur und ein kluger Städtebau adäquate Lösungen anbieten können. Es entstand ein Unikat aus Bauteilen, die in Höhe und Seite mäandern, was zur Folge hat, dass das Haus tatsächlich, wie im Wettbewerb versprochen, tolle Ein- und Durchblicke spendiert. Dabei bleibt die Komposition von vier verschiedenen, parallelen Riegeln von außen zunächst verborgen.

This project was hotly disputed in the 1990s. Looking back, and considering how rapidly Hamburg has been transformed through the Hafencity, the criticism now seems excessive. Particularly the Green Party (GAL) in Altona's district assembly fought tooth and nail to block this building because it meant that yet another office building would spoil the view for those already living along the Elbe. However, the finished product shows that architecture which responds sensitively to its environs combined with smart urban planning can provide appropriate solutions. This building is one of a kind, meandering both vertically and horizontally, with the result that it actually delivers on its promise to offer superb views into and through the volume. Composed of four different parallel volumes, it presents a somewhat oblique face to the outside. It is only when one engages with it from

1

2

1 Blick über den alten Fischereihafen mit den neuen Bauten am Holzhafen, in der Mitte der gläserne Wohnturm. View overlooking the old Fischereihafen with the new buildings on the site of the old Holzhafen, including the glass apartment tower in the middle.
2 Lageplan: Bürogebäude West (grün), Wohnhochhaus (rot), Bürogebäude Ost (blau) Site plan: western office building (green), residential tower (red), eastern office building (blue)

Erst wenn man sich intensiv mit ihm beschäftigt, verrät der Zauberwürfel etwas über sein intaktes Innenleben mit großzügigen Höfen und einem Atrium, das mit Kalkstein ausgelegt wurde. Ein hellroter Stein, bündig gesetzte Fenster im stehenden Format und gelegentliche farbige Akzente auf den Paneelen zwischen den Fenstern runden das Bild ab. Das Projekt besteht aus diesem ersten (östlichen) Bürogebäude (2003) sowie einem ähnlich konzipierten westlichen Bürogebäude und einem verglasten Wohnturm (2011). Er wird »Kristall« genannt und wirkt auch so. Das hat (positive) Konsequenzen auf die Grundrisse, die entsprechend viele unterschiedliche Zuschnitte ausbilden. Die Größen der Wohnungen zwischen 180 und 400 Quadratmetern – alle mit Elbblick – weisen allerdings darauf hin, dass das Problem hier nicht darin besteht, die erste Reihe zu verstellen, sondern dass auch dieses Quartier kräftig in Richtung Kaufkraft gentrifiziert. Positiv: Der ehemalige Holzhafen ist nicht zu einem reinen Bürozentrum geworden, sondern auch zum gefragten Wohnstandort.

within that this Rubik's Cube reveals something of its vital inner life; its spacious courtyards and an atrium with limestone floors. Additional features include the use of light-red stone, flush and vertically appointed windows, and occasional splashes of colour on the panelling between the windows. This project consists of an office building to the east (completed in 2003), a similarly conceived office building immediately to the west, and a glass apartment tower (2011), aptly named "Kristall", or crystal. As the name suggests, the apartments in this building are "cut" in various shapes and angles. However, merely the dimensions of these apartments (180 to 400 square metres)—all with views of the Elbe—indicate that the main problem with this volume is not its obstruction of the river view, but rather that it represents an intense process of gentrification within this area. On a positive note, the former timber docklands have not merely become a new office complex, but also a much coveted residential area.

3 Erster Bauabschnitt (West) – der »Zauberwürfel« von der Straßenseite mit Grundriss Regelgeschoss First construction phase (west) – the "Rubik's Cube" as viewed from the street with floor plan (full storeys) **4** Bürogebäude Ost (Zweiter Bauabschnitt) mit Grundriss Ebene 3 Eastern office building (second phase) with 3rd-storey floor plan **5** Wohnturm mit Grundriss 3.OG Residential tower with 3rd-storey floor plan

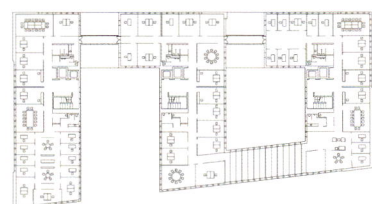

3

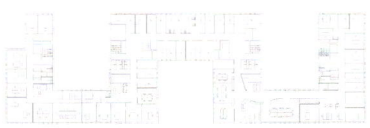

4

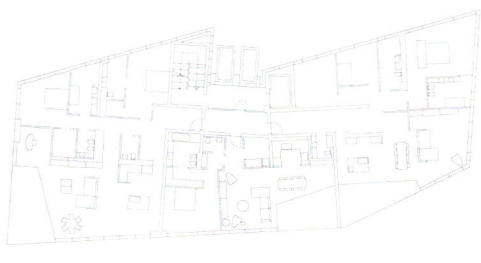

5

Hafenklang
Konzert-Location Live Music and Party Venue

Standort Location Große Elbstraße 84

Als das Gebäude des Hafenklangs um 1860 erbaut wurde, war Altona-Altstadt noch ein dichter Häuserteppich, der von der Großen Hafenstraße bis zur Palmaille reichte. Enge Straßen und verwinkelte Treppen führten den Elbhang hinab. Das Parterre diente als Stallung für Pferde, die die Straßenbahnen der Linie 30 zogen. Im Zweiten Weltkrieg sind die oberen zweieinhalb Geschosse des Hafenklangs durch Luftangriffe zerstört worden. Es blieb ein »Rest vom Hafenfest«, und echte Hamburger Kreative machten es in den letzten Jahrzehnten zum Treffpunkt für Musiker und Künstler in Hamburg. Die Gier hat die alte Kultfestung jedoch fest im Griff und eingemauert: »Hochwertig ausgestattete Büroflächen mit Hafenflair« bedrängen den neuen Hafenklang, der als Mahnmal zu verstehen ist, für eine planerische Haltung, die die wahre Urbanität einer Metropole und ihre kleinen Macken so böse ignoriert!

At the time the premises of Hamburg's iconic rock venue Hafenklang was built (around 1860), Altona's old quarter (Altstadt) was a densely populated residential district that stretched from Grosse Hafenstrasse to Palmaille. It was a warren of narrow streets and stepped lanes that wound their way down the slope to the river bank. The ground floor of this building served as stables for the horses that pulled the No. 30 tram. The top two-and-a-half storeys of the building were destroyed in air raids during the Second World War. In recent decades a local collective turned it into an important rendezvous for musicians and artists. However, commercial interests got their hands on this bastion of alternative culture, and now well appointed offices with a certain dockland flair are crowding out the old Hafenklang. This development may be seen as a reminder that urban planners ignore at their peril the little kinks and quirks that define a truly metropolis.

Die Neubauten haben die alte Kultfestung »Hafenklang« eingemauert. New buildings now surround the legendary alternative venue "Hafenklang".

Große Elbstraße 138
Bürohaus Office Building

Standort Location Große Elbstraße 138 **Architekten Architects** SEHW Architekten, Hamburg **Bauherr Client** Vineta Erste Projektverwaltungsgesellschaft mbH **Bauzeit Date built** 2005–07 **Bruttogeschossfläche Gross floor area** 1800 qm (sqm)

E.23

Hier, westlich der großen »Klunker« wie dem Stilwerk, ist der Ort der kleinen Schritte, der feinen Maßnahmen. Der Grundriss zeigt, wie schwierig es war, funktionierende Nutzflächen zu generieren. Zudem liegt das Bürohaus am Hang, was allerdings den Vorteil hat, dass sehr unterschiedliche Höhen und bewegte Hausansichten entstehen. Vorn herrschen Edelstahl und getönte Gläser vor – stärker könnte der Kontrast zum benachbarten Gelbklinker nicht sein. Da das Wetter in Hamburg bekanntlich wechselhaft ist und sich der Himmel von grüngrau im Regen bis stahlblau bei Sonnenschein auslebt, nimmt die Fassade dieses Spiel auf – und erscheint auch mal funkelnd rot im Abendlicht. Von unten an der Uferstraße, der Großen Elbstraße, ist die wichtige fünfte Fassade, die Dachterrasse, leider nicht einzusehen. Im Sommer ist sie – durch Sonnensegel besetzt und geschmückt – fast zu schön für ein Bürohaus.

Here, to the west of giants such as the Stilwerk building, is a place where superb architecture is created on a much smaller scale. From the ground plan it is clear that it wasn't easy to generate a functioning and usable floor space on this site. Moreover, this office is built on a slope, though this also lends the building greater dynamism and a more interesting floor plan. Stainless steel and toned glass are the dominant features of the facing façade, and it's hard to imagine a starker contrast to the neighbouring yellow clinker. The weather in Hamburg is notoriously erratic, with skies that change their mood from green-grey on a rainy day to steel-blue when the sun shines, and this façade plays along masterfully. It even dons a scintillating red mantle at sunset. Unfortunately, the fifth façade (the roof terrace) is not visible from the riverside road, Grosse Elbstrasse. In summer, when the sail-like awning are unfurled, this is almost too pretty for an office building.

1

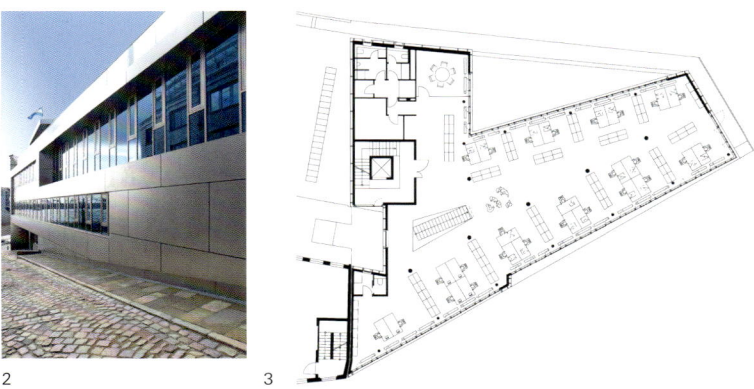

2
                                    3

1+2 Bürohaus mit Terrasse und Elbblick: fast zu schön, um hier nur zu arbeiten Office building with terrace and view of the river: almost too pretty just to work in **3** Grundriss Büros Floor plan, offices

Ehemaliges Fährterminal
Former Ferry Terminal

Standort Location Van-der-Smissen-Straße 1–3 **Architekten Architects** medium Architekten, Hamburg/Alsop Lawrie Ltd. trading as ALL Design, London **Bauherr Client** Sellhorn Ingenieurgesellschaft, Hamburg, Nutzer User: DFDS Deutschland GmbH, Hamburg **Bauzeit Date built** 1990–93 **Bruttogeschossfläche Gross floor area** 11 600 qm (sqm)

Das Fährterminal der früheren England-Fähre ist zwischenzeitlich zum normalen Bürogebäude geworden, weil die Schiffsverbindung nach Harwich gestrichen wurde. Billigflieger machten die Seeverbindung überflüssig. Deswegen wirken die Anspielungen auf die Architektur der anlegenden Fähren mit Bullaugen und Reling, insbesondere auf der Flussseite, schon wie sentimentale Nostalgie, doch immer noch produzieren tanzende Stützen maritime Ausgelassenheit und gute Stimmung. Das Büro des Bauherrn in der oberen Etage am östlichen Ende gehört zu den bevorzugten Film-Sets in der Hansestadt. Das Restaurant unten erinnert an kalifornisches Ambiente. Beiden gemeinsam ist der schönste Blick auf den Elbstrom, der sich hier in die Kurve legt und von lauter Hamburgensien gekrönt wird. Von hier aus wird man den schönsten Blick auf die Elbphilharmonie haben und auf den neuen Nachbarn ...

The terminal building of the old Hamburg-Harwich ferry was converted to offices for a while, following the discontinuation of this route, which could not compete with budget airlines. For those old enough to remember the old England ferry, references such as the portholes and railings that face the river may evoke some nostalgia. The jaunty yet graceful concrete and steel columns that define this building are largely responsible for the sense of maritime exuberance and good humour that it engenders. The client's own offices on the top floor are among the most popular film locations in the city. The restaurant below has a relaxed, Californian ambience. Both spaces enjoy one of the most majestic vantage points over the Elbe—which begins a slow northward curve at this point—and numerous Hamburg landmarks, including the Elbphilharmonie and the new next-door neighbour ...

E.24

1

2

3

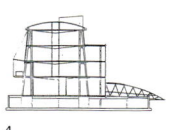 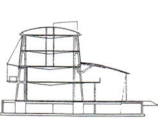  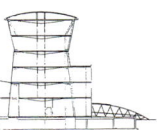

4

1 Blick über den Baukomplex in den Hafen View of the building complex and the port
2 Postmodernes Equipment Postmodern furnishings **3** Suchbild: Häuser wie Schiffe, Schiffe wie Häuser: Kreuzfahrtschiff, Dockland, Fährterminal Buildings inspired by ships inspired by buildings: cruise ship, Dockland, ferry terminal building **4** Schnitte Sectional drawings

Hamburg Cruise Center Altona

Standort Location Van-der-Smissen-Straße **Architekten Architects** Renner Hainke Wirth Architekten, Hamburg **Bauherr Client** FEG Fischereihafen-Entwicklungs-Gesellschaft mbH **Wettbewerb Competition** 2009 **Bauzeit Date built** 2010–11

Ist dieser neue Nachbar ein weiterer Dampfer? Die Grundform des Terminals spielt mit der Geometrie des benachbarten Docklands und der etwas sanfteren Form des alten England-Fährterminals. Im Übrigen ist das Cruise Center ein sehr gutes Beispiel dafür, wie man mit dem Thema Waterfront umgehen muss – gerade vor dem Geesthang, der hier Altonaer Balkon heißt. Die Höhen-geometrie des Terminals ist aus den Sichtbezügen vom Altonaer Balkon und den offenen, einladenden Gesten des Gebäudes für die Besucher vom Wasser als auch vom Land entwickelt: vom Altonaer Balkon bis tief in den Hafen und umgekehrt. Dabei wird die städtebauliche Höhenvorgabe für die Dachoberfläche bei 15,50 Metern üNN im Mittel eingehalten. Das Dach ist begehbar, die Einschränkungen des Elbblicks vom Altonaer Balkon aus werden durch die zur Elbe abfallende Dachneigung minimiert. Auf jeden Fall ein Hingucker mit hellsilbriger, eloxierter Aluminium-Verkleidung.

Is this neighbour another steamship? The basic form of the terminal plays with the geometry of the neighbouring docklands building and the somewhat gentler form of the old England ferry terminal. The Cruise Center is also an excellent example of how best to build on the waterfront—right in front of the Geest ridge, which is known at this point as Altonaer Balkon (Altona's Balcony). The stature of this building takes into consideration the visual relationship to Altonaer Balkon and makes an open, welcoming gesture to all-comers, whether they arrive from land or water. The roof altitude of 15.5 metres complies with standards set by the urban development plan. The roof is accessible to pedestrians and any obstruction to the view from Altonaer Balkon is mitigated by the slope of the roof towards the Elbe. In any case, this is a definite eye-catcher with its light-silver, anodised aluminium cladding.

1

2

1 Ansicht von der Elbe View from the Elbe **2** Ansicht von Westen mit Blick auf die Besucherplattform View from the west featuring visitor platform

Elbkaihaus
Bürohaus Office Building

Standort Location Große Elbstraße 143–145 **Architekten Architects** gmp · von Gerkan, Marg und Partner, Hamburg **Bauherr Client** GHL III – Unternehmen der HHLA-Gruppe **Bauzeit Date built** 1998–99 **Bruttogeschossfläche Gross floor area** 12 720 qm (scm)

Eine 130 Meter lange Kühlhalle aus dem Jahr 1965 wurde entkernt und erhielt wasserseitig eine Glasfront. Sie wurde in mehrere Häuser gegliedert, die jeweils durch ein Treppenhaus mit einem Aufzug erschlossen werden. Im ersten und zweiten Obergeschoss wurde über die gesamte Länge der Halle eine Stahl-Glas-Fassade vorgehängt, die den Büros einen Ausblick auf Elbe und Hafen beschert. Farblich wirken die leuchtend rot akzentuierten Wände der Treppenhäuser als edler Kontrast zu den schwarzen Fensterbändern und den dunklen, filigran wirkenden Stahltreppen. Die authentischen Pilzkopf-Säulen, nur mit einer Lasur versehen und in ihrem ursprünglichen Grauton gehalten, erinnern im Gebäude an die alte Konstruktion des Stahlbetonskeletts. Kleine Randposse: Vom Wasser sieht man den schönen Wettkampf zweier großer Hamburger Architekturbüros, in der dritten Reihe ein Haus von BRT, davor der Elbkai und vorn im Fluss das BRT-Dockland.

This cold-storage warehouse, which was built in 1965, was completely gutted and given a new glass façade facing the water. 130 metres in length, it was divided into several separate units, each of which is accessed via a staircase and an elevator. A non-bearing steel and glass façade on the second and third floors runs the full length of the building, giving those within a majestic view of the river and container docks on the opposite bank. The interior is defined by contrasting use of colour, exemplified by the red walls of the stairwells, the black window frames and the dark, filigree steel staircases The authentic mushroom-head columns which have been scumbled but retained in their original grey tone, are a reminder of the building's original reinforced concrete skeleton. From the water we can observe a handsome contest between two of Hamburg's greatest architecture firms: a building by BRT in the third row, the Elbkaihaus by gmp, and BRT's Dockland in the river.

E.26

1

2

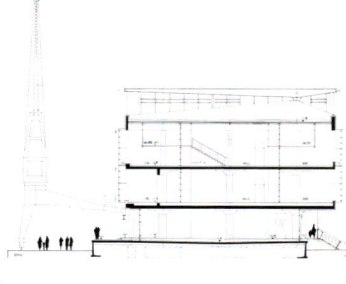

3

1 Die Front des Elbkaihauses zur Elbe; dahinter liegt der Elbberg Campus (E.28–30).
The front of the Elbkaihaus facing the water, behind it the Elbberg Campus (E.28-30).
2 Interieur Interior **3** Schnitt Sectional drawing

Dockland
Bürohaus Office Building

Standort Location Van-der-Smissen-Straße 9 **Architekten Architects** BRT Architekten LLP Bothe Richter Teherani, Hamburg **Bauherr Client** Robert Vogel GmbH & Co. KG, Hamburg **Bauzeit Date built** 2004–06 **Bruttogeschossfläche Gross floor area** 13544 qm (sqm)

E.27

Es ist die Stahl und Beton gewordene Erkenntnis: Heute wirken viele Bürohäuser in Hamburg wie Schiffe. Das ist gewollt und gar nicht so sehr einem zungenförmigen Grundstück wie beim expressionistischen Chile-Haus von 1923 geschuldet (dagegen sehen die häufig passierenden Kreuzfahrtschiffe der aktuellen Generation wie schwimmende Märkische Viertel aus). Wie eine Hochsee-Yacht der neurussischen Art liegt das Dockland-Bürohaus am Kopf des Edgar-Engelhard-Kais zwischen Norderelbe und Fischereihafen. Bemerkenswert ist die Tatsache, dass es hier im Strom direkt neben einer der weltweit am stärksten frequentierten Schifffahrtsroute gebaut werden durfte. Über viele Meter kragt der »Bug« des schiffsartigen Baus frei aus und bildet so eine dynamische Ergänzung zum »Heck« des benachbarten Fährterminals. Rund 9000 Quadratmeter Bürofläche bietet das Gebäude, das von einer Stahlrahmenkonstruktion getragen wird.

This is an original idea born in steel and concrete; these days a lot of new office blocks in Hamburg are built to resemble ships. That it takes this form is no accident, nor is it the result of a linguifcrm site, as was the case with Fritz Höger's Expressionist Chile-Haus from 1923, which borrowed the form of an ocean liner. The Dockland building, which is more like the kind of mega-yacht favoured by Russia's nouveau riche, is located at the head of Edgar Engelhard Quay between the Elbe and Altona's old fishing port. This "ship" has good company, as it juts into the waters of one of the world's busiest harbours. The "prow" projects unsupported across the water, forming a dynamic counterpoint to the "stern" of the old ferry terminal upstream. There is approximately 9,000 square metres of office space within this building, which is supported by a steel-frame structure.

1

2   3

1 Dramatische Kontur wie eine Hochsee-Yacht The dramatic contours of a yacht 2 Die Dachterrasse kann über eine öffentliche Freitreppe erreicht werden. The roof terrace can be reached via a public stairway. 3 Übersicht Overview

Elbberg Campus Altona und Lofthaus am Elbberg
Bürohäuser Office Buildings

Standort Location Lofthaus am Elbberg, Elbberg 1; Elbberg Campus Altona, Elbberg 8–10 **Architekten Architects** BRT Architekten LLP Bothe Richter Teherani, Hamburg **Bauherr Client** DWI Grundbesitz GmbH, Hamburg **Bauzeit Date built** 1996–97; 2001–03 **Bruttogeschossfläche Gross floor area** 3340 qm (sqm); 7600 qm (sqm)

Eine der ersten Maßnahmen der großflächigen Erneuerung im Fischereihafen fand auf einem spektakulären Grundstück am Elbberg statt, das seinem Namen Ehre macht und spitzwinklig zwischen Großer Elbstraße und der Straße Elbberg liegt. Was die Fassaden betrifft: ein janusköpfiges Bauwerk. An der Elbseite wurde das Haus auf schräge Pilotis gestellt und erhielt einen Ganzglas-Vorhang mit fünf Erkern. Die perfekten Biegungen des Betons und der Fenster sowie die subtil in die glatten Fassaden versenkten Sonnenjalousien und die dynamisch geschwungenen Fassaden lassen an besseres »Art déco« denken. Der Erfolg machte mutig, es folgte 2003 Teil 2 am Topos Elbhang, mit einer Staffel von Reihenhäusern im großen Maßstab für Freiberufler und einem vorgelagerten Büro-/Gewerbehaus im »Bügeleisenstil«, alles mit einer lebhaften Durchwegung am Altonaer Balkon an die Elbe angebunden.

One of the first projects in the extensive redevelopment of the Fischereihafen area was built on a spectacular but extremely narrow site between Grosse Elbstrasse and the aptly named Elbberg (literally, the hill overlooking the Elbe). This elegantly two-faced building successfully rose to the challenge posed by the unusual site. On the side facing the Elbe the building is supported by slanted pilotis, above which is an all-glass façade with five long bays. The perfect curvature of the concrete and windows, the sunscreens that can be subtly retracted into the smooth façade, and the dynamically contoured façades are reminiscent of the best Art Deco pieces. Success inspired courage, and in 2003 the second part of the Elbhang ensemble followed: a row of staggered buildings containing offices for freelancers and start-ups, and anterior office and retail premises shaped like an electric iron.

1

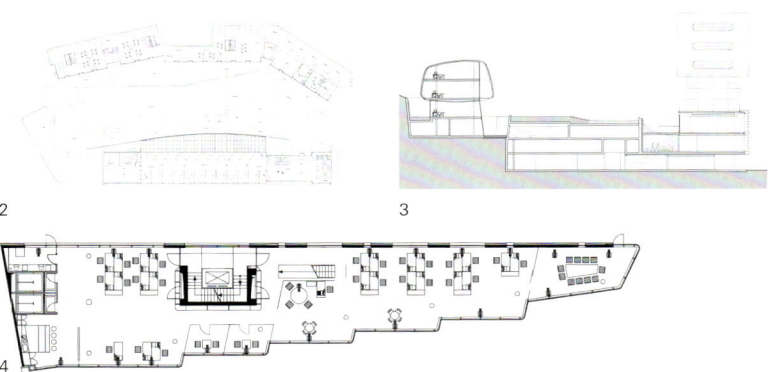

2   3

4

1 Gesamtübersicht von Süden aus der Luft: hinten links die Lofthäuser, davor das »Bügeleisen«, ganz rechts der erste Bauabschnitt Aerial overview from the south: to the rear left the lofts, in front of them the "iron" and on the far the first stage of construction
2+3 Grundriss 3. OG und Schnitt (zweiter Bauabschnitt) Floor plan, 3rd storey, and sectional drawing (second construction stage) 4 Grundriss 4. OG erster Bauabschnitt Floor plan, 4th storey (first construction stage)

Columbina Twins
Bürohäuser Office Buildings

Standort Location Große Elbstraße 273–275 **Architekt Architect** Carsten Roth Architekt, Hamburg **Bauherr Client** Aug. Prien Immobilien, Gesellschaft für Projektentwicklung mbH, Hamburg **Bauzeit Date built** 2008–09 **Bruttogeschossfläche Gross floor area** 14 500 qm (sqm)

»Die Columbia Twins sind gleichermaßen markant wie subtil, eigenständig wie kontextuell«, hieß es im Hamburger Architekturjahrbuch 2010, das mit diesen Bürohaus-Zwillingstürmen das gesamte Buch aufmachte – ein dezenter Hinweis darauf, dass man in Hamburg stolz auf solche Architekturen sein will. Die Überschrift »Sanft schimmerndes Geschmeide« ist ein weiterer Hinweis auf den Kontext: Das hier ist eine der schönsten Perlen für Hamburgs aufgereihte Kette am Hafen. Und wenn der Text weiter von »kostbaren Schmuckstücken« spricht, dann ist das vor allem der Fassadenhaut geschuldet, die aus kleinen Metallplättchen besteht. In der Tat paaren sich hier hanseatische Akkuratesse und eine Leichtigkeit, die besonders an den Längsseiten sichtbar wird, wo der Architekt mit einer »Bügelfalte«, also einem winzigen Knick in der Optik, arbeitet. Auch im Grundriss wird sofort deutlich, dass der rechte Winkel ein wenig ausgehebelt wird.

According to the 2010 Hamburg Architecture Yearbook, "The Columbia Twins are striking and subtle in equal measure, combining autonomy and contextuality", These "twin towers" were the first buildings featured in the Yearbook. a subtle indication that Hamburg takes some pride in buildings like this. The introductory heading, "a softly shimmering jewel" provides a further contextual hint: this is one of the most beautiful pearls on the string along Hamburg's harbour-front. And when the text goes on to talk about "precious gems", this refers to the external skin, which is composed of small metal plates. This building clearly marries Hanseatic meticulousness with a lightness that is particularly visible on the long sides, where the architect rendered a "crease", a slight optical bend in the façade. From the floor plan alone it is clear that this is a design that largely dispensed with right angles.

1

2

Haus West   Haus Ost

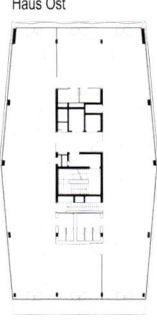

3

1 Eigenständig und trotzdem kontextuell – die Columbia Twins At once autonomous and contextually on the mark: the Columbia Twins **2** Häuser wie schimmerndes Geschmeide Buildings evocative of shimmering jewels **3** Grundriss Regelgeschosse Floor plan, full storeys

Altonaer Kaispeicher D
Kontorhaus Office Building

Standort Location Große Elbstraße 277–279 **Architekten Architects** nps tchoban voss | Architektur und Städtebau **Bauherr Client** Aug. Prien Immobilien, Gesellschaft für Projektentwicklung mbH **Bauzeit Date built** 2008–10 **Bruttogeschossfläche Gross floor area** 15 735 qm (sqm)

E.32

Der vorbildliche Umgang mit der Bausubstanz trägt hier in besonderem Maße dem Denkmalwert Rechnung – das gilt sowohl für die Altonaer Baugeschichte als auch für die moderne Architekturauffassung des ehemaligen Kaispeichers. Zwei Dinge sind bei der Erneuerung sehr gut gelungen: Erstens kann ein Teil des Bodens der vorgelagerten Terrassen als Flutschutz ausgeklappt werden. Zweitens holen die neuen Fenster mit grauen Aluminiumprofilen, die die alten kleinteiligen Holzrahmen in dunkelroter Farbe ersetzen, das alte Gemäuer eindrucksvoll in die neue Zeit. Weil das 200 Meter lange Gebäude sich im Hochwasserbereich befindet, wurden auf Höhe des ersten Obergeschosses, jeweils an den mittleren beiden Treppenhäusern, Brücken zur dahinter geplanten Polderbebauung vorgesehen, über die das Gebäude verlassen werden kann und die Feuerwehr Zutritt erhält.

The exemplary treatment of the original structure is largely due to its value as a historical building, and follows a sensitive approach that is part of Altona's architectural tradition. Two aspects of the redevelopment are particularly successful: firstly, a section of the waterfront walkway can be raised up against the building to protect against high water; secondly, the new grey aluminium window frames are larger and more contemporary than their dark-red wooden predecessors. Because this 200-metre-long building is situated in an area that is prone to flooding, bridges will connect the first floor of the Kaispeicher to the new building under construction immediately to the rear. This will allow workers to leave and the fire brigade to enter in the event of flooding.

1

2   3

1+2 Ansicht von der Elbe, die neuen Fenster bekommen dem Speicher gut. Overall view
from the water; the new windows complement the warehouse well. **3** Der Boden der Terrassen kann als Flutschutz hochgeklappt werden. The waterfront walkway can be raised
up against the building to protect against high water.

Polderbebauung Neumühlen Ost
Bürohäuser Office Buildings

Standort Location Neumühlen 11 **Architekten Architects** BHL Architekten,
Hamburg **Bauherr Client** Potenberg-STAR Immobilien **Bauzeit Date built** 2000–01
Bruttogeschossfläche Gross floor area 8000 qm (sqm)

Standort Location Neumühlen 13–15 **Architekten Architects** Grüntuch Ernst
Architekten, Berlin **Bauherr Client** Schiffahrtskontor Elbe GbR **Bauzeit Date built** 2002
Bruttogeschossfläche Gross floor area 6600 qm (sqm)

Auf einem Betonpolder mit 350 Metern Länge zum Hochwasserschutz sind vier gleiche Baukörper für Bürohäuser aufgestellt worden: vier Würfel, genauer Häuser in U-Form, die zur Elbe hin auskragen dürfen. Der bevorzugte Werkstoff ist Glas, wobei der erste Bau aus Richtung Stadt gesehen (BHL Architekten) klassisch mit Backstein verkleidet wurde. Alle vier, wollte man sie mit gängigen Dresscodes vergleichen, bedienen eine unterschiedliche Klientel. BHL arbeiten mit dem klassischen hanseatischen Tuch, d.h. Backstein. Grüntuch Ernst bringen mit einem inszenierten Glaswürfel, der abends gekühlt wirkt und glimmt, »Hauptstadt«-Eleganz an die Elbe. Besonderer Gag: Textil bespannte Leuchtkörper für das Treppenhaus.

Built on a 350-metre-long raised concrete flood-protection platform are four similar office buildings; four cubes, or more precisely U-shaped volumes, each cantilevered over the Elbe. Glass is the building material of choice in each case, though the first in line from the city side (architects: BHL) is partially faced with brick. Were we to figuratively compare these buildings in terms of common dress codes, it would become clear that each serves a different clientèle. BHL cut their "suit" from classic Hanseatic cloth, namely red brick. Grüntuch Ernst, meanwhile, bring a touch of Berlin's cosmopolitan elegance to the Elbe with a building that wears a cool, glimmering mantle by night, thanks to a special effect achieved with the aid of fabric-covered lighting elements along the stairwells.

E.33/34

1

2   3

1 Polderbebauung, gesehen in Richtung Westen mit Neumühlen und Övelgönne: Auffällig ist die einheitliche U-Form der Gebäude. Westward view towards Neumühlen and Övelgönne: the building complex with its eye-catching U-shaped cubes **2** Projekt BHL Architekten The BHL building **3** Projekt Grüntuch Ernst The Grüntuch Ernst building

Polderbebauung Neumühlen West
Bürohäuser Office Buildings

Standort Location Neumühlen 17 **Architekten Architects** Antonio Citterio Patricia Viel and Partners, Mailand **Bauherr Client** Edel Music AG, Hamburg **Bauzeit Date built** 1998–2002 **Bruttogeschossfläche Gross floor area** 11 700 qm (sqm)

Standort Location Neumühlen 19 **Architekten Architects** BRT Architekten LLP Bothe Richter Teherani, Hamburg **Bauherr Client** Hermann Ebel c/o Hansa Treuhand Schiffsbeteiligungs AG, Frank Leonhardt c/o Leonhardt & Blumenberg **Bauzeit Date built** 2001–02 **Bruttogeschossfläche Gross floor area** 6900 qm (sqm)

Antonio Citterio bringt »edles Mailänder Tuch« in die Stadt. Wie schon mit seinem Stadthaus am Neuen Wall und im Komplex am Brooktorkai (vgl. S. 156–159) zaubert er im Detail, lässt Dächer und Baukörper schweben, Material und Licht tanzen. Bothe Richter Teherani liefern hingegen Hafen-Hightech ab – eine Mischung aus Container und Louis Vuitton Design. Besonders vom Strom aus betrachtet, hat dieses strenge Ensemble einen guten Auftritt, in der Nahaufnahme überzeugt die Freiraumplanung von Möller Tradowsky. Diese lange Polderplatte optisch an der Flussseite einzufangen ist durch mit Holz beplankte Freitreppen gelungen. Der Bodenbelag – Eisensilikatschotter mit Asphalt-Glas-Gemisch – erinnert daran, dass hier Hafenland war.

Meanwhile, Antonio Citterio's design brings the finest Milanese couture to Hamburg. As with his designs for the townhouse on Neuer Wall and the Brooktorkai complex (cf. pp. 156–159), the architect's brilliance shines in the details; the roof and shell participate in an energetic dance of material and light. For the final building in the row, Bothe Richter Teherani deliver a high-tech composition that draws equal inspiration from the container docks and Louis Vuitton design. When viewed from the water this somewhat austere ensemble pulls off a virtuoso performance; up-close the spatial planning by Möller Tradowsky is equally convincing. Along the full length of the concrete platform a flight of timber-planked steps leads down to the waterside, softening the visual impact of the concrete.

1

2

3

1+3 Projekt Citterio, möglicherweise das eleganteste der Reihe The building by Antonio Citterio, perhaps the most elegant of the series **2** Projekt BRT: Design im Stil von Louis Vuitton The BRT building with a design that references Louis Vuitton

Wohnstift Augustinum
Seniorenwohnen Retirement Residence

Standort Location Neumühlen 37 **Architekten Architects** gmp · von Gerkan, Marg und Partner, Hamburg **Bauherr Client** Collegium Augustinum **Bauzeit Date built** 1991–93

Das ehemalige Union-Kühlhaus wurde 1926 von den Architekten Elingius und Schramm und deren Mitarbeiter H.W. Müller errichtet. Die unverwechselbare Silhouette des mit Betonbändern gegliederten Backsteingebäudes und den gezackten Attikaelementen war für die Schifffahrt ein markantes Orientierungszeichen des Altonaer Hafens im ehemaligen Preußen. Deshalb wurde das Kühlhaus unter Denkmalschutz gestellt. Hinter der alten Kühlhausfassade, die mit Ausnahme der erforderlichen Fenster und einer zusätzlichen verglasten Kuppel weitgehend wieder errichtet wurde, hat ein Seniorenstift Platz gefunden. Die »Krone« im 13. Stock bildet die »einschalige« Stahlglaskuppel mit einem Durchmesser von 24 Metern und einer Höhe von acht Metern. Insgesamt eine der »Backsteinperlen am Hafenrand – ihr Alter Ego folgt stromaufwärts: der Kaispeicher A als Basis der Elbphilharmonie in der Hafencity, der allerdings nur alt aussieht, aber neu gebaut wurde.

The Union-Kühlhaus cold-storage warehouse was built in 1926 by the architecture firm of Elingius and Schramm, with particular involvement by H.W. Müller. This unique brick fortress with its defining horizontal bands of concrete and serrated parapet was an unmistakeable landmark for ships entering the formerly Prussian port of Altona. For that reason the warehouse was designated as a historical building. Behind the old façade, which has been largely restored to its original state, barring the introduction of windows and an additional glass dome, a retirement home has been established. The "climax" of this building is undoubtedly the single-shell steel and glass dome on the 13th floor. This impressive feature is 24 metres in diameter and eight in height. All in all, this is one of the Hamburg waterfront's brick gems, and a fitting counterpart to the city's newest landmark—a relatively recent warehouse from 1963—which forms the base of the new Elbphilharmonie.

1

2   3

1 Ansicht vom Strom – die Kuppel ist zum Teil öffentlich und bietet den schönsten Hafenblick weit und breit. View from the water – part of the dome is open to the public and offers far and away some of the most spectacular views of the harbour around. **2** Restaurant unter der Glaskuppel Restaurant under the glass dome **3** Schnitt Sectional drawing

Elbchaussee 139
Büro- und Wohnhaus Mixed Use Building

Standort Location Elbchaussee 139 **Architekten Architects** gmp · von Gerkan, Marg und Partner, Hamburg **Bauherr Client** Meinhard von Gerkan **Bauzeit Date built** 1987–92 **Bruttogeschossfläche Gross floor area** Büro: 2000 qm (sqm, office building); Wohnhaus: 480 qm (sqm, residential building)

E.38/39

Das örtliche Baurecht schrieb auf dem Terrain der ehemaligen Hartens-Elbterrassen eine Mischung aus Restaurant, Büro- und Wohnhaus vor. Nach Abriss des Vorgängerbaus aus dem 19. Jahrhundert (bis auf den Kopfbau an der Elbchaussee) sind jetzt sämtliche Bauaufgaben auf zeichenhafte Einzelbaukörper verteilt worden. Von der Elbchaussee aus gesehen fasst rechter Hand das Bürogebäude, das sich aus einem typischen Gründerzeitaltbau als Riegel wie ein »Dampfer« zum Strom hin entwickelt, ein trapezförmiges öffentliches und autofreies Aussichtsplateau ein. Das schräg in die Achse gestellte Pendant auf der linken Seite ist das Wohnhaus des Architekten Meinhard von Gerkan. In der Mitte erreicht man bei prächtigem Elbblick eine Rampe, die haarnadelspitz wendet und hinab zur Edelgastronomie führt. Die sich darüber türmende Rotunde nimmt die Chefbüros und Besprechungsräume auf.

Local planning law dictated that this site at what used to be the Hartens Elbe Terraces would become home to a combination of restaurant, residence and offices. Following the demolition of the predecessor building from the 19th century (all but the front section facing onto Elbchaussee was torn down) each of these three functions have been delegated to individual volumes. Seen from Elbchaussee the office building to the right—which embarks from the typical late-nineteenth-century villa like a ship from a slipway—borders an open, publicly accessible trapezoid viewing plateau. The diagonally positioned building in the left corner, which counterbalances the office-restaurant ensemble, is the home of the architect Meinhard von Gerkan. A ramp that begins between the two main buildings leads, via a hairpin bend and surrounded by magnificent panoramic views of the Elbe, to the gourmet restaurant below. The rotunda that towers above the ensemble accommodates the executive offices of gmp.

1

2

3

1 Das Ensemble – gesehen von der Elbchaussee: vorn
der Altbau, dahinter die Erweiterung The ensemble
as viewed from Elbchaussee: in the foreground the
historic building, behind it the expansion 2 Blick aus
der »Brücke«, dem Besprechungsraum View from
the conference room 3 Wohnhaus Residential building
4 Aufsicht Top view

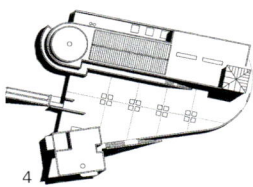

4

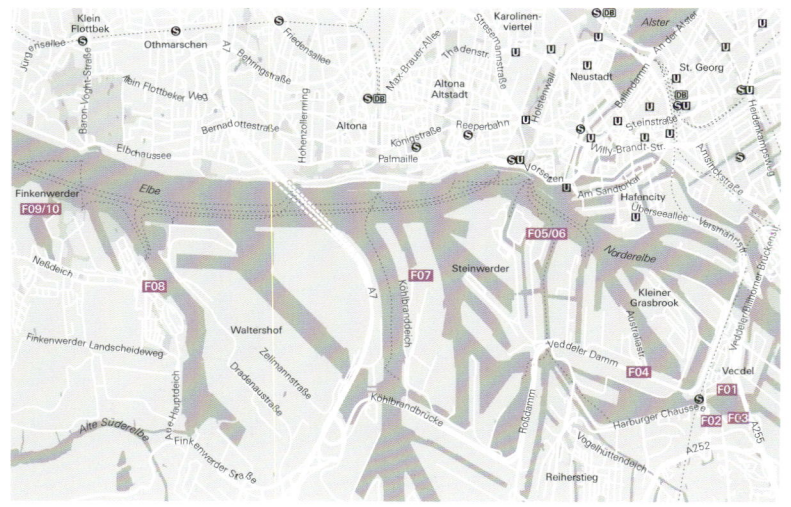

Sprung über die Elbe

The Leap Across the Elbe

Die andere Waterfront
The Other Waterfront

Die südliche Norderelbseite ist anders, ganz anders. Weder städtisch noch dörflich, sie ist einfach nur Hafengebiet. Noch! Eine Mischung aus Arbeit, Poesie und Fantasie, immer anders, je nach Tages- und Jahreszeit kann sie im Nebel versinken, weich wie ein See im Morgenlicht sein oder hart wie eine Mondlandschaft. Das Gegenüber von Hafencity, Alt- und Neustadt, St. Pauli, Altona und den Elbvororten zeigt sich nicht geschlossen, sondern ist ein Versprechen auf eine andere Welt: Das sind fremde Landschaften. Vielleicht liegt ja das Meer dahinter, das der Fremde in Hamburg sucht?

Das ist anders als in Düsseldorf, Wien oder Köln – und macht Hamburg einzigartig. In Wirklichkeit sind es übrigens Inseln, die dort liegen. Wilhelmsburg ist eine von ihnen und die größte Flussinsel Europas. Sie liegt zwischen Norder- und Süderelbe. HPA (Hamburg Port Authority) und die Hafenwirtschaft haben dafür gesorgt, dass der Hafen ein Hafen bleibt und die Seefahrt und Logistik nicht gestört und unterbrochen werden. Trotz-

The south bank of the Elbe is different, very different. Neither urban nor rural, these are docklands, pure and simple— at least for now! A fusion of industry, poetry and imagination, this is an area that changes its complexion depending on the season or time of day; alternatively soft as a fog-shrouded lake at dawn, or harsh as a lunar landscape. The south bank is not just situated opposite Hafencity, Altstadt and Neustadt, St. Pauli, Altona and the leafy suburbs on the north bank; it is, in a sense, the very antithesis of those areas. It is a kind of alternative cityscape; this could be the coastal city that so many visitors expect to find in Hamburg.

No other German city has such a split personality. That's what makes Hamburg unique. The southern waterfront is actually a collection of islands between the northern and southern branches of the Elbe. The main island, Wilhelmsburg, is Europe's largest river island. Hamburg Port Authority and the shipping industries have made sure that Hamburg has retained not just the

dem ist es gelungen, das ein oder andere Einsprengsel einer normalen Hamburger Zivilisation als Botschafter der Stadt im Hafen zu etablieren: Die Hamburger Musicaltheater beispielsweise, der Südzugang des Alten Elbtunnels. Und weiter im Westen der frühere Hamburger Yachtclub, der in ähnlich vollendeter Reformarchitektur dort steht wie in der weiteren Nachbarschaft das berühmte Lotsenhaus von Fritz Schumacher.

Es gibt also keine städtische, keine architektonische Wasserfront dort und trotzdem kann, muss man über sie berichten. Denn Hamburg setzt die Entwicklungsrichtung nach Süden fort, die durch »Perlenkette«, Hafencity und die (nicht erfolgreiche) Olympiabewerbung begonnen wurde und plakativ »Sprung über die Elbe« genannt wird. Dieser landet zunächst im schwierigen und stigmatisierten Stadtteil Wilhelmsburg. (Er war von der verheerenden Sturmflut 1962 am stärksten betroffen; später wurde er als »sozialer Brennpunkt« bekannt.) Hamburg hat 2013 versucht, diese Aufgaben mit einer internationalen Bausstellung (IBA) und einer gleichzeitig stattfindenden internationalen Gartenschau (igs) zu lösen. Einige Bauten werden hier vorgestellt.

character but the function of a port city; the requirements of shipping and logistics have top priority here. At the same time, efforts have been made to add a sprinkling of normal Hamburg life, like ambassadors from the city, within the docklands. Examples include new musical theatres and the south entrance to the old Elbe Tunnel. Further to the west we find further architectural tidbits such as the old Hamburg Yacht Club and Fritz Schumacher's famous Lotsenhaus (pilot station), both accomplished examples of Reform Architecture.

Hamburg's southern waterfront is neither urban nor particularly architectural, and yet it deserves, even demands our attention. That is because Hamburg's next phase of development will be to the south. The impetus came from the Hafencity and "Perlenkette" developments, as well as through Hamburg's (unsuccessful) Olympic bid, and has been boldly titled "Sprung über die Elbe" or "Leap across the Elbe". It is ostensibly a leap into the difficult and socially stigmatised district of Wilhelmsburg (it was the area worst hit by the devastating storm surge of 1962, and later gained a reputation as social flashpoint). In 2013 Hamburg attempted to tackle these issues with an International Building Exhibition (IBA) and a simultaneous International Garden Show (igs). Some of those buildings are shown here.

IBA Dock
Arbeiten und Präsentieren Work and Display

Standort Location Am Zollhafen 12 **Architekt Architect** Prof. Han Slawik Architekt, Hannover/Amsterdam **Bauherr Client** ReGe Hamburg Projektrealisierungsgesellschaft mbH in Vertretung für Internationale Bauausstellung, IBA Hamburg GmbH ReGe Hamburg Projektrealisierungsgesellschaft mbH on behalf of IBA Hamburg GmbH **Bauzeit Date built** 2009–10 **Bruttogeschossfläche Gross floor area** 1835 qm (sqm)

Das zuerst fertiggestellte Bauprojekt der IBA Hamburg ist Programm und wurde zunächst in eigener Sache genutzt: in hybrider Ausrichtung zum Arbeiten und Präsentieren; eine Terrasse direkt am Wasser erweitert die Möglichkeiten, hier kleine Kongresse durchzuführen. Das Dock ist schwimmfähig und in Teilen ein offen zugängliches Haus mit Cafeteria. Erreichbar ist es über einen Steg, ähnlich einer Zugbrücke an Wasserburgen. An Symbolik wurde nicht gespart: Die äußere Anmutung erinnert an die Modularität von Schiffscontainern und deren Flexibilität beziehungsweise an eine Art Baukasten. Die gute Nachricht: Das Haus übertraf bei Inbetriebnahme die Energiesparvorschriften um etwa fünfzig Prozent ins Positive, vor allem durch das Beheizen mit einer Wärmepumpe, die durch einen Wärmetauscher die Wärme des Hafenwassers nutzt. Einhundert Quadratmeter Solarzellenflächen auf dem Dach decken den Strombedarf.

The first building project completed under the auspices of the IBA was both policy and platform. This is a hybrid creation, designed for work and display, complete with a waterside terrace that is ideal for small conferences. Sections of this floating dock are open to the public, and accessible via a jetty that resembles the drawbridge to a moated castle. This structure is not short on symbolism: while evoking shipping containers and the flexibility they allow, it also resembles a box of toy building blocks. The good news: when this building came into operation it exceeded Hamburg's energy saving requirements by about 50%. It achieved this largely through a heat pump connected to a thermal bridge that takes advantage of the warmth of the harbour water. It is also equipped with 100 square metres of solar panels.

1

2

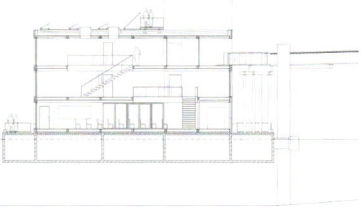

3

1 Das IBA-Dock schwimmt mit den Gezeiten auf und ab. The IBA Dock rises and falls with the tides. **2** Der Zugang zum Dock erfolgt über eine Brücke. The floating dock is accessed by a bridge. **3** Schnitt Sectional drawing

Ballinstadt
Auswanderermuseum Emigration Museum

Standort Location Veddeler Bogen 2 **Architekten Architects** nps tchoban voss | Architektur und Städtebau **Bauherr Client** ReGe Hamburg Projektrealisierungs-gesellschaft mbH **Bauzeit Date built** 2006–07 **Bruttogeschossfläche Gross floor area** 2950 qm (sqm)

Heimwehtourismus ist in Mode. Hafenstädte als Aus- und Einwandererzentralen profitieren davon – und auch Hamburg hat etwas Besonderes zu bieten. Kreuzfahrer, Musicaltouristen und alle anderen Besucher erreichen die Ballinstadt von den Landungsbrücken direkt übers Wasser mit der Linie A und erleben die Stadt, wie jene es tun, die von der Südspitze Manhattans nach Ellis Island fahren.

In einem der Pavillons, die einst Auswanderern als Schlafhallen dienten, schlagen sie in einer Liste unter fünf Millionen Namen ihre Urgroßeltern nach – und erfahren, von welchem Ort in Osteuropa sie sich auf den Weg in die Vereinigten Staaten machten. Architektonisch blieb das Konzept bescheiden. Die Planung basiert auf den historischen Anlagen von 1906. Es wurden drei Gebäude und ein Technikhaus rekonstruiert. Ziel war es, das äußere und innere Erscheinungsbild der ursprünglichen Bebauung wieder herzustellen.

Nostalgia tourism is all the rage, and port cities, as the places so many migrants were drawn to and departed from, play a central role. Hamburg has something very special to offer in this regard. Cruise passengers, musical-goers and all other visitors to the city can reach Ballinstadt directly from the St. Pauli landing bridges via harbour ferry, just like visitors to New York, who take a ferry from Battery Park to Ellis Island.

In one of the pavilions, which once served as dormitories, visitors can search a list of 5 million names to find out from which Eastern European city their great-grandparents came before making the crossing to the United States. From an architectural perspective this is a modest design, based on the original historical blueprints from 1906. Three new halls plus a machine house were constructed. The aim was to reproduce the external and internal appearance of the original structures. In two of the buildings glass roofs

1

Bei zwei Gebäuden wurde der offene Hof nach Norden gläsern überbaut, um zusätzliche Ausstellungsflächen zu erhalten. Museen profilieren sich meistens weniger über die Architektur als über die Szenografie. Es gibt raffiniertere Ausstellungskonzepte, dennoch ist die Ballinstadt lohnenswert, auch oder gerade weil mit dem Ballinpark zwischen den rekonstruierten Pavillons von 1906 und dem Müggenburger Zollhafen wieder einmal öffentliche Grünflächen direkt am Wasser entstanden sind.

were mounted over the north-facing open courtyards, creating additional exhibition space. Museums tend to distinguish themselves more through scenography than architecture. The Ballinstadt contains a sophisticated exhibition design, and yet an equally alluring feature is the newly created Ballinpark between the reconstructed pavilions and the Müggenburg docks. Finally, Wilhelmsburg has a public green space on the waterfront.

F.02

1 (Vorige Doppelseite) Es wurden drei Gebäude und ein Technikhaus rekonstruiert. (Previous double-page spread) Three new halls plus a machine house were reconstructed.
2 Blick vom Zollhafen auf die Ballinstadt View of Ballinstadt from the docks 3+4 Innenansichten Interior views 5 Schnitte und Grundrisse Sectional drawings and floor plans

2

3

4

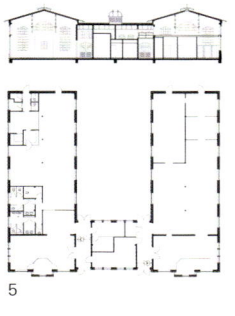
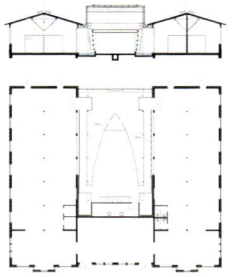
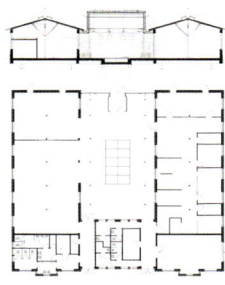

5

Haus der Projekte
Jugendzentrum Youth Centre

Standort Location Müggenburger Zollhafen, Südseite **Architekten Architects** Studio NL–D, Rotterdam **Bauherr Client** Get the Kick e.V., Hamburg **Wettbewerb Competition** 2008 **Bauzeit Date built** 2010–12

F.03

Vor der Ballinstadt, gleich gegenüber des IBA Docks am selben Hafenbecken, liegt das Haus der Projekte. Leicht und hölzern wie ein Bootshaus erinnert es an eine Arche. Die Sozial-Werkstatt des Vereins »Get the Kick« mit einer Bootswerkstatt und zur Aus- und Weiterbildung von Jugendlichen auf der Veddel ist hier entstanden. Die Heizung des Hauses wird durch Brennstoffzellentechnologie gewährleistet. Der Innenausbau (u.a. die Werkstatt und Seminarräume) wurde in Eigenleistung durch die Nutzer – als ihr erstes Projekt – selbständig gestaltet.

Die markante Bauform ist weithin sichtbar – auch von der A255/A1 in Richtung Süden. Ein gelungenes Beispiel für Eigeninitiative, weil das Projekt zu großen Teilen in Eigenarbeit der Benutzer entstanden ist.

In front of Ballinstadt, directly opposite the IBA Dock along the same harbour basin, is "Haus der Projekte". This light wooden structure has an ark-like quality. The non-profit association "Get a Kick" commissioned this building as a place where young people from Veddel can receive training in boat building. The building's heating system is based on fuel cell technology. The workshop and seminar rooms were designed by the users themselves—their first project.

Its eye-catching form is visible from afar – even from the southbound lane of the A255/A1. This building is a wonderful example of user-driven construction with much of the work undertaken by its young users.

1

2

3

1 Blick vom IBA-Dock über den Kanal auf das Haus der Projekte View of the "Haus der Projekte" from the IBA Dock across the canal **2** Schnitt Sectional drawing **3** Straßenansicht kurz vor der Fertigstellung Streetside view shortly before completion

50er Schuppen
Museum / Veranstaltungszentrum Event Location

Standort Location Australienstraße / Kleiner Grasbrook **Architekten Architects** Baudeputation, Sektion für Strom- und Hafenbau **Bauzeit Date built** 1909–12 **Bruttogeschossfläche Gross floor area** Jede der Hallen ist 271 Meter lang und 48 Meter breit. Each of the halls is 271 meters long and 48 meters wide.

Die 50er Schuppen stehen prototypisch für die große Zeit des Stückgutverkehrs im Hamburger Hafen. Sie werden bis heute genutzt. Bei einer Breite von fast fünfzig Metern werden die Dächer der dreischiffigen Hallen von beeindruckenden Fachwerkbindern aus Holz getragen. Wie gewaltig das Interior heute wirkt, kann jedermann genießen, weil Teile der Anlage als Veranstaltungszentrum dienen. Noch öffentlicher ist der Schuppen 50A als Außenstelle des Museums der Arbeit, dessen maritime Sammlungsteile hier zu besichtigen sind. Der Star bleibt aber die Aussicht: Hier werden viele Krimis gedreht und man hat den besten Blick auf Hafencity und die Nachbarn auf der anderen Flußseite. Außerdem kann man die neue Waterfront auch von Land bestaunen. Zugabe am Kai: das Ballett der historischen Kräne sowie Dampfer und ehemalige Hafenbahnlokomotiven.

The quay sheds at Kleiner Grasbrook are a relic of the golden age of the bulk cargo trade in Hamburg port. They are still in use to this day. The roof of the 50-metre-long, triple-bayed shed is borne by imposing timber cross-beams, which can be viewed by anyone who wishes, as parts of the complex double as event spaces. Shed 50A is also an outpost of the Museum of Work (Museum der Arbeit), containing its maritime collection. The star of the show, however, is the majestic view towards Hafencity. Not surprisingly, this is a popular location for crime films. It is also the ideal vantage point from which to admire Hamburg's new waterfront. The graceful ensemble of historical cranes, steamers and port railway locomotives provide a quayside encore.

1

2

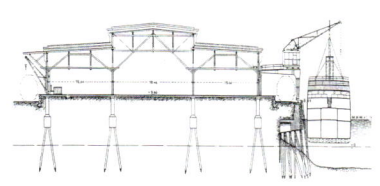
3

1 Blick über die Gesamtanlage der 50er Schuppen (vorn im Bild am Kai mit Museums-kränen) View of the quay shed complex (in the foreground the quayside featuring historic cranes) **2** Historischer Schnitt durch Schuppen 50–52 Historic sectional drawing of Sheds 50–52 **3** Kopfbau und Zufahrt Front building and access road

Theater im Hafen
Musical-Theater Musical Theatres

Theater im Hafen: Standort Location Norderelbestraße 6 **Architekten Architects** Urban-Project Raumdesign, Klaus Latuske (Umbau) **Bauherr Client** Stage Entertainment (Umbau Renovation) **Bauzeit Date built** 1994/2001 (Umbau Renovation) **Bruttogeschossfläche Gross floor area** 5000 qm (sqm)

Stage Theater an der Elbe: Standort Location Norderelbestraße 8 **Architekten Architects** AMA Group Arn Meijs Architekten BV Maastricht, Niederlande **Bauherr Client** Stage Entertainment **Bauzeit Date built** 2013–14 **Bruttogeschossfläche Gross floor area** 12800 qm (sqm)

Ein erster Kulturbotschafter am anderen Elbufer war als »Metropol-Theater« gestartet und heißt heute »Stage Theater im Hafen«. Seit 2001 ist es Heimatspielstätte für Disneys »Der König der Löwen«. Ursprünglich unter einem Zelt als temporäre Spielstätte errichtet, hat der »Altbau« später die prägnante gelbe Farbe und eine gläserne Vorsatzkanzel als Restaurant bekommen. In der Elbe spiegelt sich der markige »fliegende Bau« und inszeniert sich täglich bei wechselnden Lichtern virtuell neu. Das Theater bildet den kulturellen Vorposten des geplanten »Sprungs über die Elbe«. Es ist durch eine Fährverbindung über Wasser an die Landungsbrücken angebunden. Es ist ein Hinweis auf die Potenziale der Wasserstadt Hamburg. Die Betreiber haben das erkannt und direkt nebenan bereits ein zweites Theaterhaus gebaut, das 2014 eröffnet wird.

This building was one of the first cultural ambassadors to make the leap across the Elbe. It started out as the Metropol-Theater, and is now known as "Stage Theater im Hafen". Since 2001 it has played host to Disney's "The Lion King". It was originally built as a temporary venue beneath a marquee. Later, a raised glass cockpit for a restaurant was added and the marquee roof was given its distinct yellow colour. This mighty "tent" is reflected in the waters of the Elbe, and changes its complexion depending on the lighting conditions. The theatre is a cultural outlier for the planned "Leap across the Elbe". It is connected to St. Pauli landing bridges by a fast ferry route, giving a foretaste of how Hamburg could make more of its waterways. The operators recognised the potential and have already built a second theatre right next door, which is due to open in 2014.

1

2

1 Die Musicaltheater auf der Hafenseite der Norderelbe sind über einen Fähren-Shuttle an die Landungsbrücken angebunden. The musical theatres on the harbour side of the Elbe are linked via fast ferry to the St. Pauli landing bridges. **2** Visualisierung Visualisation

Klärwerk Köhlbrandhöft

Erweiterung und Neubau Sewage Treatment Plant (Expansion and New Construction)

Standort Location Köhlbranddeich **Architekten Architects** Architektencontor Schäfer Agather Scheel **Bauherr Client** HSE – Hamburger Stadtentwässerung **Wettbewerb Competition** 1998 **Bauzeit Date built** 1999–2007 **Bruttogeschossfläche Gross floor area** 3486 qm (sqm)

Abends strahlen sie nach Altona herüber wie übergroße illuminierte Ostereier. Und mancher Fremde fragt sich, was das denn sei. Es sind die notwendigen Imponderabilien der Stadt: Abteilung Dreck und Schmutz. Die Architekten machten aus der Not die buchstäbliche Tugend und stellten diese Fäulnisbehälter in einer Ordnung auf, als stünden sie auf einem übergroßen Eiertablett. Abends gibt es diese ungewöhnlichen Landmarken mit Beleuchtung – so schön kann der Hafen sein. Die zuständigen Architekten haben darüber hinaus einen Masterplan der Gestaltung entwickelt sowie Alt- und Zubauten in ein harmonisches Miteinander gebracht. Spektakulär ist auch ein langer schiffsähnlicher Baukörper für das Verwaltungshaus, in dem 2006/2007 viele bis dahin auf dem Werksgelände verstreute Funktionen versammelt wurden.

At night they glimmer across the water to Altona like oversized illuminated Easter eggs, causing visitors to the city to doubt their eyes. These are among the city's necessary imponderables, a facility run by the department of f lth and grime. The architects made virtue of necessity by designing and arranging these sewage containers like eggs on an oversized tray. By night these unusual landmarks are illuminated, showing once again how pretty the port can be. The architects also developed a master plan that brings the original and additional structures together into a harmonious arrangement. The most spectacular feature of this ensemble is a long shiplike building that, since 2007, houses the offices and other administrative functions of the sewage treatment plant.

1

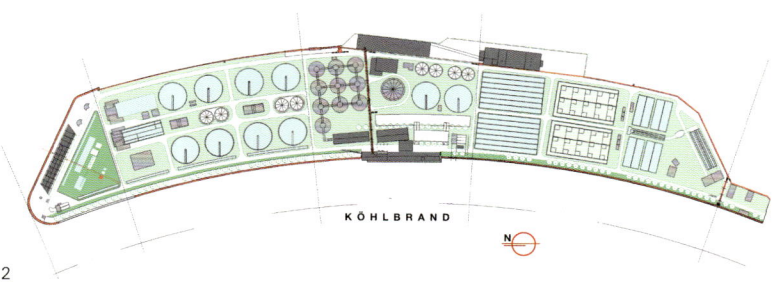

KÖHLBRAND

N

2

1 Keine überdimensionierten Vogeleier, sondern gut gestaltete und funktionierende Fäulnisbehälter. Ansicht von der Norderelbe These are not oversized eggs but well-designed, functioning sewage treatment tanks. View from the river **2** Lageplan Site plan

Marine-Center Finkenwerder
Bootswerft Shipyard

Standort Location Köhlfleet-Hauptdeich 3 **Architekten Architects** KBNK Architekten, Hamburg **Bauherr Client** Olaf Behrens **Bauzeit Date built** 2004 **Bruttogeschossfläche Gross floor area** 1920 qm (sqm)

Eine kleine Familienwerft in Finkenwerder musste erweitert werden. Die Architekten schlugen dem Unternehmen vor, neue Angebote und Betätigungsfelder zu erschließen. Deswegen entstand direkt an der Uferlinie nun ein Neubau als Hybrid für Lofts und Büros mit flexibler Nutzungsfläche, denen allen eines gemeinsam ist: ein fantastischer Ausblick auf den Strom und die Vermietbarkeit sogar für einen Tag dank eines Genius Loci, der sich aus grüner Niederelbe und kleinteiliger suburbaner Hafenlandschaft zusammensetzt. Nicht überraschend: Das rote Haus steht ganz oben auf der Liste der Location-Scouts für Events und ähnliches. Baulich sind die Gebäude im Überflutungsbereich der Elbe vor dem Köhlfleet-Hauptdeich gelegen. Die Themen Hochwasserschutz und die daran gekoppelten technischen Anforderungen standen bei der Umsetzung des Projekts im Vordergrund.

A small, family-owned boatbuilder's yard in Finkenwerder was in need of expanded premises. The architects suggested that they also expand into new markets. The result is a new hybrid-use building at the water's edge that combines a loft apartment and studio with offices, and allows for the flexible utilisation of both. All of the spaces share one great benefit—fantastic views of the Köhlfleet harbour basin. Thanks to the genius loci, which unites the greenery of the lower Elbe with small-scale sub-urban docklands, there is no problem finding tenants—even on a daily basis. Not surprisingly, this striking red house is in great demand among event location scouts. The buildings are located in a flood-prone area on the south bank of the Elbe in this former fishing village. For that reason, flood protection was a major priority of this project, both from a technical and architectural perspective.

F.08

1

2

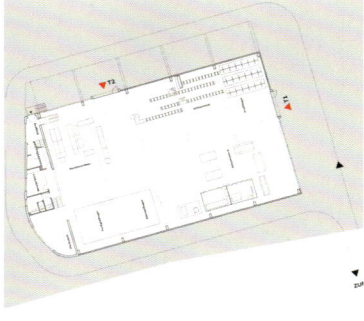

3

1 Gesamtansicht Overall view 2 In einem der Geschosse befindet sich ein Mietstudio.
One level contains a studio available for rent. 3 Übersicht Overview

Airbus A380 Montagehallen
Aircraft Assembly Halls

Standort Location Kreetslag 10, Airbus-Werksgelände Hamburg-Finkenwerder **Architekten Architects** gmp · von Gerkan, Marg und Partner, Hamburg **Bauherr Client** Airbus Deutschland GmbH **Wettbewerb Competition** 1999 **Bauzeit Date built** Gutachten Expert report 2000; 2002–05 **Bruttogeschossfläche Gross floor area** Sektionsbauhalle: 44000 qm (sqm, major component assembly hall); Ausstattungsmontagehalle: 59000 qm (sqm, interior equipment assembly hall)

Seit 2001 wird das Airbus-Werk auf Flächen erweitert, die durch Teilzuschüttungen des Mühlenberger Lochs entstanden sind. Ein politischer Akt, mit dem Hamburg bewiesen hat, dass es, wenn es ernst wird, die wirtschaftlichen Interessen vor die ökologischen stellt. In diesem Fall allerdings war es eine wichtige Entscheidung, um notwendige Industrie-Arbeitsplätze in Hamburg zu sichern. Die Industrie-Architektur, vor allem die Showseite zur Elbe und hinüber nach Blankenese, ist trotz der immensen Größe der Hallen in typischer gmp-Manier aufgebaut. Gläsern und transparent – in der Frühphase der A-380-Produktion sicherte Airbus die Glaswände nachträglich mit Abklebungen gegen Einsicht und Industriespionage. »gmp hat sich für Schwarzbrot statt Hochzeitstorte entschieden«, kommentierte das Jahrbuch Architektur in Hamburg 2001 – eine Anspielung darauf, dass vermeintlich aufregendere Entwürfe im Wettbewerb unterlegen waren.

The Airbus plant has been undergoing continuous expansion since 2001 on an area of land that was reclaimed from the river. The decision to fill this section of freshwater wetland was highly political, and demonstrated Hamburg's will, when necessary, to put economic considerations before environmental ones. In this case, the decision played a vital role in safeguarding Hamburg's future as an industrial base. The industrial architecture, particularly the waterfront side that is visible from the opposite bank in Blankenese, bears the impressive hallmarks of a gmp creation. The steel and glass façade indicates transparency, though in the early production phase of the A380 airplane, the glass walls were taped up to protect against industrial espionage. According to the 2001 Hamburg Architectural Yearbook, with this building "gmp has opted for black bread rather than a wedding cake," an indication perhaps that the competition included more exciting designs.

1

2

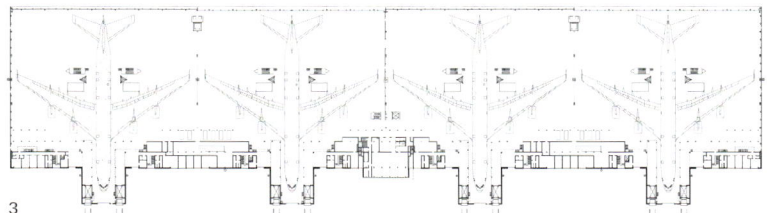

3

1 Innenansicht Hallen Interior view of the hangars 2 Ansicht vom Nordufer der Elbe View from the northern bank of the Elbe 3 Grundriss Floor plan

Airbus A380 Lackierhalle
Aircraft Paint Hangar

Standort Location Kreetslag 10, Airbus-Werksgelände Hamburg-Finkenwerder **Architekten Architects** PSP Architekten Ingenieure, Hamburg **Bauherr Client** Airbus Deutschland GmbH **Wettbewerb Competition** 2001 **Bauzeit Date built** 2003–04 **Bruttogeschossfläche Gross floor area** 45 000 qm (sqm)

Im Zipfel der neuen Halbinsel steht die Lackierhalle. Die Aufgabe war nicht leicht, denn hier wird in Hightech-Manier das größte Passagierflugzeug lackiert. Das bedeutet, es kommt auf absolute Präzision und jedes Gramm Farbe an, das nicht aufgetragen wird. Das Innenleben der Halle und besonders ein sehr ausgewogenes Arbeitslichtkonzept standen im Fokus. Außen ist trotzdem viel Besseres als die übliche Kiste (bei 38 Metern Höhe!) entstanden. Die »Willkommen«-Seite aus Richtung Nordsee wirkt sehr differenziert: Schlote, Lüftungsanlagen, Feuerleiter, dazu außen liegende Fachwerkträger über dem Dach machen aus der Industriekiste ein würdiges Industriegebäude. Es besitze, so das Hamburger Architekturjahrbuch 2007, die guten Ingenieursbauten innewohnende Maschinenästhetik.

At the tip of the newly created river peninsula stands the paint shop. This was not an easy brief. This is where the world's largest passenger aircraft is painted, a process that requires fine precision and exactitude. The main focus of the design was, naturally, the interior, and more particularly the facilitation of optimal lighting. The statuesque external façades (38 metres high!) nonetheless testify to a concept that is far better than the typical factory block. The north-facing façade that greets ships arriving from the North Sea has a nuanced appearance: smokestacks, ventilations systems, fire escapes and external trussed girders combine to form an ensemble that is worthy of the designation "industrial architecture". It possesses (according to the 2007 Hamburg Architecture Yearbook) the mechanical aesthetics inherent to high-quality engineering structures.

1

2   3

1 Innenansicht der größten Lackierhalle für Großraumflugzeuge weltweit. Sie wurde nach aktuellen technologischen Umweltstandards gebaut, mit besonderem Schwerpunkt auf der Energieeffizienz. Interior view of the world's largest paintshop hangar for widebody aircraft. It was built in compliance with state-of-the-art technological and environmental standards, with a particular emphasis on energy efficiency. **2** Ansicht der Lackierhalle von Nordwesten View of the paint hangar from the northwest **3** Lageplan der Gesamtanlage des Airbusgeländes Site plan of the entire Airbus site

Bildnachweis Photo Credits

S.|p. 10: gmp Architekten, Hamburg
S.|pp. 22–23 ELBE&FLUT/Thomas Hampel
S.|p. 26: Masterpläne Hafencity 2000 und
2010: hamburgplan, Hamburg mit Christia-
anse/ASTOC, Rotterdam/Köln im Auftrag der
Freien und Hansestadt Hamburg, Stadtent-
wicklungsbehörde (heute: Behörde für Stadt-
entwicklung und Umwelt) und GHS Gesell-
schaft für Hafen- und Standortentwicklung
(heute: HafenCity Hamburg GmbH)
S.|pp. 30–33: A.01 Elbphilharmonie: Abb. 1+3:
Oliver Heissner, Hamburg, Abb. 2:
ELBE&FLUT/Thomas Hampel, Abb. 4+5:
Junius Verlag
S.|pp. 34–35: A.02 Am Sandtorkai 68:
Abb. 1+2: ELBE&FLUT/Thomas Hampel,
Abb. 3: ingenhoven architects
S.|pp. 36–37: A.03 Ocean's End: Abb. 1+2:
Klaus Frahm, Abb. 3: BLK2 Architekten
S.|pp. 38–39: A.04 H_2O: Abb. 1: ELBE&FLUT/
Thomas Hampel, Abb. 2+3: Spengler Wie-
scholek Architekten
S.|pp. 40–41: A.05 Dock4: Abb. 1+3:
ELBE&FLUT/Thomas Hampel, Abb. 2: ASP
Schweger + Partner
S.|pp. 42–43: A.06 China Shipping: Abb. 1:
Junius Verlag, Abb. 2: BRT Architekten
S.|pp. 44–45: A.07 Harbour Cube: Abb. 1:
Junius Verlag, Abb. 2+3: Marc-Olivier Mathez
S.|pp. 46–47: A.08 Harbour-Hall: Abb. 1:
Junius Verlag, Abb. 2: APB Architekten, Foto
Andreas Weiss, Abb. 3: APB Architekten
S.|pp. 48–49: A.09 Bankhaus Wölbern:
Abb. 1–3: ELBE&FLUT/Thomas Hampel
S.|pp. 50–51: A.10 Ponton mit Traditions-
schiffhafen: Abb. 1: Junius Verlag, Abb. 2:
EMBT Arquitectes Associats, Barcelona
S.|pp. 52–53: A.11 Magellan-Terrassen:
Abb. 1–3: Junius Verlag
S.|pp. 54–55: A.12 Marco-Polo-Terrassen:
Abb. 1+2: ELBE&FLUT/Thomas Hampel
S.|pp. 56–57: A.13 Pantaenius House:
Abb. 1–3: Junius Verlag
S.|pp. 58–59: A.14/15 Am Kaiserkai 4–8:

Abb. 1+3: ELBE&FLUT/Thomas Hampel,
Abb. 2: Marc-Olivier Mathez
S.|pp. 60–61: A.16/17 Oval und Kontor am
Kaiserkai: Abb. 1+2: Junius Verlag, Abb. 3
ingenhoven architects
S.|pp. 62–63: A.18 home4: Abb. 1+2: Elbe &
Flut/Thomas Hampel, Abb. 3: BRT Architekten
S.|pp. 64–65: A.19 ElbElysium: Abb. 1+2:
Klaus Frahm, Abb. 3: BLK2 Architekten
S.|pp. 66–67: A.20 Kai 12: Abb. 1–3: nps
tchoban voss | Architektur und Städtebau
(Foto: Axel Neubauer)
S.|pp. 68–69: A.21/22 Baugemeinschaft 2006:
Abb. 1: ELBE&FLUT/Thomas Hampel, Abb. 2:
Junius Verlag, Abb. 3: LOVE architecture
S.|pp. 70–71: A.23 Johannes-Dalmann-Haus:
Abb. 1+3: Martin Kunze, Abb. 2: Schenk
Waiblinger Architekten
S.|p. 73: HHLA (Gustav Werbeck)
S.|p. 75: Oliver Heissner
S.|pp. 76–77: A.24/25/26 Kaiserkai 47–57:
Abb. 1+3: ELBE&FLUT/Thomas Hampel,
Abb. 2: Junius Verlag, Abb. 4: Behrendt
Wohnungsbau
S.|pp. 78–79: A.27/28/29 Kaiserkai 35–45:
Abb. 1+2: ELBE&FLUT/Thomas Hampel, Abb.
3: Detlef Klose, Abb. 4: SEHW Architekten
S.|pp. 80–81: A.30/31/32 Quartier am Kaiser-
kai: Abb. 1+3: ELBE&FLUT/Thomas Hampel,
Abb. 2: Marcus Bredt, Berlin, Abb. 4: KBNK
Architekten
S.|pp. 82–83: A.33/34/35 Dalmann-Carrée:
Abb. 1+2: ELBE&FLUT/Thomas Hampel, Abb
3: MRLV Architekten (Foto: Klaus Frahm)
S.|pp. 84–85: A.36 Baugenossenschaft
Bergedorf-Bille: Abb. 1: ELBE&FLUT/Thomas
Hampel, Abb. 2: PFP Architekten, Abb. 3:
Klaus Frahm
S.|pp. 86–87: A.37 K1: Abb. 1–3: nps tchoban
voss | Architektur und Städtebau (Foto: Axe
Neubauer)
S.|p. 89: Junius Verlag
S.|pp. 92–95: A.38 Unilever-Haus:
Abb. 1: Roland Halbe, Abb. 2: Adam Mørk,
Abb. 3: ELBE&FLUT/Thomas Hampel,
Abb. 4+5: Behnisch Architekten, Stuttgart

S. | pp. 96–97: A.39 Marco Polo Tower: Abb.
1+2: Roland Halbe, Abb. 3–5: Behnisch Archi-
te‹ten, Stuttgart
S. | pp. 100–101: B.01 Hamburg Cruise Center
Terminal 1: Abb. 1: Christoph Gebler, Hamburg,
Abb. 2: Renner Hainke Wirth Architekten
S. | pp. 102–103: B.02 SAP Schulungs-
und Bürogebäude: Abb. 1+2: ELBE&FLUT/
Thomas Hampel
S. | pp. 104–105: B.03 Kühne+Nagel Haupt-
quartier: Abb. 1+2: Junius Verlag, Abb. 3:
Störmer Murphy and Partners, Hamburg
S. | pp. 106–107: B.04 Commercial Center:
Abb. 1+2: ELBE&FLUT/Thomas Hampel,
Abb. 3: Baumschlager Eberle
S. | pp. 108–109: B.05 Katharinenschule in
der Hafencity: Abb. 1+2: ELBE&FLUT/Thomas
Hampel, Abb. 3: Spengler Wiescholek
Architekten und Stadtplaner
S. | pp. 110–111: B.06 Sandtorpark:
Abb. 1: ELBE&FLUT/Thomas Hampel,
Abb. 2+3: Junius Verlag
S. | pp. 112–113: B.07/08 Hofquartier:
Abb. 1: H.G. Esch, Hennef, Abb. 2: ASTOC
Architects and Planners, Köln,
Abb. 3: Dorfmüller/Kröger/Klier, Hamburg
S. | pp. 114–115: B.09 Baugemeinschaft Hafen-
liebe: Abb. 1+2: ELBE&FLUT/Thomas Hampel,
Abb. 3: Architekturbüro Neitmann
S. | pp. 116–119: B.10/11 Hamburg-America-
Center und Coffee Plaza: Abb. 1, 3, 4: Elbe &
Flut/Thomas Hampel, Abb. 2: Junius Verlag,
Abb. 5–7: Richard Meier & Partners Architects
S. | pp. 120–121: B.12 SKAI: Abb. 1+2: Klaus
Frahm, Abb. 3: BLK2 Architekten
S | pp. 122–123: B.13 Kibbelsteg-Brücken:
Abb. 1+2: ELBE&FLUT/Thomas Hampel,
Abb. 3: gmp Architekten, Hamburg
S | p. 125: Junius Verlag
S | pp. 128–131: B.14/15/16 Arabica, Ceylon
und Java: Abb. 1, 2, 4+5: Eibe Sönnecken,
Abb. 3: Arbeitsgemeinschaft Trojan Trojan +
Partner und Dietz Joppien Architekten AG
S. | pp. 132–133: B.17 Pacamara: Abb. 1: Junius
Verlag, Abb. 2+3: nps tchoban voss | Architek-
tur und Städtebau (Fotos: Axel Neubauer)

S. | pp. 134–135: B.18 Sumatra-Kontor:
Abb. 1: ELBE&FLUT/Thomas Hampel,
Abb. 2+3: Junius Verlag
S. | pp. 136–137: B.19/20/21 Altes Hafenamt
mit Wohnturm und Infopavillon:
Abb. 1: ELBE&FLUT/Thomas Hampel,
Abb. 2+3: Bolles + Wilson
S. | pp. 138–139: B.22 Virginia / Hotel
25hours: Abb. 1+2: Klaus Frahm, Abb. 3:
BLK2 Architekten
S. | pp. 140–141: B.23/24/25 Projekte Süd-
liches Überseequartier: Abb. 1–3: Übersee-
quartier Beteiligungs GmbH
S. | pp. 142–143: B.26 Science Center: Abb. 1:
HafenCity GmbH, Animation: Gärtner u.
Christ Architekturdarstellung, Hamburg
S. | pp. 146–147: ELBE&FLUT/Heinz-Joachim
Hettchen
S. | pp. 152–155: C.01/02 Spiegel-Verlag und
Ericus-Contor: Abb. 1, 3–5: Elbe und Flut,
Thomas Hampel, Abb. 2: Henning Larsen
Architects
S. | pp. 156–159: C.03/04/05 Germanischer
Lloyd: Abb. 1: Elbe und Flut, Thomas Hampel,
Abb. 2+4: Heiner Leiska, Abb. 3+6: gmp
Architekten, Hamburg, Abb. 5: Klaus Frahm
S. | pp. 160–161: C.06/07/08 Brücken-Ensem-
ble: Abb. 1–3: Junius Verlag
S. | pp. 162–163: C.09 Internationales Mari-
times Museum Hamburg im Kaispeicher B:
Abb. 1: ELBE&FLUT/Thomas Hampel, Abb. 2:
MRLV Architekten, Abb. 3: MRLV Architekten
(Foto: Michael Zapf)
S. | pp. 164–165: C.10 Verwaltung Gebr. Hei-
nemann: Abb. 1: Junius Verlag, Abb. 2: Ulrich
Arndt, Hamburg
S. | pp. 166–167: C.11 Hauptzollamt / Zollamt
Hafencity: Abb. 1+2: ELBE&FLUT/Thomas
Hampel, Abb. 3: Winking · Froh Architekten
S. | pp. 168–169: C.12 Ökumenisches Forum
Brücke: Abb. 1: Junius Verlag, Abb. 2+3:
Norbert Miguletz
S. | pp. 170–171: C.13 Greenpeace-Zentrale und
designxport: Abb. 1: ELBE&FLUT/Thomas
Hampel, Abb. 2+3: Bob Gysin + Partner BGP
Architekten

S.| pp. 172–173: C.14 U-Bahn-Station Übersee-
quartier: Abb. 1+3: Jens Weber Fotografie,
Abb. 2: netzwerkarchitekten
S.| pp. 174–175: C.15 HafenCity Universität
(HCU): Abb. 1: ELBE&FLUT/Thomas Hampel,
Abb. 2: code unique architekten
S.| pp. 176–177: C.16 Baakenhafenbrücke:
Abb. 1–3: ELBE&FLUT/Thomas Hampel
S.| pp. 178–179: C.17 Aussichtsturm View
Point: Abb. 1: Renner Hainke Wirth
Architekten, Abb. 2: Junius Verlag, Abb. 3:
ELBE&FLUT/Thomas Hampel
S.| pp. 180–181: C.18 U-Bahn-Station HafenCi-
ty Universität: Abb. 1–3: raupach architekten
S.| pp. 182–183: C.19 Automuseum Prototyp:
Abb. 1+3: ELBE&FLUT/Thomas Hampel,
Abb. 2: Dinse Feest Zurl Architekten
S.| pp. 184–185: C.20/21 Oberhafen-Kantine/
neues Umspannwerk: Abb. 1–3: ELBE&FLUT/
Thomas Hampel
S.| pp. 188–189: ELBE&FLUT/Thomas Hampel
S.| p. 193: Hamburg. Historische Photo-
graphien 1842-1914, Hans Meyer-Veden, Ham-
burg 1995
S.| pp. 194–195: D.01 Steckelhörn 11: Abb. 1:
J. Mayer H. Architects, Abb. 2, 3+4: David
Franck Photographie
S.| pp. 196–197: D.02 Katharinenhof: Abb. 1:
ELBE&FLUT/Heinz-Joachim Hettchen, Abb. 2:
Gössler & Schnittger
S.| pp. 198–199: D.03 Neuer Dovenhof:
Abb. 1+2: Oliver Heissner, Hamburg
S.| pp. 200–201: D.04 Deichtor-Center:
Abb. 1+3: ELBE&FLUT/Thomas Hampel,
Abb. 2: BRT Architekten
S.| pp. 202–203: D.05 Speicherblock X:
Abb. 1+3: Bernadette Grimmenstein, Abb. 2:
gmp Architekten, Hamburg
S.| pp. 204–205: D.06 Umgestaltung der
HHLA-Hauptverwaltung: Abb. 1: ELBE&FLUT/
Thomas Hampel, Abb. 2+3: Jürgen Schmidt,
Abb. 4: gmp Architekten, Hamburg
S.| pp. 206–207: D.07 Ehemaliges Freihafen-
amt: Abb. 1, 4+5: SKA Sibylle Kramer Archi-
tekten, Abb. 2+3: Klaus Frahm, Hamburg
S.| pp. 208–209: D.08 Speicherblock P:

Abb. 1+2: ELBE&FLUT/Thomas Hampel,
Abb. 3+4: Kramer Biwer Mau Architekten
S.| pp. 210–211: D.09 Kesselhaus: Abb. 1:
Junius Verlag, Abb. 2: ELBE&FLUT/Thomas
Hampel, Abb. 3: gmp Architekten, Hamburg
S.| pp. 212–213: D.10 Hanseatic Trade Center I:
Abb. 1+2: Junius Verlag, Abb. 3: gmp Archi-
tekten, Hamburg
S.| pp. 214–215: D.10 Hanseatic Trade Center
II: Abb. 1+2: Junius Verlag, Abb. 3: Kleffel
Köhnholdt Gundermann
S.| pp. 218–219: ELBE&FLUT/Thomas Hampel
S.| pp. 224–225: E.01 Aztekenkontor:
Abb. 1–3: Klaus Frahm
S.| pp. 226–229: E.02 Gruner + Jahr: Abb. 1–3:
Junius Verlag, Abb. 2, 4+5: Steidle & Partner,
München
S.| pp. 230–231: E.03 Johannisbollwerk: Abb. 1:
Junius Verlag, Abb. 2–4: APB Architekten
S.| pp. 232–233: E.04 Hotel Hafen Hamburg –
Classic & Residenz und Aufstockung:
Abb. 1–3: meyer fleckenstein architekten
stadtplaner, Fotos: Wolfgang Neeb
S.| pp. 234–235: E.05 Erweiterung des Bern-
hard-Nocht-Instituts für Tropenmedizin:
Abb. 1: ELBE&FLUT/Thomas Hampel,
Abb. 2+3: kister scheithauer gross architekten
und stadtplaner
S.| pp. 236–237: E.06/07 Wohnen an der
Hafenstraße: Abb. 1+2: Junius Verlag, Abb. 3:
Architekten-Contor Schäfer Agather Scheel
S.| pp. 238–239: E.08 Astraturm: Abb. 1: Junius
Verlag, Abb. 2: KSP Architekten (Foto: Carsten
Brügmann) Abb. 3: steidle Architekten
S.| pp. 240–241: E.09 Atlantic Haus: Abb. 1:
ELBE&FLUT/Thomas Hampel, Abb. 2+3:
Herzog + Partner Architekten
S.| pp. 242–243: E.10 Empire Riverside Hotel
und Brauhaus: Abb. 1+2: ELBE&FLUT/Thomas
Hampel, Abb. 3: Junius Verlag
S.| pp. 244–245: E.11 Baugenossenschaft
Bergedorf-Bille I: Abb. 1+2: Ralf Buscher,
Hamburg, Abb. 3: PFP Architekten
S.| pp. 246–247: E.12 Wohnblock im Brauquar-
tier: Abb. 1: Junius Verlag, Abb. 2: Reinhard
Görner, Abb. 3: steidle Architekten

S.|pp. 248–249: E.13 Baugenossenschaft Bergedorf-Bille II: Abb. 1–3: Junius Verlag
S.|pp. 250–251: E.14 Tanzende Türme: Abb. 1+2: Junius Verlag, Abb. 3: BRT Architekten
S.|pp. 256–257: E.15/16 Dock 47 und Pinnasberg 45: Abb. 1+2: Spengler Wiescholek Architekten und Stadtplaner, Abb. 3: ELBE&FLUT/Thomas Hampel
S.|pp. 258–259: E.17 Stadtlagerhaus: Abb. 1: ELBE&FLUT/Thomas Hampel, Abb. 2: Junius Verlag, Abb. 3: Störmer Murphy and Partners, Hamburg
S.|pp. 260–261: E.18 Stilwerk: Abb. 1: ELBE&FLUT/Manfred Wigger, Abb. 2: Junius Verlag, Abb. 3: ELBE&FLUT/Thomas Hampel
S.|pp. 262–265: E.19/20/21 Holzhafen: Abb. 1+5: H.G. Esch, Hennef, Abb. 3+4: Elbe & Flut/Thomas Hampel, Lageplan und Grundrisse: ASTOC Architects and Planners, Köln
S.|pp. 266–267: E.22 Hafenklang: Junius Verlag
S.|pp. 268–269: E.23 Große Elbstraße 138: Abb. 1: Junius Verlag, Abb. 2: SEHW Architekten (Foto: Andreas Fromm), Abb. 3: SEHW Architekten
S.|pp. 270–271: E.24 Ehemaliges Fährterminal: Abb. 1,2,4: Alsop Lawrie Ltd. trading as ALL Design, London, Abb. 3: ELBE&FLUT/Thomas Hampel
S.|pp. 272–273: E.25 Hamburg Cruise Center Altona: Abb. 1: Christine Delius, Abb. 2: Klaus Frahm
S.|pp. 274–275: E.26 Elbkaihaus: Abb. 1: ELBE&FLUT/Thomas Hampel, Abb. 2: Jürgen Schmidt, Abb. 3: gmp Architekten, Hamburg
S.|pp. 276–277: E.27 Dockland: Abb. 1: ELBE&FLUT/Thomas Hampel, Abb. 2: Junius Verlag, Abb. 3: BRT Architekten
S.|pp. 278–279: E.28/29/30 Elbberg Campus Altona und Lofthaus am Elbberg: Abb. 1: ELBE&FLUT/Thomas Hampel, Abb. 2–4: BRT Architekten
S.|pp. 280–281: E.31 Columbia Twins: Abb. 1+2: Klaus Frahm/arturimages, Abb. 3: Carsten Roth Architekt
S.|pp. 282–283: E.32 Altonaer Kaispeicher D:

Abb. 1–3: nps tchoban voss|Architektur und Städtebau (Fotos: Axel Neubauer)
S.|pp. 284–285: E.33/34 Polderbebauung Neumühlen Ost: Abb. 1: ELBE&FLUT/Manfred Wigger, Abb. 2+3: Junius Verlag GmbH
S.|pp. 286–287: E.35/36 Polderbebauung Neumühlen West: Abb. 1: Klaus Frahm, Hamburg, Abb. 2+3: Junius Verlag GmbH
S.|pp. 288–289: E.37 Wohnstift Augustinum: Abb. 1: ELBE&FLUT/Thomas Hampel, Abb. 2: Klaus Frahm, Hamburg, Abb. 3: Schnitt gmp Architekten, Hamburg
S.|pp. 290–291: E.38/39 Elbchaussee 139: Abb. 1+2: Heiner Leiska, Abb. 3: Jürgen Schmidt, Abb. 4: gmp Architekten, Hamburg
S.|pp. 296–297: F.01 IBA Dock: Abb. 1+2: ELBE&FLUT/Thomas Hampel, Abb. 3: Prof. Han Slawik
S.|pp. 298–301: F.02 Ballinstadt: Abb. 1, 3, 5: nps tchoban voss|Architektur und Städtebau, Abb. 2+4: Daniel Sumesgutner, Hamburg
S.|pp. 302–303: F.03 Haus der Projekte: Abb. 1+3: IBA Hamburg GmbH (Fotos: Martin Kunze), Abb. 2: Studio NL–D, Rotterdam
S.|pp. 304–305: F.04 50er Schuppen: Abb. 1: ELBE&FLUT/Thomas Hampel, Abb. 2+3: Reinhold Liebermann
S.|pp. 306–307: F.05/06 Theater im Hafen: Abb. 1+2 Stage Entertainment
S.|pp. 308–309: F.07 Klärwerk Köhlbrandhöft: Abb. 1: Daniel Sumesgutner, Hamburg, Abb. 2: Architektencontor, Hamburg
S.|pp. 310–311: F.08 Marine-Center Finkenwerder: Abb. 1+2: Markus Bredt, Berlin, Abb. 3: KBNK Architekten, Hamburg
S.|pp. 312–313: F.09 Airbus A380 Montagehallen: Abb. 1+2 Heiner Leiska, Hamburg, Abb. 3: Grundriss gmp Architekten, Hamburg
S.|pp. 314–315: F.10 Airbus A380 Lackierhalle: Abb. 1+2: Oliver Heissner, Hamburg, Abb. 3: PSP Architekten, Hamburg

Dirk Meyhöfer geb. 1950, Dipl.-Ing., arbeitet seit 1987 selbständig als freier Journalist (DJV), Architekturkritiker, Publizist,
Kurator und Hochschullehrer in Hamburg.
Seine Themenschwerpunkte sind Architektur, Städtebau, Design, Wohnen und
Denkmalpflege.

Dirk Meyhöfer, born 1950, holds a di-
ploma in architecture and has worked as
a freelance journalist (DJV), architectural
critic, publicist, curator and university
lecturer in Hamburg since 1987. His the-
matic focus is on architecture, urbanism,
design and cultural heritage preservation.

Impressum Imprint

Junius Verlag GmbH
Stresemannstraße 375
22761 Hamburg

ELBE&FLUT Edition
Hampel und Hettchen GbR
Lastropsweg 1
20255 Hamburg

© 2014 by Junius Verlag GmbH /
ELBE&FLUT Edition
Alle Rechte vorbehalten.
All rights reserved.

Übersetzung Translation:
Stephen Roche, Damian Harrison, Carolyn
Kelly, networktranslators.de, Hamburg
Gestaltung Book design:
Andy Lindemann, ELBE&FLUT
Umschlag Cover design:
qart Büro für Gestaltung, Hamburg

Satz Typesetting: Junius Verlag GmbH
Druck und Bindung Printing and binding:
Rasch Druckerei und Verlag GmbH,
Bramsche
Printed in Germany
ISBN 978-3-88506-481-7
1. Auflage 2014

Bibliografische Information der
Deutschen Nationalbibliothek:
Die Deutsche Nationalbibliothek verzeichnet
diese Publikation in der Deutschen Natio-
nalbibliografie; detaillierte bibliografische
Daten sind im Internet über http://dnb.d-nb.
de abrufbar.
Bibliographic information published by the
Deutsche Nationalbibliothek:
The Deutsche Nationalbibliothek lists this
publication in the Deutsche Nationalbiblio-
grafie; detailed bibliographic data are available on the Internet at http://dnb.dnb.de.